The Discourse of Broadcast News

"As a study of broadcast news in particular, this book is the first of its kind; as a study of media discourse in general, this book is undoubtedly the best of its kind."
  Paul Simpson, *Queen's University, Belfast, UK*

"A groundbreaking study of broadcast news that focuses on it as live-to-air institutional talk ... highly recommended for all serious students of radio and television news."
  Paddy Scannel, *University of Michigan, USA*

In this timely and important study, Martin Montgomery unpicks the inside workings of what must still be considered the dominant news medium: broadcast news. Drawing principally on linguistics, but multidisciplinary in its scope, *The Discourse of Broadcast News* demonstrates that news programmes are as much about showing as telling, as much about ordinary bystanders as about experts, and as much about personal testimony as calling politicians to account.

Using close analysis of the discourse of television and radio news, the book reveals how important conventions for presenting news are changing, with significant consequences for the ways audiences understand its truthfulness. Fully illustrated with examples and including a detailed examination of the high-profile case of ex-BBC journalist Andrew Gilligan, *The Discourse of Broadcast News* provides a comprehensive study that will challenge our current assumptions about the news. *The Discourse of Broadcast News* will be a key resource for anyone researching the news, whether they be students of language and linguistics, media studies, or communication studies.

Martin Montgomery is Director of the Scottish Centre for Journalism Studies and Reader in Literary Linguistics at the University of Strathclyde. He is the author of many titles including the Routledge books *An Introduction to Language and Society* (2nd edition, 1995) and *Ways of Reading* (3rd edition, 2006, co-authored).

The Discourse of Broadcast News

A linguistic approach

Martin Montgomery

Routledge
Taylor & Francis Group

LONDON AND NEW YORK

First published 2007
by Routledge
2 Park Square, Milton Park, Abingdon, Oxon OX14 4RN

Simultaneously published in the USA and Canada
by Routledge
270 Madison Ave, New York, NY10016

Routledge is an imprint of the Taylor & Francis Group, an informa business

© 2007 Martin Montgomery

Typeset in Sabon by Keyword Group Ltd.
Printed and bound in Great Britain by Antony Rowe Ltd,
Chippenham, Wiltshire

British Library Cataloguing in Publication Data
A catalogue record for this book is available from the British Library

Library of Congress Cataloging-in-Publication Data
Montgomery, Martin.
   The discourse of broadcast news / Martin Montgomery.
      p. cm.
   Includes bibliographical references and index.
   1. Mass media and language. 2. Discourse analysis. I. Title.
   P96.L34M66 2007
   306.44–dc22   2007015387

ISBN 10: 0-415-35871-X (hbk)
ISBN 10: 0-415-35872-8 (pbk)

ISBN 13: 978-0-415-35871-2 (hbk)
ISBN 13: 978-0-415-35872-9 (pbk)

Contents

Figures

Acknowledgements

It seems as if this book began to take shape a long time ago but in fact it's only about three years since I first discussed it with Louisa Semlyen at Routledge. I'd like to thank her and Ursula Mallows for all their encouragement and support in bringing it to print. My colleagues in English Studies at Strathclyde University and in the Scottish Centre for Journalism Studies have also given much support, especially Sallyanne Duncan, Claire Black and Paul Rowinski. I'm sure they will recognise conversations in the book. In terms of intellectual debts, I owe an inestimable amount to the work and meetings of the Ross Priory Group for the Study of Broadcast Talk, with special thanks to Paddy Scannell, Andrew Tolson, Trudy Haarman and Michal Hamo who read large parts of the book in typescript and made hugely helpful comments. Others who gave valuable feedback on parts of the typescript include Philip Schlesinger, Joanna Thornborrow Deborah Cameron, Michael Schudson and Donald Matheson. I learnt a lot from John Hartley when we were colleagues at the Polytechnic of Wales, on whose very good book *Understanding News* I confess I should have relied more closely. Most of what I know about discourse analysis is ultimately derived from my time at Birmingham with Malcolm Coulthard and John Sinclair. Their work on spoken discourse was genuinely path-breaking even at that time and still offers important insights decades later. It was with great sadness that I heard of John's death as this was going to print. From him I learnt to take language seriously and, in his words, 'to trust the text'. If this book succeeds in its purpose a very great debt is due to him and I hope it might serve in some small way as a tribute. Its faults of course remain my own.

Scholarly discussion of broadcast news would be impossible without illustration, example and analysis. I'm grateful to the BBC, ITV and CNN for accepting this and for generously raising no objections to the use of images or transcripts from their broadcasts. I'm also grateful to be able to draw upon early versions of Chapter 5 and Chapter 6 which appeared respectively in Thornborrow, J. and Coates, J. (2005) *Studies in*

Narrative 6: The Sociolinguistics of Narrative. Amsterdam: John Bejamins, pp. 239–260, and in *Media Culture and Society* (2006) Vol. 28(2): 233–259. Every effort has been made to contact and acknowledge copyright holders, but if any errors remain we would be happy to correct them at a later printing.

Glasgow, June 2007

Transcription conventions

Samples of the spoken discourse of broadcast news are presented in the book according to a set of transcription conventions which may be illustrated and described using the following passage.

Extract 8.7.5

```
 1 INT'VIEWER:   do you accept any responsibility at all
 2               for the death of Dr David Kelly
 3 BLAIR:        (2.0) (hhhh) (1.5) it was a terrible (.) terrible thing
 4               to have happened
 5               (2.0) I don't believe we had any option however (1.0)
 6               but to disclose (1.0) his name (.)
 7               because I think had we failed (.) to do so (.)
 8               that would have been (1.0) seen (.)
 9               as attempting to conceal something from the committee (.)
10               that was looking in to this (.) at the time
11               and again (.)
12 INT'VIEWER:  do you accept any responsibility at all
13 BLAIR:                       [in relation to this (.) no I I I I've said
14               what I've said (.)
15               and I feel desperately sorry for his family
16               and indeed (.) for the terrible ordeal that they were put through
17               but as I said at the time
18               and again this has been gone into time and time again (1.0)
19               I (.) if we had concealed the fact (.)
20               cos this whole row was about (.)
21               erm the information that as as you know
22               we've been over this many many times
23               had been given to the BBC reporter (1.0)
24               he had then come forward (.) and said to his superiors (1.5)
25               this is me (.)
26               I think it's me who's responsible for having given this story
27               there was a Foreign Affairs Select Committee
28               (.) Report going on at the time
```

```
29          I think if we'd concealed that from people
30          we would have been subject for a different
31          to a different (type of allegation)
32 INT'VIEWER:          [so the short answer to the question is
33          you don't accept any responsibility
34 BLAIR:   well it's a a it's not a question of not accepting responsibility
35          it is a question of simply explaining the circumstances
36 BLAIR:                              [it's a question to which
37    →     you could give a yes or no answer Prime Minister
38 BLAIR:                              [yeh but it's maybe not (.)
39          a question (.) you need to give a yes or no answer to
```

Longer passages of more than 2 or 3 lines are described as **Extract** or **Ext.** Shorter passages are described as **Example** or **Ex.** The heading for each extract or example is numbered according to its position in the book. Thus, **Extract 8.7.5** is from Chapter 8, Section 7 and is the 5th extract in that section. Subsequent citations of shorter passages from the extract identify them as such by giving the line numbers of the original extract, thus:

Ext. 8.7.5: ll. 32–33
```
32 INT'VIEWER:          [so the short answer to the question is
33          you don't accept any responsibility
```

The transcript is divided into lines which, for ease of readability, correspond as much as possible to major syntactic units – usually the clause.

Each line of the transcript is numbered on the left-hand side and the speaker is identified by name (e.g. BLAIR) or role (e.g. INT'VIEWER) at the beginning of their turn or stretch of speech.

Since punctuation in speech is performed prosodically, standard written punctuation marks such as commas, full-stops and colons are not applied in the normal way.

Full-stops are used to indicate pauses of relatively short duration (half a second or less), are separated by a space on either side and usually enclosed within parentheses. Longer pauses are given an approximate timing mostly in half seconds, thus:

```
1 INT'VIEWER:   do you accept any responsibility at all
2          for the death of Dr David Kelly
3 BLAIR:   (2.0) (hhhh) (1.5) it was a terrible (.) terrible thing
4          to have happened
5          (2.0) I don't believe we had any option however (1.0)
6          but to disclose (1.0) his name (.)
```

Colons are used to indicate extended syllables, as in the following:

```
5          do we not need more time (.) to:: (.) check Gaddaffi out
```

An audible intake of breath is indicated by hhhh. Conversely, breathing out audibly is indicated by the use of parentheses: (hhhh). For instance, at the beginning of line 3 in Extract 8.7.5 above, the speaker pauses for two seconds, breathes out audibly, pauses for further one and half seconds and then begins his turn. (It is noticeable in the transcripts – especially where speech is unscripted – that hesitation phenomena tend to cluster around clause boundaries and so may be found more commonly at the beginnings and ends of lines.)

Where one speaker overlaps with another, the extent of the overlap is captured by off-setting the line of one speaker to coincide with the relevant point in the speech of the other and using a square bracket to indicate the onset of overlap. In the following section of the transcript Blair and the interviewer overlap in several places. At line 32 the interviewer begins to speak before Blair has finished his turn. And at lines 36 and 38 Blair begins to speak before the interviewer has finished.

```
30          we would have been subject for a different
31          to a different (type of allegation)
32 INT'VIEWER:      [so the short answer to the question is
33          you don't accept any responsibility
34 BLAIR:   well it's a a it's not a question of not accepting responsibility
35          it is a question of simply explaining the circumstances
36 BLAIR:                                    [it's a question to which
37    →     you could give a yes or no answer Prime Minister
38 BLAIR:                              [yeh but it's maybe not (.)
39          a question (.) you need to give a yes or no answer to
```

Where one speaker begins to speak precisely as another finishes (so-called "latched turns") an equals sign is used at the end of one turn and at the beginning of the latched turn.

```
36 INT'VIEWER:   isn't that everybody's responsibility including yours=
37 A. IZZADEEN:  =I think it's much more (.) wider than that
38          we're facing in the UK a complete attack (.)
```

Where a feature or a line in the transcript has been singled out for discussion an arrow is used to identify it: →

```
35    →     you could give a yes or no answer Prime Minister
```

Stretches of speech where there is uncertainty about the accuracy of the transcription are enclosed within parentheses:

```
30          we would have been subject for a different
31          to a different (type of allegation)
```

If transcription was impossible the stretch is left blank within parentheses.

Double parentheses are used for gloss or comment on the speech. In the following lines information about the pace of delivery has been given in double parentheses. The interviewer speeds up in line 27, slows down in lines 28 and 29 and speeds up again in line 30.

26 INT'VIEWER:	and indeed there's a very helpful calculator on your website
27 ((fast))	which enables you to work out
28 ((fast))	whether you'd be better or worse off (.)
29 ((slow))	and they would in fact (.)
30 ((slow))	be four hundred and twenty nine pounds (.) worse off
31 ((fast))	that's enough to take a holiday

Labels enclosed within square brackets denote discourse structure or function, as in:

Extract 7.3.1.10
[Evaluation]

1	I remember holding on to it with my left hand and saying
2	"I've gotta keep focussed I've gotta keep focussed"

Or as in:

1 ANNOUNCER:	this is the news at one from ITN		
2	with Leonard Parkin		[PRE-OPENING]
3 PRESENTER:	hello good afternoon		[GREETING]
4	after the coup in Uganda General Tito Okello	[NEWS ITEM]	

In Chapter 5 the onset of a new shot or a cut has been indicated in the transcript either by the symbol ▶ or the symbol I. The symbol / is used in this chapter to divide the verbal track into clauses.

Quick guide

(.)	pause of half a second or less
(1.5)	pause timed in seconds
(only partly intelligible)	uncertain transcription
((fast))	contextual gloss – usually manner of speech
[	beginning of overlapping stretch of speech
=	introduces latched turn
:	extended syllable
hhhh	inhalation
(hhhh)	aspiration
[GREETING]	discourse coding
→	indicates line which is the focus of comment or discussion

Structural notations

A ➡ B + C	'A consists of/is expounded by B plus C'
B + C	'B is followed by C'
(B)	'B is an optional element'
A (+B)	'A is optionally followed by B'
A < B >	'B is embedded inside A'
A{B + C}	'A contains B followed by C'
*	An initial asterisk is used to denote an ill-formed sequence
* C + C + A	'This sequence is ill-formed'
B^{1-n}	'B can be repeated several times'

1 Broadcast news

Journalism, in its various forms, is clearly among the most influential knowledge-producing institutions of our time

(Ekström, 2002, p. 259)

As the sense-making practice of modernity, journalism is the most important textual system in the world

(Hartley, 1996, p. 32)

1.0 Introduction

Journalism has claims to be the most important textual system of modernity because of its continuous and ubiquitous reach, because of the consistency, productivity and relative autonomy of its protocols, and because of the depth of its daily penetration into popular consciousness. In its sheer prevalence as a textual or discursive system it can be considered a knowledge-producing institution as important as science or religion. The central, prototypical output of the journalistic system is news; and its dominant platform at the present time is no longer print, nor yet the world-wide-web, but broadcasting.

Most major studies of the news, however, tend to focus on the practices that surround and underpin its production. There have, for example, been important landmark studies of the production structure of radio and television news, including the stop-watch culture of broadcast news journalists (Schlesinger, 1978/1992); important studies of the relations between journalists and their sources and how such factors influence and structure the news (Gans, 1979/2004); and important studies of how news organisations and the professional ideologies of news-workers shape news as a product (Tuchman, 1978). Here, for instance, is how Tuchman begins her classic study, *Making News*:

This book looks at news as a frame, examining how that frame is constituted – how the organisations of newswork and of newsworkers are put together. It concentrates upon newspapers and television stations as complex organisations subject to certain inevitable processes, and upon newsworkers as professionals with professional concerns.

(Tuchman, 1978, p. 1)

And, true to her aim, her book provides important insights about the micro-processes of the daily production of the news and the kinds of practical reasoning adopted by journalists – the importance to them, for instance, of notions of facticity and the aspiration to objectivity.

In addition to studies of news production there have been many important studies of news content, perhaps the most notable in the field of broadcast news being those of the Glasgow (University) Media Group in a string of publications such as *Bad News* (1976), *More Bad News* (1980) and *War and Peace News* (1980). A constant concern of this work has been with the capacity of broadcast news to deliver fidelity to the real. The early work set out to demonstrate that the news was systematically skewed or biased in favour of the prevailing power structures. In later work, such as *Bad News from Israel* (Philo and Berry, 2004; see also Philo, 2002), the concern with systematic bias has been married to exploration of the sense-structures that audiences bring to bear upon the news.

While this rich sociological tradition has provided many insights into both how the news is shaped and how well it maps the world it represents, it takes for the most part the texts and the language of news programmes for granted. By comparison with the depth and quantity of the sociological stud-ies there has been little systematic inquiry into the structures of the language of broadcast news. Linguists, it is true, have long been interested in the language of journalism but by far the largest part of their detailed analyses have been carried out on newspaper texts and newspaper language (see, for example: Bell, 1991; Caldas-Coulthard, 1997; Fowler, 1991; Richardson, 2006; Van Dijk, 1988a,b; White, 1997, 2000; Bednarek, 2006). By con-trast, systematic and comprehensive accounts of broadcast news as discourse are few and far between, existing for the most part as occasional articles or chapters (see, for example: Bentele, 1985; Lerman, 1985; Hartley and Montgomery, 1985; Graddol, 1994; Meinhof, 1994; Bondi Paganelli, 1990; Haarman, 1999, 2004, 2006). Only one area of broadcast news discourse has received detailed and sustained attention and that is the news inter-view (see, for example, Blum-Kulka, 1983; Clayman, 1991; Harris, 1991; Greatbatch, 1998; Heritage and Greatbatch, 1991; Fetzer, 2002; Clayman and Heritage, 2002). But these studies tend to focus somewhat narrowly on interviews with political figures, treating the interviews usually in isolation from the specific and immediate news contexts in which they occur.

Given the easy availability of print journalism for analysis it is hardly surprising that it has been the subject of such sustained and detailed study. Yet it seems clear that broadcasting, by radio or television, must draw upon a set of verbal practices quite different from those deployed in print. It is not just a question of contrasting media – graphic versus audio-visual – and the different forms of sensory and cognitive processing which they require. The communication situation of broadcasting is radically different from print. While both are 'one-or-few-to-many' forms of mass communication, print forces a separation not only in space but also in time between the moment of encoding and the moment of decoding, the latter taking place for the most part in individualised singularity. Broadcasting, on the other hand, allows for simultaneity in transmission and reception so that audiences experience it often as 'live' communication alongside an implied, if invisible, community of others. In this respect, broadcasting is much closer to the real-time co-presence of speech than other forms of mass communication. And, indeed, a substantial element of broadcasting, both within news programming and across the schedules more generally, is precisely that: 'speech' or 'talk'.

Print journalism produces texts that are fixed on the page but that audiences may sample in their own time and at their discretion: they may overlook some items and concentrate on others; they may scan items, returning to them later, or skip to others that catch their interest. Broadcast journalism, by contrast, produces texts which are 'evanescent', to use Crisell's term (1994, p. 86). The temporal flow of the broadcast is not typically subject to the audience's control. Items are sequenced by the broadcaster and experienced and decoded in 'real time' by the audience, who may attend more closely to one item rather than another, but who are not in a position to sample the news bulletin in the manner of a newspaper reader. To some extent this suggests that the individualised consumer of print journalism is in more control than the broadcast audience. And in one fundamental respect broadcasters lack control over their audiences: as the news is broadcast, audiences may choose to watch this programme or another or not to watch or listen at all. As Scannell points out: "the relationship between broadcasters, listeners and viewers is an *unforced* relationship because it is unenforceable" (Scannell, 1996, p. 23). This places special obligations on broadcasters: the live, ephemeral, evanescent and unforced quality of modern broadcasting gives it, argues Scannell, its special communicative ethos – one oriented towards sociability rather than instrumentality, to universal accessibility rather than towards privatised or sectionalised interests (see also Peters, 1999).

The differences between the print and broadcast media are therefore quite profound and we should not expect the discourse of broadcast news to exhibit the same properties or qualities that can be discerned in the discourse of newspapers. This study, then, seeks to provide a comprehensive account of the everyday discourse of broadcast news: it brings to bear those analytic procedures and disciplines that have evolved to describe the forms and the structures of spoken discourse in a variety of situations – including everyday conversation, medical practice, the classroom, the law courts, or broadcast talk more generally – and applies them to the discourse of broadcast news.

1.1 Defining news

We may define broadcast news initially in circular fashion as what viewers and listeners expect to see and hear when they switch on or switch
channel at the appropriate moment in the broadcast schedule to catch a
news bulletin programme (usually on the hour or half-hour); news is what
news organisations have selected for inclusion within the pre-determined slot
and is what gets broadcast within it. Usually what gets broadcast as news
has claims to offer, as Ekstrom puts it, "reliable, neutral and current factual information that is important and valuable for citizens in democracy",
presented "on a regular basis" (Ekstrom, 2002, p. 274). The reference to
democracy, however, seems perhaps a little gratuitous. As Schudson notes,
"I am reluctant to smuggle 'democracy' into the very definition of journalism" (2003, p. 14), offering instead a broader formulation: "information
and commentary on contemporary affairs taken to be publicly important",
though even here he concedes that "in any day's newspaper or radio or television 'news' broadcast, there is a great deal of material that is interesting
but not important" (op. cit. pp. 14–15). Adopting the most inclusive perspective, then, news can be defined as information about current or recent
events, happenings or changes taking place outside the immediate purview
of the audience and which is considered to be of likely interest or concern to
them. **Broadcast** news consists of the mediated and regular presentation of
this material to a mass public.

In some respects, news, like conversation, is a form of reality maintenance.
In the case of conversation –

> one may view the individual's everyday life in terms of the working
> away of a conversational apparatus that ongoingly maintains, modifies
> and reconstructs his subjective reality ... [T]he greater part of reality
> maintenance in conversation is implicit, not explicit. Most conversation
> does not in so many words define the nature of the world. Rather it
> takes place against the background of a world that is silently taken for
> granted ... At the same time that the conversational apparatus ongoingly
> maintains reality, it ongoingly modifies it. Items are dropped and added,
> weakening some sectors of what is still being taken for granted and
> reinforcing others.
>
> (Berger and Luckmann, 1971, pp. 172–173)

In case of the news, however, the realities that it maintains are not the realities
of concrete, direct experience but are realities of the world 'out there' beyond
the immediate purview and the concrete relationships of the viewer/listener.
News constructs a taken-for-granted world of others, of 'them', of people
whom we do not expect to encounter as part of our daily life, in places where
we are not. But they are second-order realities. The news describes for us and
takes for granted imaginary communities, perhaps at the level of the nation,

but increasingly at the global level – communities to which we may feel bound but for the most part we experience in no other way. And rather than the ordinariness of the conversational world, news describes its world in extraordinary terms. In accounts of disasters, scandals, elections, accidents, wars, summits, famines, glamour and privation, sporting victories and defeats it creates and affirms a world beyond our own which in the constant daily news round it routinely reaffirms and modifies: the extraordinariness of the events at a distance brought to us by the news serves to confirm and stabilise the routine ordinariness of the close at hand in which we are immersed.

When individuals become swept up in a particular news event (a sporting occasion, a mass demonstration) their routine reaction to the news is often one of alienation. The second-order news depiction seems to represent askew the first-order event in which they took part, as they find themselves depicted in terms normally reserved for the distant other. A common reaction of all who by accident get caught up in the news is: 'but it was not like that'. So, where we have undergone the experience at first hand, reality seems drained from the representation even though it seems to run so strongly in the rest.

1.2   News values

If news may be defined as events or information of likely concern to the audience, how does one define 'of likely concern'? Not every event or piece of information counts as news. News has to be notable according to particular principles of selection, paradigms of relevance, and frames for including and excluding material. As Hall has pointed out:

> Journalists speak of the news as if events select themselves. Further they speak as if which is the 'most significant' news story, and which 'news angles' are most salient, are divinely inspired. Yet of the millions of events which occur every day in the world, only a tiny proportion ever become visible as 'potential news stories': and of this proportion, only a small fraction are actually produced as the day's news in the news media.
>
> (Hall, 1981, p. 234)

Principles of exclusion and inclusion may be summed up under the heading of 'news values'. Following the pioneering work of Galtung and Ruge (1965a,b) these may be outlined in the following way. Events become news to the extent that they satisfy the following criteria.

1.2.1   Recency/Timeliness

News, as the name implies, deals by definition with 'the new' ("new information of recent events", as the *Shorter Oxford English Dictionary* puts it). News has particular temporal rhythms dominated until recently by the dailiness of a 24-hour time-frame (see Schlesinger, 1978/1992). 'Yesterday's news' ceases quickly to be news at all. "What was live news becomes cold fact" (Park, 1999, p. 12). Or, as Tuchman (1978) observes, "news is a depletable consumer product that must be made fresh daily". Developments in information technology and the increasing prevalence of rolling 24-hour news outlets may be shortening and accelerating the news cycle. The retro-spective emphasis on 'today's top stories' is being replaced by the prospective 'upcoming in the next hour'. Accordingly, news items have a limited life-cycle with their news value dwindling rapidly over time.

News organisations have traditionally emphasised the importance of being the first outlet to carry the story (a 'scoop' or 'exclusive') and, more recently, the extra importance of the 'news flash' and the 'breaking story'. In prac-tice, however, for most of the time, most broadcast news is **not** 'first-time', breaking news, nor is it exclusive to the broadcaster. The same material is being, and most likely has been, carried in not very different terms by several other news outlets. For this reason, most news material exists in a kind of half-life, with news outlets struggling to find something new to say about it. Once material has 'broken' there is pressure either to add detail or to increase its interpreted significance each time it receives further mention. But unless the 'depletable product' can be radically refreshed it is difficult to extend the life of a news item beyond a 3 or 4 day life-cycle.

1.2.2   *Intensity/Discontinuity*

The sharper and more temporally bounded the event the easier it is to inte-grate it into the temporal rhythms of news. Events that unfold over a long duration are difficult to integrate into the increasingly short cycles of news publication. Thus, coastal erosion, agricultural failure, climate change or the business cycle lack newsworthiness until they 'go critical' and a slow process can be condensed to a narrow event such as economic slump, famine or the melting of an ice-cap. Events in a series of stable, steady-state occurrences are less newsworthy than an event which represents a sudden deviation from the norm. If cancer deaths as a proportion of early mortality remain annually at 35 per cent this is less newsworthy than if they suddenly increase in a year to 45 per cent (or decrease to 25 per cent).

1.2.3   *Scale/Scope*

Events need to be of a scale large enough to warrant attention. "The stronger the signal, the greater the amplitude, the more probable that it will be recorded as worth listening to" (Galtung and Ruge, 1965a, p. 64). Thus, a Tsunami that kills 150,000 people is more newsworthy than an earthquake that kills 150 people. Like all news values, however, the notion of scale is situationally sensitive. An earthquake in Los Angeles is more newsworthy than a similar sized earthquake in Iran – for reasons relating to proximity and cultural relevance outlined below.

1.2.4 Conflict

Conflict between opposing parties is newsworthy. Strikes, breakdowns in negotiations, divorce, war, election campaigns are all high in news value. In each case material can be structured in terms of binary oppositions (Hartley and Montgomery, 1985). Strong oppositions serve not only to dramatise individual events but also provide overarching frames for organising diverse material. "The Cold War" and more recently "the War on Terror" provided a continuous frame for myriad news items over several years. Typically oppositions are multi-layered and overlapping with an implicit or presupposed valorisation of one side of the offering over the other: we know in the presence of an opposition, without thinking, 'whose side we are on'. And when oppositions are strong they are 'generative', offering clear if understated spaces for projection and identification. "The War on Terror", for instance, is between West and East, Freedom and Tyranny, Civilisation and Barbarism, Progress and Reaction, Reason and Fundamentalism, Good and Evil, Us and Them .... One opposition with its clear value structure folds into another with cumulative force.

1.2.5 Personalisation

People have news value in a way that processes do not. They are concrete, they provide points of identification, and they help to dramatise conflict. "News has a tendency to present events as sentences where there is a subject, a named person or collectivity consisting of a few persons, and the event is then seen as a consequence of the actions of this person or these persons" (Galtung and Ruge, 1965a, p. 66). The pace, rhythm and presentational qualities of broadcast news accentuate the tendency to personalise (even though, of course, this long predates TV and radio). TV's emphasis on close-up and radio's contrapuntal blending of voices bring human reactions dramatically into play. In mediating the news they make human interest profoundly inescapable. A Tsunami in the Indian Ocean, through on the spot accounts for radio and especially television, is quickly dramatised into images of 'distant suffering' (Boltanski, 1999; Chouliaraki, 2006) with an impact far beyond purely literal or statistical description.

1.2.6 Power

The salience of news material is enhanced if it involves people with power – however this may be defined. The actions of presidents, princesses, prime ministers and popes attract more notice than those of plumbers, porters, park-keepers and pensioners. Habermas (1989) describes this, bleakly, in terms of the re-feudalisation of the public sphere. News offers repeatedly images of the actions and demeanour of the powerful emphasising the show of power rather than the intricacies of its hidden processes. But it is not just people in power who attract attention in the news media. It is also powerful organisations, powerful nations and power blocs of various kinds. Thus in the major metropolitan centres of the Northern hemisphere the US is more likely to make the news than Uzbekistan, Germany or Japan rather than Nigeria or Moldavia, the EU rather than the OAS. The collapse of Enron carries more news value than the opening of a workers' cooperative in Peru.

1.2.7   Negativity

Bad news makes good news. War reporting is one of the earliest historical examples of news; but crime, fatal accident, famine, earthquake, execution, epidemic and disaster are staple elements of the news. Galtung and Ruge (1965a and b) comment that negative events tend to unfold more quickly than positive events and that the meaning of negative events is more emotionally charged, more clear-cut, less ambiguous. In this way 'negativity' as a news value interacts with other values such as intensity, discontinuity, conflict and personalisation. The dominant news items of the 21st century – 9/11, war in Iraq, the Indian Ocean Tsunami, climate change – are all examples of extremely bad news. They are also classic, prototypical news stories that would be difficult if not impossible to exclude from any news agenda.

1.2.8   Unexpectedness

Routine events are difficult to assimilate to the news, which favours the novel, the atypical and the unusual. As the old joke has it: 'Man bites dog' is a more likely news item than 'Dog bites man'.

1.2.9   Consonance

At the same time, there are certain classes of event that trigger a 'news script' that strongly determines the shape of coverage. Major accidents, for instance, while newsworthy insofar as they are unexpected (as well as negative, for instance, and discontinuous), often trigger a logic (or 'script' – see Schank and Abelson, 1977; Montgomery *et al.,* 1989; Garton *et al.,* 1991) in which coverage focuses first on the scale of the casualties and fatalities, then on the skill or heroism of the emergency services, then on the fortitude or courage of the survivors, then on the possibility of human error and then on the ascription of blame. Even the unexpected event can in its coverage assume familiar contours.

1.2.10   Proximity/Cultural relevance

The further removed an event from the news centre the less relevance it has for the news outlet. This is partly a question of literal, geographical distance, so that to a London- or Washington-based broadcaster, events in Ulan Bator will lack salience. Questions of geographical remoteness, however, interact with the considerations of the habitual reach of the broadcaster: a broadcaster which defines its reach in global terms (e.g. CNN or BBC World) is more likely to carry a story from Ulan Bator than a regional or national broadcaster (such as, for example, BBC Scotland). Distance may also be understood metaphorically, in cultural terms, as well as literally. Societies and figures that are remote in cultural terms from the norms of broadcasters feature less prominently than those which have a great deal in common with the news centre. In the aftermath of the Indian Ocean Tsunami, initial coverage in the UK focused on the plight of Western holidaymakers, tourists and backpackers in Thailand, Bali and Sri Lanka. Two or three days passed before the plight of local indigenous populations became the focus.

1.2.11 *Meaningfulness/Unambiguity*

Cultural relevance is to some degree a guarantee of the meaningfulness of material. To BBC Scotland the role of Scottish regiments in the occupation of Iraq had a particular news value over and beyond the occupation itself. But in more general terms, news has a predilection for material whose meaning can be presented as if clear-cut and unambiguous rather than cloudy and complex. "An event with a clear interpretation, free from ambiguities in its meaning, is preferred to the highly ambiguous event from which many and inconsistent implications can and will be made" (Galtung and Ruge, 1965a, p. 64)

1.2.12 *Composition/Fit*

In any bulletin particular slots carry particular values. It is common, for instance, for some broadcasters to finish their bulletin with a relatively quirky, 'upbeat', human-interest story. In the final slot such material is likely to take precedence over an accident or injury story. There may also be considerations of balance within a bulletin as a whole between, for example, domestic news and international news, political news and sporting news. News values may also be encoded differentially into different news media. Television has an obvious predilection for actuality footage. A news story with strong pictures is likely to take precedence over one without footage, all else being equal.

Galtung and Ruge describe these news values as 'factors' which must inhere in material for it to be deemed newsworthy: the more factors displayed by material the greater its 'amplitude' and the more likely it is to be registered or noticed. And it is these particular factors rather than others that define the interest of an item. Their account is an illuminating way of thinking about the newsworthiness of news but raises several important questions.

1.3   The epistemological status of news values

The epistemological status of the 'factors' is somewhat ambiguous. Galtung and Ruge (1965) arrived inductively at their picture of the factors inform-ing the news on the basis of a survey of actual news coverage. It is possible, therefore, that the factors which they identified are potentially skewed by the kind of coverage which they surveyed – three major international crises (Congo, Cuba and Cyprus). A more recent study of three British national daily newspapers by Harcup and O'Neill argues that the original values need to be adjusted to take account of "day-to-day coverage of lesser, domestic and bread-and-butter news" and should include areas such as entertainment and celebrity (Harcup and O'Neill, 2001, p. 276).

From another perspective the factors are often discussed as if they con-stitute a framework or filter employed by journalists in constructing the news, for example, as "inferential frames" (Glasgow University Media Group, 1980), in which case they can be understood as elements of the commonsense practical reasoning that journalists draw upon in identifying newsworthy material. Like all modes of commonsense reasoning, however, they must be situationally sensitive and indexical. 'Scale', for instance, can only be a relative rather than an absolute category and has to be interpreted always in terms of the context in which it is applied, interacting with other factors such as 'proximity', as well as with the predilections of the particular news organisation or platform involved (broadcast versus print journalism, or popular versus quality press).

Third, news values are often handled – whether explicitly or implicitly – as a critical analytical framework the purpose of which is to demonstrate the arbitrary nature of the news as the outcome of a naturalising production process in which the values (or factors or frames) operate perhaps uncon-sciously in an unacknowledged (and ideologically laden) fashion to include some segments and versions of reality while excluding or 'ex-nominating' others (see, for example, Allan, 1999, pp. 60–64; Fiske, 1987, p. 290). It seems just as likely, however, that the news selection, far from being natu-ralised and unconsciously ideological, is an inescapable and necessary aspect of the social process in general, and of news production in particular, where the values or frames – far from being a rigid strait-jacket for the determi-nation of news – help to underpin a complex and self-conscious practical accomplishment.

> Frames enable journalists to process large amounts of information quickly and routinely: to recognise it as information, to assign it to cognitive categories, and to package it for efficient relay to their audi-ences. Thus for organisational reasons alone, frames are unavoidable, and journalism is organised to regulate their production.
>
> (Gitlin, 1980, p. 7)

As Allan himself recognises, news values and frames are the "subject of often intense negotiation between journalists and their editors as well as their sources" but nonetheless "help to render an infinity of noticeable details into practicable repertoires" (op. cit. p. 64).

Broadcast news, in short, has no option but to make the world manifest in quite particular ways. It models reality 'out there', but assembles it through certain kinds of routine practices for drawing form out of the potentially chaotic plenitude of undifferentiated occurrences in ways that seem to meet the concerns and interests of its audience.

1.4   Broadcasting standards: the regulation of broadcast news

News values tell us something about the content of news programmes and the routine editorial practices of those who make the news. But broadcast news is also affected and shaped by other pressures. Because broadcasting plays such a prominent role in the self-consciousness of contemporary societies, broadcast institutions are commonly subject to national regulatory frameworks; and these will often stipulate terms within which news should be broadcast. In the UK, for instance, broadcasters are subject by law to the provisions of the Communications Act 2003, as well as Article 10 of the European Convention on Human Rights; and a particular body, 'The Office of Communications', or *OfCom*, has responsibility for publishing guidelines (the *OfCom Broadcasting Code*) based upon the relevant legislation and ensuring that these are adhered to. Here are some of the provisions of the code as they apply specifically to the news.

1.4.1. News, in whatever form, must be reported with due accuracy and presented with due impartiality.

1.4.2. Significant mistakes in news should normally be acknowledged and corrected on air quickly. Corrections should be appropriately scheduled.

1.4.3. No politician may be used as a newsreader, interviewer or reporter in any news programmes unless, exceptionally, it is editorially justified. In that case, the political allegiance of that person must be made clear to the audience.

1.4.4. Programmes must exclude all expressions of the views and opinions of the person providing the service on matters of political and industrial controversy and matters relating to current public policy (unless that person is speaking in a legislative forum or in a court of law).

1.4.5. Due impartiality on matters of political or industrial controversy and matters relating to current public policy must be preserved on the part of any person providing a service.

1.4.6.   Views and facts must not be misrepresented. Views must also be presented with due weight over appropriate timeframes.

1.4.7.   Any personal interest of a reporter or presenter, which would call into question the due impartiality of the programme, must be made clear to the audience.

1.4.8.   Presenters and reporters (with the exception of news presenters and reporters in news programmes), presenters of 'personal view' or 'authored' programmes or items, and chairs of discussion programmes may express their own views on matters of political or industrial controversy or matters relating to current public policy. However, alternative viewpoints must be adequately represented either in the programme, or in a series of programmes taken as a whole. Additionally, presenters must not use the advantage of regular appearances to promote their views in a way that compromises the requirement for due impartiality. Presenter phone-ins must encourage and must not exclude alternative views.

1.4.9.   A personal view or authored programme or item must be clearly signalled to the audience at the outset. This is a minimum requirement and may not be sufficient in all circumstances.

1.4.10.   In addition to the rules above, due impartiality must be preserved on matters of major political and industrial controversy and major matters relating to current public policy by the person providing a service in each programme or in clearly linked and timely programmes.

1.4.11.   In dealing with matters of major political and industrial controversy and major matters relating to current public policy an appropriately wide range of significant views must be included and given due weight in each programme or in clearly linked and timely programmes. Views and facts must not be misrepresented.

1.4.12.   Broadcasters should not give undue prominence to the views and opinions of particular persons or bodies on matters of political or industrial controversy and matters relating to current public policy in all the programmes included in any service taken as a whole.

(Adapted from the Ofcom Broadcasting Code,
which came into effect on 25 July 2005)

To some extent, the provisions enshrined within the code reflect routine virtues commonly demanded of journalism everywhere – for instance, the commitment to factual accuracy. But in other respects the code reflects traditions of good practice particular to broadcasting in modern democracies. The emphasis on impartiality (and 'fairness', handled elsewhere in the code) is quite specific to broadcasting the news. (It would not apply to the press, where individual newspaper titles will often be highly partisan.) In addition the provisions are designed to forestall the use of news programmes as an editorial platform for the views of a broadcaster or for the views of only a restricted section of the public or of a special interest group. Provisions of this kind give broadcast news a distinctive character – especially when compared with the press. Some broadcasting in the UK – particularly the BBC – is funded from the public purse and is expected to broadcast for the public benefit and in the public interest, obligations which have always been interpreted to include news and current affairs. But even commercially funded broadcasters (such as Channels 4 and 5) are considered to have public service obligations, especially in these areas, where *Ofcom* has in the past set formal quotas for hours of programming. The stipulations of the code show quite clearly that the implied model of the news at stake is very much one defined by the public interest, with a corresponding effort to prevent it becoming a vehicle for sectional interests.

1.5   The relative importance of broadcast news to audiences and producers

It is perhaps for this reason that television, in particular, remains the primary source of news for most people most of the time in the industrial democracies of Europe or North America, despite fluctuations in ratings and in measurements of audience share. In Britain, a fairly recent study of news audiences by Hargreaves and Thomas could claim:

> Television is now the supreme news medium, in the sense that it is used and respected by almost everyone. It is the only news medium presently capable of reaching across the whole of British society. Most people (91%) say they find television a useful source of news compared with 73% for newspapers, 59% for radio, 15% for the internet and 13% for magazines.
>
> (Hargreaves and Thomas, 2002, p. 4)

Figures published the following year confirmed a long-term trend in which broadcasting – especially television – continues to consolidate its position as a major source of news for most people most of the time (see Figures 1.1 and 1.2).

In the UK (with a population of 58 million) the combined audience for evening news on the five terrestrial television channels is over 10 million (see Figure 1.3) – comparable to the combined national daily newspaper circulation. In the USA (with a population of 300 million) as many as 30 million people watch evening news on one of the three network television stations NBC, ABC or CBS. News is a staple and significant component of the broadcasting schedule. BBC One is the main public service channel on British television, accounting for approximately a quarter share of all television viewing (ITV1 accounts for 23.7 per cent). On BBC One alone, about 30 per cent of output consists of news programming. News is about

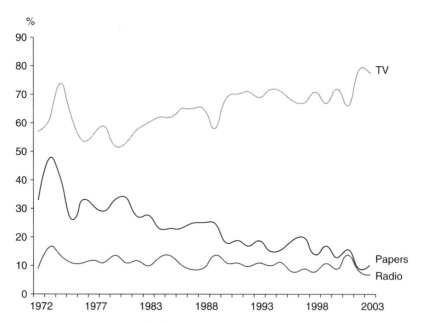

Figure 1.1 Primary source of world news amongst the general UK population (Source: Ofcom: 'Review of PSB', 2004).

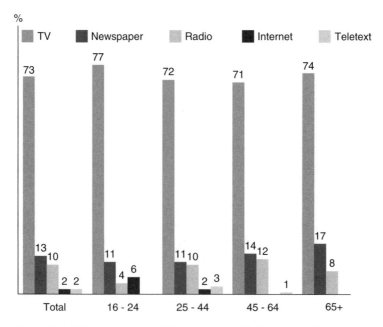

Figure 1.2 Primary source of UK news in 2003 (Source: OfCom: 'Review of PSB', 2004).

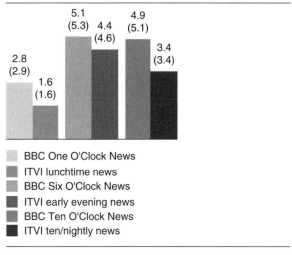

BBC One O'Clock News
ITVl lunchtime news
BBC Six O'Clock News
ITVl early evening news
BBC Ten O'Clock News
ITVl ten/nightly news

Source: BARB, TNS/Infosys
Note: Figures for 2002/2003 appear in brackets

Figure 1.3 Average audiences for network news bulletins 2003/2004 (millions).

36 per cent of all output on the BBC's main channels, One and Two, with over 3000 hours of programming in 2003/4. News programming is also a significant element of the other four main terrestrial channels (BBC Two, ITV1, Channel 4 and Channel 5), including the latter three commercial channels, who by franchise agreements with the government have public service obligations which include news provision. Although the most popular programmes on British television are soap operas, such as *Coronation Street* and *Eastenders* (with audiences as high as 11 million and 9 million respectively), and drama, such as *Casualty,* news programmes account for up to ten of the top 30 programmes on all terrestrial television in the UK (e.g. the week ending 6th February 2005). Audience figures for BBC's *The Six O'Clock News* and *The Ten O'Clock News* are regularly over 5 million.

Radio, although traditionally carrying a large element of music in its programming, counts news as its second most significant category of output. BBC Network Radio, for instance, produces overall around 70,000 hours of programme output in a year (2003/4: 76,752; 2002/3: 63,740); and, while over half of this is music, in 2003/4 11,718 hours – over 15 per cent of total output – were devoted to news. BBC radio has a dedicated news channel, Radio 5 Live. But, even so, BBC Radio 4, its main spoken-word radio channel, devoted 30 per cent of its output to news. (The number of radio listeners in the UK has in any case just reached a record high, with the latest industry figures showing that more than 45 million people tune in each week – the highest number recorded since the UK industry body, RAJAR, began monitoring listening habits in 1992.)

So news is a highly significant element of broadcast output on both radio and television. Furthermore, at the same time as it draws significant audiences, news is relatively inexpensive to produce. Drama, on BBC (terrestrial) television, for instance, costs about £518,000 an hour to produce. Entertainment costs £200,600. Sport costs £162,400 per hour. News, however, is the cheapest category of content, costing a mere £40,600 per hour, only half the cost of the other cheapest category of content – children's television. Indeed, it could be argued that for the major networks, if news did not exist, they would need to invent it as perhaps the most cost-effective way of engaging audiences.

For some years, however, concern has been expressed at declining audiences for network news, particularly in the USA, where the three main network news providers, NBC, ABC and CBS, have been losing audience share steadily for the last 20 years; and it is true that the number of viewers watching evening news has dropped from over 50 million in 1980 to less than 30 million in 2004. In whatever way audiences can be measured the falls in the USA can seem dramatic. As one report puts it:

> In 1980, the three commercial network nightly news broadcasts had a combined 37% rating, and a 75% share. And at their historic peak, in 1969, they had a 50% rating and an 85% share. The November 2004 figures mean that ratings have fallen almost 59.6% since 1969, and 45.4% since 1980. Share has fallen 55.3% since 1969 and 49.3% since 1980.
>
> (Journalism.org: *The state of the news media 2004*)

Put bluntly, the ratings in the USA for all three nightly news broadcasts combined have fallen by almost a half in 14 years. The figures for local TV news show a similar picture. From 1997 to 2004 local TV news in the USA dropped from nearly 20 per cent of audience share to 16 per cent. The picture in Britain is less dramatic but there are still some signs of a decline in audience. In 1997 an average of 6 million were watching the main ITV news bulletin. In 2005 the popular early evening news on ITV was drawing about 4.5 million viewers. The Six O'Clock BBC One news programme was watched by about 6 million in 1997, but this had dropped to 5.16 million in 2005.

These figures might be interpreted as evidence of a generally declining appetite for news, especially when considered alongside falling readership figures for newspapers; but the full picture is more complex. With the development of digital free-to-view broadcasting in Britain and the rise of cable and satellite broadcasting on both sides of the Atlantic, coupled with the growth of web-based platforms for news, there has been a proliferation in the ways news can be delivered to people. Thus, decline in audience for mainstream television news bulletins ('network TV' in the USA) can be linked to some degree with the rise of dedicated news channels such as CNN, Fox or Sky on cable and satellite. The match, however, is not precise. The growth in audience for dedicated news channels is not as fast as the decline for mainstream television news and seems in any case to be slowing if not to have reached a plateau in the USA. In Britain the audience for 24-hour rolling news channels still remains comparatively small: Sky News and BBC News 24, for instance, command respective shares of the overall television audience in the UK of around 3–4 per cent. In the USA prime-time viewing of cable news (including, e.g., Fox and CNN) was 2.6 million in 2004 – small compared with nearly 30 million watching the networks. Fox, considered to be America's most popular cable news provider, attracts only a small fraction of the US television audience, gaining at best up to half a million viewers in prime time.

The audience for news may not be declining so much as changing. It is noticeable, for instance, that audiences for mainstream – especially prime time, evening – news programmes tend to be older than the audience for rolling, dedicated news channels – and for online news. In the US some evidence also suggests that morning, 'breakfast' news is attracting larger audiences as the evening programmes are losing them. These changes are driven by a complex array of factors, including lifestyle changes: as the working day grows longer, people prefer to take their news before they start work rather than after they finish. Indeed, fewer people of working age are home in time for 'prime time'. Younger people in any case are less interested in 'news by appointment'. They are more selective: they prefer to take the news that they want, when they want it – online, or from a 24-hour news channel. And if audiences are more prone to pick and choose the news they want, 'grazing' a larger number of news sources rather than relying habitually on one, they still react to major events. The invasion of Iraq, the destruction of the World Trade Centre, the death and funeral of John Paul II, the Indian Ocean Tsunami, events such as these lead to intense peaks in viewing figures – especially for forms of continuous news delivery. The graph in Figure 1.4, for instance, shows television viewing on three channels in multichannel households – two of them 24-hour news – during the beginning of the Iraq war and the months preceding it. (The invasion of Iraq took place on 20th March, 2003.)

There are significant peaks, especially for Sky News and BBC News 24, to coincide with the invasion of Iraq in March 2003. During the war Sancho and Glover (2003) report:

> news viewing in analogue terrestrial homes rose by 84%, from 171 minutes per week to 315 minutes per week after war broke out ... [and] .... news viewing in cable and satellite homes underwent a huge 145% increase, up from an average of 118 minutes per week prior to the outbreak of war, to 289 minutes.
>
> (Sancho and Glover, 2003, p. 5)

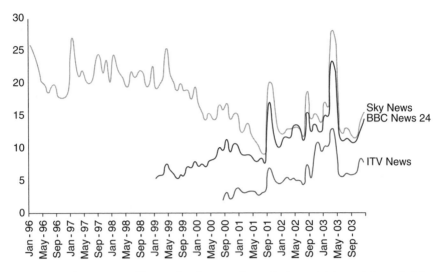

Figure 1.4 Average weekly reach of news channels in multichannel households, 1996–2003 (Source: OfCom).

So, despite evidence that audiences for broadcast news may show some signs of fragmenting in the wake of digitisation and with the rise of a multi-channel environment, the overall picture continues to be one in which television and radio together remain the primary means for communicating the news to the general public. And the largest audiences by far are still for prime-time bulletin news programmes provided by the networks (in the USA) or by the main broadcasting channels (in the UK). There is little sign that this situation will change in the immediate future.

1.6   Conclusion

Given the significance attached to broadcast news both by audiences and by broadcasters, there is a compelling case for devoting its discourse to the same degree of careful analysis as has been devoted to the language of newspapers. The focus in this study, therefore, will be on bulletin news of the kind carried by major terrestrial broadcasting channels. This is the news that most people see or hear and that most are familiar with: it is the main source of the news for most of the people most of the time. Accordingly, while some attention is given to rolling news, as well as to extended magazine news programmes, many of the examples in this book are drawn from prime-time half-hour news bulletin programmes such as those on BBC One at 6.00 p.m. or 10.00 p.m. or ITV at 1.30 p.m., 6.30 p.m. or 10.30 p.m. These are, admittedly, by no means all the news that gets broadcast; and 24-hour dedicated news channels have clearly become an increasingly significant form of news output. Indeed, there are signs that bulletin news is beginning to assimilate to itself some of the discursive practices of rolling news. Nonetheless the dominant model of broadcast news discourse remains, and may be found most clearly in, bulletin news. While print journalism may be easily available for analysis, this is hardly a reason to allow it to catch our undivided analytical attention, especially since broadcast news is without doubt the primary mode of communicating knowledge about the world of the present and passing moment.

2   Broadcast news and discourse analysis

2.0   Introduction

There are several possible ways of studying broadcast news as discourse and this book will draw upon more than one tradition of research. The main traditions of work represented here will include (socio-)linguistics (discourse, genre and pragmatic analysis)[1], sociology (conversation and interactional analysis)[2], media studies (the study of broadcast talk)[3] and a body of interdisciplinary research now known as critical discourse analysis[4]. The goal of analysing the discourse of broadcast news is to display its structure as situated communicative action under conditions of mediation in the specialised domain of news broadcasting. The pursuit of this goal resembles the long-established sociolinguistic and ethnographic concern with 'who speaks what, to whom, when, and how?' (see Hymes, 1977/2001; Saville-Troike, 2003); but it is explored here in relation to a communicative situation that involves much more than spontaneous speech, in which it is difficult to define the limits on audience, in which the technical possibilities for recording and relaying communication have been significantly and rapidly enhanced and in which graphic and visual elements play a powerful and integrated role. Such complexities pose challenges to any descriptive schema and it is difficult to meet the demands of the task without resorting to the insights of more than one discipline or research tradition. Nonetheless, at the heart of the complexity is a communicative act, broadcast news, that is daily experienced and easily recognised as fluent, intelligible versions of the world. The aim of analysis is to display how this is accomplished, by attempting to answer the question of how the communicative parts hold together in a meaningful and intentional fashion in a unified act of communication.

Stated in this fashion, the aim of analysis may seem narrowly descriptive when applied to the news, which – given its high status as a form of public discourse – is often subject to critique. Indeed, most reflective commentary on the discourse of broadcast news – whether from the theoretically informed perspective of academic research or from the more informal perspective of the engaged audience – concentrates on issues of bias, (mis)representation, inaccuracy, distortion, ideology, 'dumbing-down' and the selective construction of reality. In its most distilled form, comment can be reduced to the criticism that the news does not reflect or construct the world truthfully; rather it constructs the world in such a way as to conform to an image shaped by partial interests – typically those of the powerful.

These are clearly fundamental issues to address in relation to such a salient public genre. Often, however, they are raised with only very selective attention to the discourse itself, which is treated as if its primary or only purpose was accurately to map reality. But discourse – language in use – does much more than map reality and convey information. A common thread that runs through the separate traditions of research cited at the beginning of this chapter is that discourse is a mode of interaction, a bridge between self and other, as well as a mode of representation – even in the case of the news where the latter function seems so strongly foregrounded. Thus, exploring the discourse of broadcast news entails much more than examining it as a mode of constructing reality and mediating the world. It means taking seriously its full communicative potential as a mode of interaction constitutive of its audience at the same time as it depicts or constructs reality.

Indeed, many of the criticisms of broadcast news require or presuppose a much more rounded examination of it as discourse in order to be effective: the focus on bias, for instance, may be seen as giving priority to the representational at the expense of the social-relational. Scannell (1998) identifies two contrasting stances that may be adopted by research on language and the media. One he describes as a hermeneutics of suspicion and the other as a hermeneutics of trust. The hermeneutics of suspicion assumes as its starting point that "the media and language are both systems of representation that, in ordinary practice and use, misrepresent the reality which they re-present" (p. 256). By contrast a hermeneutics of trust approaches language and media as social phenomena "– as things that simply, routinely and ordinarily *work* (whether for or against human interests is not, *in the first instance*, at issue)" (p. 257). The task for the researcher in the latter case is to display the kind of work being done and show how it is done. The two lines of inquiry may seem at first sight opposed to each other; but the hermeneutics of trust versus suspicion may be viewed as complementary. If we wish to understand and explain the news as a phenomenon we need thorough analysis of how it works. Criticism of the news is best conducted on the basis of adequate description of its discourse in which the full range of its communicative purposes is captured. The remainder of this chapter is devoted to core concepts in the study of discourse on which the analyses in succeeding chapters depend.

2.1 The linguistic approach to discourse analysis

From the perspective of linguistics, discourse is patterning of language beyond and between sentences (or utterances). Discourse from this perspective is a discrete level of linguistic organisation similar to sound patterning (studied as phonology) or sentence structure (studied as syntax). Indeed, some approaches to discourse analysis (Coulthard and Brazil, 1992; Sinclair and Coulthard, 1975; Stubbs, 1983; Willis, 1992) extrapolate analytic methods from the description of other levels of linguistic organisation and extend them upwards to the domain of inter-sentential patterning. And, more generally, a fundamental premise of (linguistic) discourse analysis is that principles of linguistic organisation do not stop with the sentence but shape the way we combine sentences together into discourse.

There is still debate about the exact nature of these principles of organisation that govern the shaping of utterances or sentences into discourse. One of the founding proponents of linguistically oriented discourse analysis posed the problem thus: "The fundamental problem of discourse analysis is to show how one utterance follows another in a rational, rule-governed manner – in other words, how we understand coherent discourse" (Labov, 1972, p. 252). And several decades later the question is not neatly resolved (see, for example, Widdowson, 2004). Since the beginnings of work on the linguistic organisation of discourse most researchers have been at pains to point out that morphological, lexical or syntactic links between one sentence or utterance and another are not sufficient to account for coherence in discourse. For instance the following turns between the interviewer (BBC's Jeremy Paxman) and a politician (Michael Howard) are coherent as discourse even without obvious lexical, morphological or syntactic cues or links between one turn and the next:

Ext. 2.1.1
1 PAXMAN: so the the choice at this election
2   between you and Mr Blair is between (.)
3   a leader who supports a war (.)
4   and has sway in the White House (.)
5   and a leader who supported the war
6   and has no sway in the White House (.)
7 HOWARD: I would have (.) a perfectly good working relationship
8   with with President Bush
9 PAXMAN: [they won't even let you in through the door=
10 HOWARD: =look if I'm the Prime Minister of this country ... .

The coherence of the exchange depends upon recognising that the initial turn by the interviewer (ll. 1–6) is a kind of question and that the initial turn by the politician is a kind of answer to that question. But the surface signals of these actions are not clear. The turn by the interviewer does not contain formal grammatical markers of a question and the turn by the interviewee has few overt lexical (or grammatical) links with the prior question. If the exchange had proceeded along the following lines the explanation of its coherence would be easier.

Ext. 2.1.2
1 PAXMAN: given the fact that
2   the White House was closed to you on a recent visit to Washington
3   if you became Prime Minister
4   what kind of working relationship
5   would you have with President Bush?
6 HOWARD: I would have (.) a perfectly good working relationship
7   with with President Bush
8 PAXMAN: [they won't even let you in through the door=

Here the politician's turn is in direct response to a turn marked grammatically as a question ('what … would you have …'); and there is close grammatical and lexical overlap between the two turns in the repetition of the expressions 'would have', 'working relationship' and 'with President Bush'. The exchange is thus not just coherent but also cohesive in its surface forms. The original extract (2.1.1), however, is not cohesive in this way at all – even though it is perfectly coherent. For it to be heard as coherent, elaborate inferential machineries must be invoked in order to explain how Paxman's declarative is really a question (or challenge) and that "a working relationship with President Bush" has some kind of semantic equivalence with "holding sway with the White House", so that invoking the latter can be heard as a riposte to the challenge of lacking the former.

Because inferential machineries may need to be invoked to explain the relationship between turns, discourse analysis necessarily lies at the interface of the linguistic and the social. Indeed, when elaborating the principles of organisation that underpin the coherence of discourse, it is difficult if not impossible to disentangle the social from the linguistic – especially when studying spoken dialogic or interactional discourse, as opposed to the extended monologic discourse of writing or lengthy speeches. And yet the challenges of spoken discourse as an area of inquiry are important precisely because language itself as a system of communication arises out of social and verbal interaction.

2.2   Discourse as social action

It is difficult to disentangle the linguistic from the social, primarily because the founding insight of discourse analysis is that language is a form of action, a way of 'doing things with words' (Austin, 1962). This is a different emphasis from our everyday models of language which conceptualise it primarily as providing a map or representation of reality. When, however, language is seen as a form of action, mapping or constructing reality becomes one form of action among many. Language does not simply inform or depict, but provides the means to compliment, thank, joke, promise, insult, greet, announce, boast, and so on. These are actions that we perform in discourse, sometimes – as in the case of greeting or departing – with little referential or propositional content. Language is the action; and it is difficult to conceive how promising or apologising or insulting could else be done except in words. But while such actions depend completely on language for their performance they are also underpinned by social content and structure. For one thing, the performance of an action through linguistic means is dependent on features of context in which the utterance takes place: the same utterance may realise different actions in different contexts. In addition, the actions have a social impetus, shape and influence and in themselves constitute the building blocks of social interaction. When discourse is seen from the perspective of action as well as – or including – representation it is seen as constitutive of social relationships. In the terminology of Halliday, it is interpersonal in its function as much as ideational (Halliday, 1978, 1985).

Doing things with words includes actions such as announcing, reporting, greeting, challenging and so on, all of which are characteristic of the discourse of the news. But in addition there are significant elements of broadcast news discourse that are devoted to managing the discourse itself. There is a high degree of metadiscursivity, discursive reflexivity and intertextuality. There are various reasons for this – but perhaps a key determinant resides in the tightly regulated nature of the production context in which broadcast news discourse is situated. Broadcast news, especially in bulletin programmes, must run to schedule; and the discourse must work to fit this schedule. Thus, key discourse actions include attention to the temporally constrained nature of the discursive regime as, for instance, in moves such as, "that's all we have time for today". Closings to communicative events may be arbitrarily enforced: "I'm sorry I'm going to have to cut you off there". Moreover, some aspects of discursive management and reflexivity are related to the publicly sensitive and sometimes contested nature of news discourse, particularly in interview: "that is being frank with the electorate is it?"; "is that a yes or a no?"; "It's a question to which you could give a yes or no answer Prime Minister"; "Yeah, but it's maybe not a question you need to give a yes or no answer to." For reasons such as these, the kinds of action performed in the discourse of broadcast news are not only interpersonal or social-interactional but textual to a significant extent.

2.3   Discourse practice

Discourse acts do not take place in isolation but as part of chains of action in which individual acts are shaped in the light of the preceding or succeeding acts, one act played off against another: questions set up implications for answers, jokes anticipate laughter, headlines introduce bulletins. Discourse unfolds in time as collaborative activity between interlocutors and between producers and their audience. To some extent the state of the discourse at any one point in time will be unique and its evolution unpredictable: the news stories of the day should by definition be 'new'. But at another level the discourse of broadcast news – like any institutionalised discourse – runs along well-worn grooves. Certain sequences of action are produced over and over again. News bulletin programmes, for instance, always have headlines and greetings near their onset. News reporters nearly always 'sign off' their reports in protocols such as, "Brent Sadler, CNN, Grozny". Interviewees are always introduced: "With me on the line from Westminster is the opposition spokesperson for education". Such practices may seem relatively devoid of content. Who, after all, really notes that the voice over the report has been Brent Sadler, that he's been working for CNN and the location of the voice has been Grozny? Such routines, however, are part of the way in which closing a report or opening an interview gets done. In themselves they may not seem too highly wrought an interactional accomplishment but they are sedimented solutions to a range of interactional problems such as coordinating the transition from pre-recorded news material to the next item in a sequence. They are part of the way in which utterances and actions follow another in broadcast news in an intelligible fashion. Some of the most obvious and recognisable discourse practices can be associated with the peculiar difficulties of a communicative event that is assembled from discourses – some 'live', some recorded – that are dispersed across space and time and that must be managed as a self-contained whole within a predetermined slot in a broadcast schedule. But other discourse practices constitute almost naturalised and imperceptible routines. An example of this would be the practice of 'withholding' receipt tokens during news interviews as a way of maintaining neutrality (Heritage and Greatbach, 1991), discussed in more detail in Chapter 7. Discourse practices may be defined, then, as the regular sequential arrangement of recognisably similar discourse acts to serve institutionalised communicative purposes.

2.4 Discourse structure

The discourse of broadcast news can be seen as a structured set of discourse units, in which smaller units, such as discourse acts, cohere into larger units such as completed news items or interactional exchanges within a news interview. In the context of a news interview, for instance, discourse acts such as questions implicate answers; and these together may cohere as an exchange within the interview. Structures, therefore, build in terms of constituency upward from smaller to larger units (or conversely larger units may be regarded as analysable in terms of combinations of smaller units). Thus, broadcast news may be described in terms of the discourse acts (such as a headline) which combine together to form news presentation or news report; and these may be described as units which combine together with other units to make up the bulletin news programme. (Alternatively, the news programme may be treated as a whole divisible into progressively smaller units.) Whether the discourse is seen in terms of the largest unit broken down into smaller units or building from the smaller to the larger is simply a choice in the procedure of description. Either way, however, the discourse is conceptualised as the articulation of elements which are tacitly recognised by users of news as a genre (whether they be producers or consumers) as part of the routinely well-formed way of putting it together. This sense of structure pervades the discourse up and down the scale of units and is particularly salient around their boundaries. Anyone who is engaged in news programme making as a participant and anyone who watches or listens to much news knows, for instance, when a two-way interview between studio presenter and correspondent is coming to a close – and this before the close is reached – partly through the temporal rhythms of news programmes but also because of a series of paralinguistic signals 'given off' by the correspondent – signals such as slowing and descending through the pitch range. And, of course, some transitions around the boundaries of some units are explicitly lexicalised in standard phrases such as, "**We now go to our correspondent in Shanghai, Lindsey Hulsum**". Members of the community of practice of broadcast news, both producers and audience, orient to news as a discursive construct, in which parts fit together into a discursive whole; and if the parts do not fit together in recognisably well-formed ways the intelligibility and coherence of the enterprise is at risk.

2.5   Discourse genre

A genre of discourse is a specific and recognisable configuration of discourse elements realising a particular communicative purpose or set of purposes and usually known amongst a language community by a widely shared label, such as 'advert', 'sermon', 'gossip', 'joke', 'lecture'. 'News' is one such genre. The label is widely understood; and instances of broadcast news are instantly identifiable as such to audiences. Indeed, as suggested in Chapter 1, news has claims to be the most widely dispersed and understood discourse genre of modern times. There are, it must be noted, generic variations between radio news and TV news and between bulletin news and rolling news. And in any case news as a genre is woven out of sub-genres such as the news report, the news interview, or the news headline. Indeed, the structural composition of news discourse may be seen in terms of the chaining together of units each of which is realised by a different sub-genre. Like structure, genre as a concept also faces two ways. "The constructional value of each and every element of a work can be understood only in relation to genre ... It is genre that gives shape and meaning to ... a whole entity, and to all the elements of which that entity is comprised" (Medvedev, 1928, quoted in Titunik, 1973).

Genre is both the stabilisation or sedimentation of a particular set of discourse practices and the enabling framework from which discursive change and innovation take place. Indeed, a major source of difficulty in defining and applying the term genre is that some genres, at least, are unstable, in flux, with the boundaries dividing one from another tending to be indeterminate. In print journalism, for example, the notion of a 'news piece' is understood as generically opposed to 'feature'. The latter tends to be longer, less compressed, with less emphasis on current incident, more personal, with more focus on human interest and with greater allowance for the personal viewpoint of the journalist. Despite this there seems to be no contradiction involved in describing hybrid or intermediate cases as a 'news feature'.

So genre describes more than a patterned, recurrent configuration of elements or unit but also encompasses shared understandings between producers and audiences about forms and the purposes they serve. In this sense although genre is textually manifested in discourse it may also be considered a process beyond the discourse itself involving a promise, by producers, and recognition, by audiences, of the type of discursive activity being performed. Genre is a set of generative and interpretative procedures, a 'horizon of expectations' (Todorov, 1990, p. 18) against which any specific generic instance must be set[5].

While genre is at once the sedimentation and routinisation of a set of practices and a backdrop against which innovation and change can take place, it should also be noted that well-defined discourse genres such as the lecture, the sermon, the debate, legal cross-examination, or the medical consultation are often embedded in strongly institutionalised domains of social life such as medicine, education, law, politics and religion. They derive their purpose from their institutional position, at the same time as being the discursive embodiment of the institution. The productivity of genres, however, also allows for their migration across domains as models for newly discovered communicative purposes. Thus 'the lecture', 'the debate' and 'cross-examination', which have all had a life in broadcasting (Scannell and Cardiff, 1991), sometimes become transformed into new genres such as the studio discussion or the political interview.

2.6   Discourse domain

Discourse genres arise in discourse domains. The notion of discourse domain overlaps with the well-established sociolinguistic or ethnographic interest in 'context' (of situation) or 'setting' (see Malinowski, 1946; Firth, 1957; Halliday, 1978; Hymes, 2001; Saville-Troike, 2003). It has long been accepted that language or discourse is a contextualised activity and that any instance of discourse or language in use bears the trace of its context. The notion of discourse domain builds upon this insight but seeks to take account of the way in which an increasing range of contexts – especially in modern societies – have become institutionalised. It seeks also to acknowledge the way in which discourse is increasingly embedded in settings or contexts characterised not by immediate spatial co-presence but by mediation.

A discourse domain may be defined as an institutionalised area of social life dependent upon recognisably distinct discourse practices and genres. Law, politics, medicine, religion and journalism are all discourse domains to the degree that they involve institutionalised practices that take discursive form. In some cases the domain may be constituted in part by particular spatio-temporal configurations: activity within the domain takes place embedded within semiotically infused arenas incorporating symbolic and material elements which perform the same kind of proxemic and organisational work from one occasion to another: one thinks of the lecture theatre, the law court, the classroom, or even the hospital ward. But the notion of domain can be applied to institutional configurations that transcend the limitations of physical location because of the possibilities for the dissemination and exchange of messages effected by mechanical reproduction and, more recently, digitalised communication. In domains such as literature, broadcasting, film, or advertising the discourse takes shape for the most part under conditions of mediation rather than embedded in immediate co-presence, with the moment of consumption temporally or spatially separated from the moment of consumption. In all cases, however, what marks a domain as a domain is its institutionalised character.

Although the defining characteristic of a discursive domain is that it is constituted in and by discourse, the domain itself is informed and shaped by social practices that are partly discursive and partly extra-discursive. In other words, domains assume their characteristic disposition from a variety of supporting practices, some of which may be economic or technological in character. Performance in domains is stipulated to some degree in advance, often by training, so that repertoires of behaviour become specialised and pre-specified and are differentially allocated to participants whose roles in domains may become narrowly defined. Broadcast journalism as a domain, for instance, at present depends upon the demarcation of roles (e.g. 'presenter', 'reporter', 'correspondent', 'editor' and so on) and relies upon the routine enactment and deployment of quite specific genres (for instance, the report, the interview, or the discussion) which incorporate practices influenced by regulatory and commercial pressures, enabled by certain kinds of technology (the satellite phone, for instance, or the autocue) and shaped by specific characteristics of the arrangements for production and consumption. Discursive domains are thus held in place by a variety of institutional supports (e.g. training) and pressures (e.g. economic, commercial and regulatory).

2.7   Order of discourse

The mutual interaction of discourse practice, discourse genre and domain constitute an overarching 'order of discourse' (Foucault, 1966/1970/2001, 1969/1972/2002; Fairclough, 1995, 2003; Mills, 2004). There is an interlocking relationship between these different layers of abstraction, between action, practice, structure, genre and domain. The discourse domain specifies and produces the range of genres that we find within it. Genres are stipulated in part by the kinds of structure that occur within them. Structures are constituted in terms of sequences of particular kinds of practice and these in turn are composed by particular selections from the total repertoire of discourse acts. In this way the separate layers within an order of discourse interact, so that any specific discursive component carries within it the imprint of the whole. A simple discourse fragment such as " / Matt Frei / BBC News / Washington / " spoken as three tone units in a descending pitch sequence, is instantly recognisable as a fragment of a news programme. It is, in short, completely sui generis and will not be confused by habitués of the domain (whether audience or producers) with the output of any other order of discourse. As a fragment it is multiply generated by the action of the discrete layers. At the level of discourse action it is: self-identification + news organisation identification + locational formulation. At the level of discourse structure and prosody it clearly signals a closing. At the level of genre it is part of the distinctive way in which reports from the reporter in the field return the discourse to the studio. The fragment is thus a projection of the detailed specifications of the differing layers of broadcast news discourse. The interlocking layers combine in its production and in so doing generate it as the output of an overarching order of discourse – the discourse of broadcast news.

2.8   Participation framework and broadcast news

Broadcast news as a particular order of discourse embedded within a discursive domain places users of the discourse in a distinctive set of roles. Unlike simple dialogic speech situations which involve minimally a speaker and a hearer, with recurring alternation of roles between the two, broadcast news takes shape out of complex production formats and participation frameworks (Goffman, 1981) in which the discourse is sometimes scripted, sometimes relatively spontaneous, sometimes spoken, sometimes written, sometimes written to be spoken, sometimes single-authored, sometimes multiply authored, sometimes dialogue and sometimes monologue. From the perspective of the shaping of the utterance, Goffman (1981) usefully distinguishes between 'author', 'animator' and 'principal'. The author is the one who has "selected the sentiments that are being expressed and the words in which they are encoded". The animator is the one who gives voice to the words that have been selected, sometimes by someone else. The principal is whoever is potentially held to account for the sentiments expressed. In many situations the three roles coalesce; but in bulletin news programmes, for instance, the presenter who reads the news from the autocue may merely be animating a script authored elsewhere, by the editorial team, and the ultimately accountable source for the discourse – the principal – may be the organisation itself. Thus, in the case of a BBC bulletin it may be the director general or members of the board of trustees who resign their positions should a bulletin be called into question and not necessarily the news editor and certainly not the news presenter[6].

And, just as various alignments are possible in terms of the production of broadcast news discourse, important distinctions apply in its reception where the potential participation framework is equally complex. As Goffman observes: "an utterance does not carve up the world beyond the speaker into precisely two parts, recipients and non-recipients, but rather opens up an array of structurally differentiated possibilities, establishing the participation framework in which the speaker will be guiding his delivery" (Goffman, 1981, p. 137). Broadcast news is oriented to its audience in at least two distinct ways. While the overarching order of discourse is for an audience in the 'mass', with a potential reach of several million, parts of the discourse may well be conducted as interchanges between direct interlocutors. Discourse of this type may take place within the studio between a presenter and an 'editor' or 'reporter', between a presenter and an interviewee, but it may also take place between the studio and the news field in the form of live two-way exchanges. We may thus distinguish between discourse between immediate interlocutors that is designed to be 'overheard' by the broadcast audience (vox pops, for instance) and discourse that is directly and solely addressed to it (headlines, for example). Thus, in posing an interview question to an interviewee, the discourse of the interviewer is bidirectional. It is oriented in the first instance to the interviewee; but the design of the question will also be shaped by the assumed concerns of the broadcast audience beyond. Headlines, on the other hand, are designed exclusively for the broadcast audience. The switch between these two different kinds of orientation – the bidirectional and the unidirectional – may be described, in the terminology of Goffman, as a shift of footing which he describes as follows: "A change of footing implies a change in the alignment we take up to ourselves and others present as expressed in the way we manage the production or reception of an utterance" (1981, p. 128). When a news presenter switches within a news programme from reading the news to interviewing a correspondent or reporter about it there is a subtle but perceptible change of alignment. On television this may be marked by different visual arrangements and postural shifts; but in addition a different relation is adopted by the presenter to his or her utterance. The presenter moves for animating an utterance to apparently authoring it, from reading a script to speaking extempore, from address to the audience to address to a colleague. A comprehensive account of the discourse of broadcast news must take into account not only the patterns and structures of the discourse but also the complex participation framework of the news.

2.9   Scripted discourse and improvised discourse in broadcast news

The complex participation framework of the news entails shifts in footing and these in turn entail different kinds of utterance production, seen most basically in alterations in the degree of scriptedness. It is a known or widely assumed fact that large portions of news programmes are tightly scripted, and this for a variety of reasons. First of all, news bulletin programmes operate within the exacting constraints of the broadcast schedule. They are time-limited; and scripting is a way of ensuring that there is neither too little material (leading in extreme cases to 'dead air'[7]) nor too much for the allotted time slot in the schedule. Second, given the time constraints, speakers cannot afford to forget what they were going to say nor 'take time out' to plan the next piece. They need to be able to speak on cue and fluently to occupy the slot. Third, the discourse is to a mass public and governed by legal and statutory constraints (designed, for instance, to exclude libel and bias). For this reason prior scrutiny of the discourse will routinely occur in order to reduce the likelihood of legal redress. Scripting, therefore, is a way of reducing risks of various kinds – of inaccuracy, of temporal slippage, of legal challenge and so on.

Nonetheless, it is also clear that broadcast news discourse is not all scripted to the same extent. Interviews, live-two ways, certain kinds of studio-based exchange may be only loosely scripted and sometimes not at all. Limited departure from a script is possible as long is it does not compromise the overall timings of the programme. And sometimes, of course, critical and major news events can lead to the temporary suspension of the schedule and the waiving of time constraints. In the extreme case of some kinds of breaking news there may be insufficient time to prepare anything but a sketchy and limited script and broadcasters must resort to extempore and improvised speech. It is important, therefore, to recognise that various kinds of improvisatory departure from script are not only clearly present in the news but, especially in rolling news, increasingly salient. Their presence in this most careful of public discourses may further be seen as a necessary concession to those tendencies to informalisation and conversationalisation that are an increasing feature of all public discourse (discussed in Chapter 8).

The notion of scriptedness, of course, should not be restricted to the extreme case of reading aloud from a prepared text. There are fixed formulae for transitions between one phase, episode or footing and another – signatures and greetings, for instance. And there are various kinds of 'loose' scripting. In the case of interviews, for example, the questions may on occasion (though not always) be known or discussed in advance[8]; and some kinds of experienced interviewee have almost definitely rehearsed (like good exam candidates) the broad outlines of response to likely questions. Finally, certain kinds of news content tends to follow broad 'scripts' or schema. Narratives of survival, for instance, which featured in the news after the London bombings, independently tended to share certain common 'schematic' characteristics (see Chapter 7).

Degrees of scriptedness, therefore, become a feature of note in any study of the discourse of broadcast news, especially since variations in the reliance on a script interact with other considerations such as informalisation, shifts of footing and transitions from one kind of structural element of news discourse to another.

2.10   Modality and the speaker's alignment to the discourse

Modality in linguistics designates those resources available within language systems for expressing the speaker's attitude towards and assessment of the truth of the propositions being uttered. There are three main kinds of modality: deontic modality, epistemic modality and evidentiality. Most significant from the perspective of news discourse are evidentiality and epistemic modality[9]. Epistemic modality refers to the resources available within language to allow speakers to "signal stronger and weaker commitment to the factuality of statements" (Saeed, 1997, p. 125). Generally news discourse is assumed to be in a veridical relationship to the truth and so there is no need to modalise degrees of commitment to the factuality of its statements. Thus in the following example propositions are presented without attenuation of their claim to truth:

Ex. 2.10.1
President Hugo Chavez of Venezuela has won a third term in office, securing a clear lead over rival Manuel Rosales.

Epistemic modality choices in the example are unmarked and the proposition regarding the outcome of the election is offered as a simple statement of fact or averral.

Alternative choices in (epistemic) modality, however, could have expressed much weaker commitment to the assertion of the proposition, as the following examples illustrate.

Ex. 2.10.2
President Hugo Chavez of Venezuela *may* have won a third term in office ...

Ex. 2.10.3
President Hugo Chavez of Venezuela *might* have won a third term in office ...

Ex. 2.10.4
President Hugo Chavez of Venezuela has *possibly* won a third term in office ...

Ex. 2.10.5
President Hugo Chavez of Venezuela is *most likely* to have won a third term in office ...

The two main ways of registering doubts about the certainty of a proposition using marked epistemic modality are through modal verbs (such as *may* or *might*) and lexical expressions such as *probably, possibly, certainly,* and so on. By and large these are not particularly common in the presentational discourse of broadcast news.

However, where the voice of the institution in the discourse of broadcast news in the person of the presenter gives way to or interacts with reporters, correspondents, public figures or simply members of the public we find that assertions are much more prone to marked modality choices. These may include personal point of view prefaces such as "I think", "I guess", "I suppose" and various markers of evidentiality (Chafe and Nichols, 1986; Marriott, 2007). Evidentiality refers to those resources available to speakers for communicating degrees of reliability in the sources of information that may underpin an assertion. Different languages differ in the degree to which evidentiality is encoded within the grammar. But some of the distinctions habitually encoded include whether or not the factual basis of the proposition has been experienced directly by the speaker, whether it is an inference based on evidence, or whether it is 'quotative' – i.e. information supplied in a statement from another speaker. In the following example we have two clauses (a) and (b).

Ex. 2.10.6
(a) Pope Benedict has returned to Rome at the end of his first visit to a predominantly Muslim country
(b) having apparently successfully defused criticism that he views the Islamic faith as "violent".

The modality of the first clause (a) is mostly unmarked (except for *predominantly*) and its proposition about the return to Rome of the Pope is presented as a simple statement of fact. The modality of the second clause (b), however, is much more complex. There are at least four propositions embedded – Russian doll-like – in the clause. Beginning with the most embedded, these are:

> The Islamic faith is violent
> The Pope views the Islamic faith [as being violent]
> The Pope is criticised [for viewing the Islamic faith as violent]
> The Pope has successfully defused criticism [that he views the Islamic faith as violent]

However, the reliability of each proposition is governed in turn by the reliability of the next higher proposition in the chain. And here there are two main kinds of evidentiality at work in the way these propositions are asserted: the use of *apparently* and the quotative 'violent'. In the case of the latter, the quotative makes it uncertain whose word was *violent*. (And so the criticism that he views Islam as such to be violent may be seen as ill-founded.) In the case of the former, the use of *apparently* suggests that the claim (about criticism having been defused) is a matter of inference rather than fact. In this way, the modal complexity of the second clause provides answers to several kinds of objection that might be raised against the embedded propositions. Illustrative objections (with their associated defence) could be raised as follows:

(But) the Pope did <u>not</u> say in his own words that Islam is violent.
(Defence: *and that is why* 'violent' *is quotative*.)
(But) the criticism of the Pope was <u>not</u> successfully defused.
(Defence: *the text only claims* 'apparently'.)

Thus, the second clause with its modal complexity is one designed to anticipate various kinds of objection and guard against overstatement.

While this kind of intricate counterpoint about the epistemic and evidential status of propositions does occur in broadcast news, it tends particularly to be a feature of unscripted contributions by certain kinds of speaker in certain places in the structure of broadcast news. It is, for instance, most unlikely to occur in headlines. Generally, shifts in the patterning of modal choices – from unmarked to marked – overlap with shifts of footing and transitions from one phase of the news discourse to another. The closer the discourse approximates to the unqualified voice of the institution the more the modality choices become unmarked. This adoption of unmarked modality in the discourse of news presentation expresses its particular epistemological status: it is a public discourse striving to be beyond objection, authoritative (but almost 'authorless'), impersonal, neutral.

2.11   Institutionalised discourse roles and participation framework

The discourse of broadcast news occurs within a tightly defined domain to which access is regulated on the basis of certain kinds of entitlement. Not only are there temporal restrictions but also constraints on who can speak when and how. Access to the discourse is mostly restricted to professional news people, or to recognised public figures and members of the public endowed with a particular warrant to speak because of their involvement, as a participant or witness, in the news. Thus, topics and speakers are restricted to those featuring appropriately within the news agenda.

In both the UK and the USA there is a repertoire of professional, institutionalised roles or identities that figure in broadcast news. Perhaps the most salient is that of *Presenter*. Presenters typically are responsible for reading the news but they may also manage the transitions into and out of reports and interviews/discussions as well as conducting them. Other terms in widespread use are *Newscaster*, *Newsreader* and *Anchor*. In some kinds of programme, typically the news magazine programme, the roles of *News Presenter* and *Newsreader* may be separate. In UK news bulletin programmes, the role of *Presenter* usually subsumes that of *Newsreader*. In the USA *News Anchor* is the more common term for *News Presenter* but the nomenclature is not precisely interchangeable, since many *News Anchors* are also involved in writing and/or editing the news for their programmes to a greater degree than their British counterparts. In this book *Presenter* is used as the generic label for *Newscaster, Newsreader* and *Anchor*.

Other significant institutional roles are those of *Reporter, Correspondent* and *Editor*. All of these hold entitlements to speak in broadcast news programmes because of their professional affiliated status within the news organisation. In effect all act as an authorised conduit between the news organisation and the news event or field, though there are slight differences in status. In British usage the *Reporter* brings no particular expertise to bear upon the task except his or her journalistic skills and competence. A *Correspondent*, however, will have a specialised field of competence, or responsibility for a particular field, as in Arts Correspondent, Business Correspondent, Washington Correspondent or China Correspondent (see Schlesinger, 1978/1992, pp. 153–154). In the context of news broadcasting, both the BBC and ITN also use the term *Editor* for senior journalists with special expertise – as in World Affairs Editor, Foreign Affairs Editor, Political Editor, Senior Home Affairs Editor, Economics Editor and so on. Despite the 'back office' connotations of the term 'editor', these figures have speaking roles within the news programme. They are distinguished from *Reporters* and *Correspondents* by enjoying greater freedom to interpret and comment on the news sometimes in an extempore fashion.

The different professionalised roles or identities occupy different slots within the news discourse and have associated with them differing fashions of speaking. The genre or style of news presentation, for instance, is different from the genre or style of news editor/correspondent: one will tend to unmarked modality, the other to marked. In this sense there is a strong congruence between the institutionalised role or identity (e.g. *Reporter* or *Presenter*) and discourse role (doing 'news presentation' or reporting). A discourse role is a specific repertoire of discourse practices that have become normative for a specific slot in the news discourse. Presenters, for instance, 'aver' or 'assert' but rarely 'comment' or 'speculate', practices more appropriate to Correspondents or Editors. Although particular discourse roles may be coincident with particular institutional/professional roles and identities, it is worth separating them analytically because of occasions in practice when a single individual will rotate through a variety of roles. Thus, although it is rare, it is still possible for a single individual to function variously as reporter, correspondent and presenter as they move between programmes, each change demanding a difference in the ensemble or repertoire of discourse practices appropriate to the different discursive spaces or slots.

Changes in performative roles between different discourse slots in discourse structure overlap with alterations in degrees of scriptedness and with corresponding changes in terms of participation framework. *News presentation*, for instance, is largely, though not always, scripted; live two-ways between the *presenter* and the *correspondent/editor* are much less so. Throughout the news, therefore, there are changes of alignment towards the utterance and towards the audience. And these shifts of alignment or footing – alterations in the participation framework – from simply animating a script to speaking as a source of expertise and opinion correspond with alterations from one kind of discourse role to another (for instance, from presenting to interviewing or being interviewed). In this respect it is worth comparing ways in which speakers identify themselves or are identified in the context of broadcast news. A correspondent, for instance, as we noted earlier, is likely to self-identify by name and location in closing their report, as in " / Matt Frei / BBC news / Washington / ". News presenters, on the other hand, are less likely to do so, although they may well be identified by caption near the onset of the programme and/or by voice-over from an unseen continuity announcer: "This is the ITV lunchtime news with Katie Derham and . . . ." Thus, *news presentation* is conducted in the voice, transcendently, of the broadcast institution, whereas the words spoken by the *Correspondent* belong to a greater degree to them as well as to the institution.

2.12 Summary

This chapter has outlined some of the core concepts for the study of broadcast news as discourse. The relationships between them may be summarised schematically as follows:

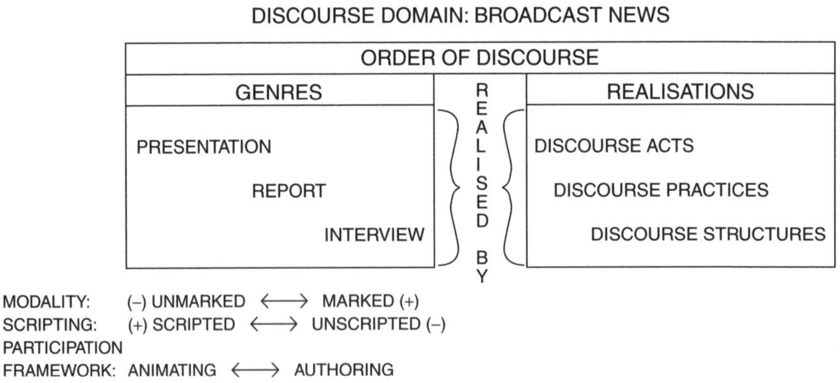

DISCOURSE DOMAIN: BROADCAST NEWS

ORDER OF DISCOURSE			
GENRES		R E A L I S E D	REALISATIONS
PRESENTATION			DISCOURSE ACTS
	REPORT		DISCOURSE PRACTICES
		INTERVIEW	DISCOURSE STRUCTURES
		B Y	

MODALITY: (–) UNMARKED ⟷ MARKED (+)
SCRIPTING: (+) SCRIPTED ⟷ UNSCRIPTED (–)
PARTICIPATION
FRAMEWORK: ANIMATING ⟷ AUTHORING

Figure 2.1 Components of a discourse model for broadcast news.

2.13 Conclusion

News is a textual phenomenon. It takes shape in words – in news presentation, reports and interviews. It is also offered to the public on a variety of platforms, purveyed in a variety of media, each of which constitutes audiences for its words in quite different ways. Each medium has its own particular verbal preferences, its own protocols and its own kinds of verbal economy. Broadcast news, through the radio or television bulletin reaching indeterminately large audiences, adopts and draws from a particular set of verbal repertoires which constitute its distinctive order of discourse. This book examines the particular discursive practices through which news is broadcast and in so doing describes how broadcast news functions as an order of discourse. In the following chapters we look at different aspects of the order of discourse of broadcast news beginning with the structure of news programmes and then considering in turn news presentation, news reports and news interviews.

3   The discourse structure of broadcast news

3.0   Introduction: broadcast news and discourse structure

Bulletin news unfolds as a sequence of elements where strong constraints govern the order in which elements can occur: as work by van Dijk (1988a and b), Bentele (1985) and Haarman (1999) would suggest, not anything can happen in any order. Thus, there is a clear expectation that headlines will precede studio presentation of items and that reports will be introduced from the studio (not vice versa). It is not just that the separate structural elements of a news programme will be intrinsically different from each other (headlines, for instance, are recognisably different from reports) but that the elements are defined in part by their place in sequence.

The movement from one element to another will often necessitate quite deliberate discursive work to signpost the transition – from, for instance, the news *presentation* of an item to a *report* from a *correspondent* or a *live two-way*. The following example shows a news presenter managing the transition to a *live two-way* with a *correspondent*.

Ex. 3.0.1
1 PRESENTER: well our correspondent Stephen Sachar was at that court hearing
2   this afternoon
3   we can talk to him now in Sweden

Thus, the way in which the news unfolds as an ordered sequence of elements is often the focus of deliberate discursive work at their boundaries. This chapter will frequently rely upon this discursive work in offering an analysis of the discourse structure of broadcast news.

If news on television and radio can be considered an *order of discourse*, it is one composed of interrelated *genres* and *sub-genres*, each associated with elements within a temporally unfolding whole. The structure of news discourse is most marked in examples of the half-hour scheduled *bulletin programmes* where the news of the day is given some kind of comprehensive but summary treatment. It is most fluid – least marked – in the 24-hours running news programme where temporal constraints are relatively relaxed, especially in response to a breaking story or item. The 24-hour, running-news channel may be seen as characterised by open (relatively flexible) discourse structures, whereas the scheduled half-hour programmes are characterised by closed (relatively rigid) discourse structures. In what follows we consider the closed type of structure first, before moving on to consider more flexible, less constrained types of structure.

3.1 The overall discourse structure of a news bulletin programme

The overall discourse structure of a news programme can be stated in the most basic terms as follows. The programme opens with signature opening visuals, followed by headlines, which in turn are followed by a succession of discrete news items, and concludes with a signing off from the presenter followed by closing visuals and credits. In one common variant the opening headlines precede or are embedded within the opening visuals in a structure which can be stated formally as follows[1].

NEWS PROGRAMME

OPENING SIGNATURE VISUALS + HEADLINES (+ SIGNATURE VISUALS) + NEWS ITEMS(1-N) + CLOSING VISUALS

An alternative to this variant opens the programme with the headlines, elevating them to the first place in the structure as follows.

NEWS PROGRAMME

HEADLINES + OPENING SIGNATURE VISUALS + NEWS ITEMS(1-N) + CLOSING VISUALS

The core elements of a news programme, of course, are the *news items*; and these in turn display a regular structure. The essential details of each *news item* are delivered by a *presenter* (or *newscaster*) usually in a studio setting; and these may then be elaborated in a pre-recorded *news report* from a *reporter/correspondent*. The *news item* may then conclude with a *two-way interview* with the *correspondent*, usually in the field but sometimes in the studio.

The essential details of the *news item* presented from the studio may be termed the *news kernel*. In structural terms this element is obligatory, whereas the other elements of the *news item*, the *report* and the *two-way*, are subsidiary, or optional, and dependent on the prior *kernel*.

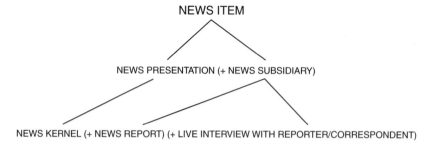

Thus, a *news item* consists minimally of *news presentation* of a *news kernel* typically delivered from the studio by the *news presenter*:

1. NEWS ITEM ➡ NEWS PRESENTATION

It may also consist of a sequence composed of a *news presentation* of a *news kernel* from the studio, coupled with additional optional subsidiary material in the form of a *news report*.

1a. NEWS ITEM ➡ {NEWS PRESENTATION (+ NEWS SUBSIDIARY)}

where

2. NEWS PRESENTATION ➡ NEWS KERNEL
3. NEWS SUBSIDIARY   ➡ NEWS REPORT

This sequence may be elaborated by adding a live *two-way interview* with the news *reporter* (whose voice typically will have provided commentary in the news report).

3a. NEWS SUBSIDIARY ➡ {NEWS REPORT + (LIVE 2WAY INTERVIEW)}

In these statements of structure, sequential constraints are implicated. Thus, it is not possible within the standard grammar of television bulletin news to begin a *news item* directly with an *interview* between *studio presenter* and *newsreporter*. In other words, a live *two-way interview* or a *report* **must** be preceded by studio presentation. At one level, this sequential constraint reflects the simple requirement to contextualise a news interview for the broadcast audience – to provide in some way for its relevance 'now' at this point in the programme. But it could also be seen as reflecting the hierarchy of news discourse – that all of the voices of the news are subordinate to its institutional voice delivered from the regular deictic zero point of enunciation, the news studio. Thus we do **not** find sequences such as the following –

*NEWS ITEM ➡ NEWS SUBSIDIARY {LIVE 2WAY/INTERVIEW + NEWS REPORT} + NEWS KERNEL

On the other hand, it is possible (and increasingly common) to embed a *news report* within a live *two-way interview* between the *news presenter* and the *news correspondent/reporter*. In other words the *news item* can be introduced by the *news presenter* from the studio and followed by a *two-way interview* with the *reporter/correspondent* which is then used in turn to introduce a video-recorded *report*. The item then concludes with a resumption of the *two-way interview*. Thus, in these cases the subsidiary element takes a rather different form –

NEWS SUBSIDIARY ➡ LIVE 2WAY< NEWS REPORT >

Overall, then, broadcast news as discourse is highly structured: it unfolds as the accomplishment of predictable sequences of discourse activities, each one differentiated from another. Indeed, the transition from one place in sequence to another is itself an occasional focus of the discourse. This may be seen most obviously in those utterances which explicitly project forward in the programme's structure, such as: "... coming up later in the programme ..." or "... after the break ..."

But it can also be seen in those micro-details of the discourse which have a punctuative role such as prosodic markers involving pace and pitch.

3.2   Opening the news bulletin programme

News programmes, even when they occupy a fixed, recurrent position within the schedule of a mixed programme channel, rarely arrive without some prior notice. A continuity announcer quite typically will mark the transition from the prior programme in the schedule to the news programme with the following kind of announcement, taking place **before** the news programme begins.

Ext. 3.2.1
CONTINUITY ANNOUNCER:
[shot of zen martial arts exercise against background of Scottish scenery with dreamy flute melody and voice-over]

1	This is BBC One Scotland.
2	Now the news and reporting Scotland
3	with Fiona Bruce and Jackie Bird.
4	It's ten o'clock.

The continuity announcement serves various functions. In the first instance, this utterance is about identification – of present channel, of upcoming programme, of upcoming speaker(s), and of present time. Second, however, it is about punctuation – signalling where we have reached in the flow of the schedule. Third, it is about temporal projection. Strictly speaking, there are still seconds remaining to *The News* and to the time of ten o'clock. The announcement, however, anticipates the event, making possible certain kinds of elliptical opening when the programme itself does actually begin. The opening signature visuals and title logo, for instance, can be moved 'down' the sequence (as noted above). Instead, the news programme can be made to open with a summary of the lead *news item* and *headlines* as happens in this extract (with the headlines here interspersed with a signature drum beat) as follows:

Ext. 3.2.1 (Continued)

5 PRESENTER: Sir Mark Thatcher is charged
6   in connection with an alleged plot to stage a coup.
7   The son of Margaret Thatcher's accused of helping a bid
8   to topple the government of Equatorial Guinea in West Africa.
9   After appearing in court he's now under house arrest in South Africa.
10   He says he's innocent of all the charges.
11   Also tonight
12   Drum beats: ♪ ♪
13   Russia investigates whether terrorists caused two passenger jets to crash.
14   Drum beats: ♪ ♪
15   The head of British Airways tells us
16   he's sorry for the chaos but the cost-cutting must go on.
17   Drum beats: ♪ ♪
18   And the cyclist who's become the first British man in nearly a century
19   to win three medals at the same Olympics.
20   Drum beats: ♪ ♪

These headlines alternate between a mid-shot of the presenter reading a news summary or headline in direct address to camera and a clip of exemplary news footage to support the statement. The visual elements are thus in contrapuntal rhythm – a shot of studio news presentation alternating with a shot of the news field. The signature visuals themselves, the theme tune and logo then follow, with the programme already in flow.

Network news in the UK also features a segment at the end of the programme with items broadcast to local audiences in the English regions or from Scotland, Wales or N. Ireland. Headlines for these items follow the main headlines at the beginning of the programme. In the case of Scotland, for instance, their headlines follow those from London with the same signature tune and background drum roll, as follows:

Ext. 3.2.1 (Continued)

21 PRESENTER: And here in Scotland:
22   guilty of one of the worst-ever wild-life crimes yet
23   this game keeper is allowed to walk free from court.

24	Drum beats: ♪ ♪
25	And bullying:
26	why is there a huge increase
27	in the number of school-children calling Help-line?
28	Drum beats: ♪ ♪

Although, these are conventionally described as headlines, there are several differences between broadcast headlines and newspaper headlines. In the latter case there is an immediate and close spatial juxtaposition of headline and story, with the newspaper headline acting as invitation to read whatever story is adjacent to it or 'headed' by it. In the case of broadcast headlines, however, there may be an interruption of several minutes between a headline and its corresponding news item. For this reason, they are better understood as news item 'trailers', projecting forward temporally into the programme, providing clues to its overall structure and providing the audience with reason to keep viewing or listening.

It is noticeable that most of the temporal marking at the beginning of the programme – especially tense, for example – draws everything into the immediate present. In Extract 3.2.1 above, for instance, we find:

This **is** … **Now** … It**'s** ten o'clock … **is** charged … **is** accused … he**'s now** under house arrest … he **says** … Russia **investigates** … the head of B.A. **tells** us … this game-keeper **is** allowed to walk..

Headlines are followed by signature music, signature graphics and logo (such as spinning globe or map) which blend channel-identification with notions of both time and space. In Figure 3.1 we see the signature graphics and logo of the BBC's Six O'Clock News, blending time and space in the spinning globe with the hour at its centre.

The use of time and space in the logo are generic markers of news almost wherever it is broadcast. Figure 3.2 shows the equivalent graphic signature from NBC in the USA.

Figure 3.1 Signature graphics and logo for the BBC's Six O'Clock News.

Figure 3.2 Opening signature and graphics for NBC's Nightly News.

Similar techniques – especially references to clock time or the use of the spinning globe – are adopted by many broadcasters, as Figures 8.1 and 8.2 demonstrate.

Following the signature graphics, music and logo, there is typically a con-textualising shot of the news presenter – for example, a crane shot of the studio setting with news presenter(s) shown in long shot in position (usu-ally sitting at a desk but increasingly seen standing). This is followed by a zoom-in to the news presenter(s), now given face-on to camera, and will end with a mid-shot (head and shoulders) of the news presenter(s). This in turn will be the cue for a presenter to greet the audience in direct address and begin presentation of the first news item of the bulletin.

Ext. 3.2.1
5 PRESENTER: Good evening.
6   Sir Mark Thatcher the son of the former Prime Minister
7   is under house arrest tonight … .

From the initial headlines to the onset of the first news item may take well over a minute, especially if timed from the onset of the 'pre-announcement'. This multi-layered material is placing the programme within the schedule, inserting it into the broadcast flow, signalling the channel and the genre, stitching the particular presentation of news events into a landmark temporal moment (ten o'clock, one o'clock, six o'clock – early evening, late evening), anticipating the structure of the programme and projecting forward into it. Openings, therefore, amount to a complex introduction to the structured nature of the anticipated programme.

3.3   Closing the news bulletin programme

By comparison closing the programme is almost perfunctory, taking perhaps half the time – or less – of the opening. Common elements in closing are as follows:

(a) some kind of *reprise* of the main news item or items, for example:

Ex. 3.3.1
1   The Royal Mail has failed to deliver on its key targets
2   but says the service is improving.
3   And at least twelve people have been killed
4   in a series of explosions in Bir Sheva in southern Israel.

(b) the *reprise* may be preceded by a *reprise preface* to distinguish the *reprise* itself from other news items, for example:

Ex. 3.3.2
1   Go back now to tonight's headlines

or

Ex. 3.3.3
1   Our main headline tonight

(c) a *closing*, which indicates that there are no further news items to come, for example:

Ex. 3.3.4
1   And that's all for now

or

Ex. 3.3.5
1   That's all from the one o'clock news this Tuesday lunchtime

or

Ex. 3.3.6
1   That is Channel Four news

or

Ex. 3.3.7
1   And that's all from me for the moment

(d) a *trailer*, looking forward to later bulletins, such as

Ex. 3.3.8
1   I'll be here with an update of all the main news at one o'clock
2   Kirsty Young's here at five thirty and seven tonight

Ex. 3.3.9
1   We now join the BBC news teams across the United Kingdom

Ex. 3.3.10
1   I'm back with our next bulletin
2   That's at ten twenty five after the ten o'clock news

Ex. 3.3.11
1   Well don't forget the England rugby team coming back five a.m. Heathrow
2   the news at noon will have the first news conference and much more

Ex. 3.3.12
1   We're back at noon therefore and again at seven

(e) the last words from the presenter are usually an explicit farewell or *leave-taking*, as in the following examples,

Bye for now; So it's goodbye from me; Goodbye; Good evening;
Until then enjoy your evening; Good night ...

(f) and these are followed by the final signature graphics, logo and credits which round off the programme.
    Not every element need occur. An example of a simple closing section from UK *Channel 5* morning news with no *reprise* is as follows:

Ext. 3.3.1

1 CLOSING And that's all from me for the moment	Delivered
2 TRAILER I'll be here with an update of all the main news at one o'clock	standing
3 Kirsty Young's here at five thirty	in
4 and seven tonight	direct address.
5 ♪	Fade up music
6 LEAVE-TAKING Bye for now	
7 SIGNATURE GRAPHICS ♪ ♪ ♪ ♪ ♪	Credits
8 ♪ ♪ ♪ ♪ ♪ ♪ ♪ ♪ ♪ ♪	and music.

Leave-taking and *closing*, on this basis, would appear to be obligatory structural elements while some elements, such as the *reprise*, are optional.

The structure of the closing section may be summed up as:

CLOSING SECTION

(REPRISE-PREFACE) (+ REPRISE) + CLOSING (+ TRAILER) + LEAVE-TAKING + FINAL SIGNATURE GRAPHICS

Let us consider in more detail what each of these elements entails and the kind of work that they are performing. First of all, *leave-taking*.

Leave-taking is a function of direct visual address where the *presenter* speaks with the direction of gaze apparently towards the audience. Only programmes with *presenters* routinely finish by taking leave of the audience. As well as news programmes, sports programmes, cookery and gardening programmes and some kinds of wild-life programmes use recognisable and familiar presenters; and these routinely adopt the convention of the presenter saying goodbye to the audience[2]. However much the broadcast news programme may be delivered in impersonal terms it is still delivered to the audience in direct visual address (see further discussion in Chapter 4 below). Doing so is part of establishing and projecting a continuing personal relationship with the viewer/listener – one in which the politeness of leave-taking is supposedly relevant. It is noticeable, therefore, that ending the programme is seen as akin to temporarily breaking co-presence with the audience.

It is often conducted alongside of, or in the wake of, a *trailer*, in which some reference is made to a later version of the programme.

Ex. 3.3.13
1 PRESENTER: I'll be here with an update of all the main news at one o'clock.
2   Kirsty Young's here at five thirty and seven tonight.

Ex. 3.3.14
1 PRESENTER: Well don't forget the England rugby team
2   coming back five a.m. Heathrow.
3   The *News at Noon* will have the first news conference
4   and much more.
5   We're back at noon therefore
6   and again at seven.

Ex. 3.3.15
1 PRESENTER: I'm back with our next bulletin.
2   That's at ten twenty five
3   after the ten o'clock news.
4   Until then
5   enjoy your evening.

Sometimes there will be specific reference to content (for example: "more on that story at nine o'clock"). Fundamentally, however, trailers invoke the notion of a return of the speaker at a determinate time. If the opening of the programme sutures it into the schedule, the closing invokes the schedule again at its end by predicting the speaker's (or the programme's) own return: departures are only temporary; returns are recurrent and at appointed times. In their closing, therefore, the news programme invokes the dailiness (Scannell, 1996) of news or at least the cyclical nature of the news round (so significant an element of the daily round of broadcasting). Simultaneously, the reference to 'being back' reinforces the way in which the news issues not only from a defined and enduringly recognisable individual, the named *presenter,* but also from a deictic zero point – 'here' – to which 'we' – it is presumed – will return again and again. The 'here' is both a reference to the studio (this place) but also a reference to the channel (this broadcaster).

The *closing* element itself in its simplest form proclaims "that's all": there is nothing left. It can be everything from the speaker, "That's all from me". Or it can be everything from the programme: "That's all from the one o'clock news". Or it can be everything at this point in time: "And that's all for now". There are two significant dimensions to the act of closing, one which might be called topical and the other temporal. From the perspective of timing, *closing* provides a discursive solution to a technical problem: for the programme must be made to finish exactly at a predetermined moment in order to implement the onward movement of the schedule. From the perspective of topicality, however, the notion of "that's all" may seem an arbitrary way to declare closure, as curious in its own way as the (apocryphal?) tale of the early BBC news programme that simply announced "there is no news tonight". By what criterion, it might be asked, is there now nothing further left of any significance to report? By implication the news is about something, but its content for the purposes of the broadcast programme is almost always treated as finite in a quite definitive way. In the production of a *closing*, the news has completed itself. Everything of interest has apparently been exhausted, at least for the purpose of this programme at this point in time, whatever other competing topical pressures might be in play.

Note also in these endings a kind of mirror reflection of a move that takes place at the beginning. In opening a news programme, the emphasis falls on the proximate form "this is ... (the news at ten ...)". In opening, the projection is forward from the present. In closing, however, the reference is through the distal form back from the present: "that's all for now".

3.4   Opening a bulletin news item

Whilst the opening and closing of news programmes is managed through quite explicit mechanisms the transition from one news item to another is marked in less explicit ways. News presenters, for instance, do **not** routinely mark the transition from one item to another with phrases such as "and now to our next story...". Instead one item succeeds another with little or no lexical marking. There are, however, prosodic, paralinguistic and visual markers of the transition. Take, for example, the following simple, hourly, news bulletin from the music radio station *Classic FM* where one item moves quite rapidly on to the next. (The complete bulletin takes less than 5 minutes.)

Ext. 3.4.1: Classic FM News

Its eleven o'clock
I'm John Adderly
(.) (hh)
A day before her traditional Christmas message the Queen's been praising the work of Britain's armed forces (.) (hh) Her majesty's made a special radio address to them on the British Forces' Broadcasting Service saying they're doing a vital job (.) (hhh) She also says that she understands the danger service men and women are putting themselves in (.) (hh) The Queen paid tribute to the work the armed forces are doing in war zones
[.. audio clip ..]
The former head of the Royal Navy says the armed forces are in danger of being reduced to a gendarmerie incapable of defending the country's interests (hhh) (.) In a Sunday newspaper interview Admiral Sir Allan West says the re-shaping of the armed forces to wage anti-terror operations in countries like Iraq and Afghanistan could be jeopardising Britain's (.) long term security
(hhhh) (2.0)
Police have been given more time to question three men over the murder of thirty-two year old Darren Hargreaves who died of severe head injuries (hh) after being attacked in Stoke on Trent on Friday (.) (hhh) Eight other people who'd been arrested (.) have been released on bail
(hhhh) (1.5)
First it was planes now the turn of trains to cause potential Christmas travel misery. A strike by staff at Central Trains could leave thousands of rail users in the Midlands stranded (.) (hhh) There has been some much needed relief for passengers at Britain's busiest airports after days of cancellations due to freezing fog services are returning to normal at Heathrow (.) Sheila Ranger from the RAC foundation told Classic FM drivers could now be the ones to suffer
[.. audio clip ..] (1.0)
Charlie Drake who was branded one of the last great slapstick comedians has died at the age of eighty one (.) (hh) He starred in

a string of TV shows in the sixties and seventies (hh) Charlie Drake
passed away in his sleep at a retirement home for entertainers (.) (hh)
at Twickenham in South West London
(hhhh) (2.0)
Sunday trading laws may ... ...

Where these radio news items include an audio clip, this always comes at the end of the item and the item does not resume after the audio clip. Where there is no audio clip, the boundary between one item and the next is marked by a significant pause (one second or more) and an audible intake of breath (hhhh). Pauses do occur elsewhere – usually at the boundaries of what might be called a spoken sentence – but these are less significant. In addition there are prosodic cues. The conclusion of an item is delivered with a slowing of the syllable rate and with a gradual stepping down in the pitch of the voice. At the onset of the next item the speaker steps up in pitch and the rate of delivery. The force of this prosodic transition is to suggest that one piece of spoken discourse has finished and another is beginning: the pauses, coupled with the prosodic marking, are unmistakable signals that the speaker is moving on from, loosely, one spoken paragraph to the next – from one news item to the next.

Televised news adds further visual/semiotic cues to these prosodic features, using captions for example to accompany a change from one item to the next, while extended items mark transitions with more complex visual changes. A fully elaborated news item will commonly feature recorded footage with voice-over from a reporter or correspondent in the field, as discussed in Chapter 5, perhaps followed by a live two-way. Returning the discourse from the *reporter* in the field to the *news presenter* in the studio typically coincides with the onset of the next item – a transition reinforced by the substitution of a new caption. Closing an elaborated or extended news item, therefore, will coincide with a range of shifts, including change of speaker and change of visual frame. In Figures 3.3 and 3.4 we see the end of a news item involving a live two-way and the beginning of the next item delivered in news presentation from the studio.

The onset of a televised news item will, therefore, often entail not only prosodic cues but also postural shifts by the *news presenter*, semiotic signals such as caption replacement and shifts of visual frame such as those entailed by switching from the news field to the news studio and from subsidiary recorded footage or live two-way to studio presentation.

3.5   Opening and closing a bulletin news report

Some news items consist simply of a news kernel read by the news presenter. More typically, however, they will feature a report from the news field – as well as, in some cases, an interview with the reporter or correspondent.

Figure 3.3 End of news item on Prince William's girlfriend. BBC correspondent Nicholas Wichell is seen in one half of a live two-way from Buckingham Palace.

Figure 3.4 Beginning of the next item about USA air strikes in Somalia. Presenter George Aligaiah in studio.

As we noted above, therefore, the full structure can be represented as follows:

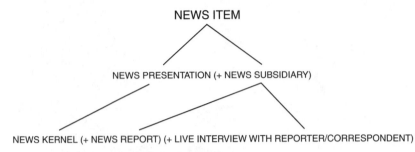

NEWS ITEM

NEWS PRESENTATION (+ NEWS SUBSIDIARY)

NEWS KERNEL (+ NEWS REPORT) (+ LIVE INTERVIEW WITH REPORTER/CORRESPONDENT)

The onset of the *news report* is principally a matter of transition from one kind of discourse to another, from studio *news presentation* of a *kernel* to *report*[3] (usually pre-recorded) from the news field involving both (a) change of speaker and (b) change of visual frame from the studio to a depicted scene or object elsewhere. It also involves a switch from a speaker who presents in direct visual address to the audience through the camera to a speaker who indirectly addresses the audience in voice-over to picture. These shifts are anticipated and managed by the *presenter* in two ways: (a) by explicitly introducing/identifying the next speaker by name – for example, "Lisa Baldini reports"; and (b) by a form of kinesic/postural 'handover' – i.e. the *presenter* breaks direct visual address to camera and looks away from the audience and down as if to watch the upcoming report. How this is managed discoursally may be illustrated in the following two examples.

Ex. 3.5.1

1 PRESENTER: … he will be sentenced this afternoon. Lisa Baldini reports.
  [Presenter looks down to her right. Cut from studio shot to picture of accused.]
2 REPORTER: Fifty-three year old Harvey had previously denied the charges

Ex. 3.5.2
1 PRESENTER: … but first Adam Parsons on the team's triumphant return
2   to a greeting of thousands of flash bulbs.
  [Presenter looks down to her right. Cut from studio shot to picture of taxiing jumbo jet.]
3 REPORTER: The plane had been re-named 'sweet chariot' …

From these examples it can be seen that the transition in bulletin news from presented *news kernel* to subsidiary *news report* may also be accompanied by a shift in the time reference of the discourse from present or future in the discourse of presentation to past in the discourse of the report. As well as identifying the next speaker by name the presenter will routinely refer to their location, thus reinforcing the transition from the space of presentation to the space of the reported news field, as in: "our reporter Bill Maclaren reports from Allerdyce" or "Andy Tie was in court".

Closing a news report is effected principally through the reporter or correspondent "signing off" using a widely adopted verbal protocol involving the speaker in self-identification by personal name, identifying their broadcast institution and naming their location: // SPEAKER'S FIRST NAME + LAST NAME // + NAME OF BROADCAST INSTITUTION // + LOCATIONAL FORMULATION //

This kind of verbal protocol is accompanied with a distinctive set of prosodic cues, which involve a stepping down in pitch level by the speaker, an increase in the distribution of prominence, with a corresponding decrease in the syllable rate (slowing down the delivery). In the following example of signing off, the prominent syllables have been rendered in upper case and the text divided into tone-units by the use of //.

Ex. 3.5.3
1 REPORTER: . // HE himself // does NOT appear //
2   to have MADE up his MIND yet // about iRAQ //
3   // MATT FREI // BEEbeecee NEWS // WASHington //

Closings of reports thus are signalled lexicogrammatically, and prosodically through a kind of rallentando effect.

3.6   Opening a live two-way with a reporter/correspondent

The standard structural format of the news bulletin programme places any *live two-way interview* with a correspondent or reporter in a subsidiary position after the presentation of a *news kernel*. Most typically they follow the *report*, though sometimes a two-way exchange with a reporter will be used as a way of framing the *report*. Very occasionally, in *news items* which feature a senior correspondent or editor, there will be a live two-way without a report. With or without a report, however, the live two-way is always somehow subsidiary to and dependent upon presentation of a news kernel. As noted earlier it is impossible to begin a news item with a live two-way exchange or for such an exchange to be the news item itself. We may represent these structural constraints in a tree diagram as follows:

NEWS ITEM

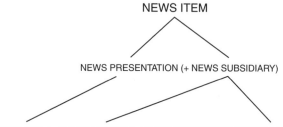

NEWS PRESENTATION (+ NEWS SUBSIDIARY)

NEWS KERNEL (+ NEWS REPORT) (+ LIVE INTERVIEW WITH REPORTER/CORRESPONDENT)

Or as re-write rules:

1. NEWS ITEM   ➡   NEWS PRESENTATION (+ NEWS SUBSIDIARY)

2. NEWS PRESENTATION   ➡   NEWS KERNEL

3a. NEWS SUBSIDIARY   ➡   NEWS REPORT (+ LIVE 2WAY)

or

3b. NEWS SUBSIDIARY   ➡   LIVE 2WAY < NEWS REPORT > (where the report is embedded within a live 2-way)

or (very occasionally)

3c. NEWS SUBSIDIARY   ➡   LIVE 2WAY

It is always the case, therefore, that the news presenter effects the transition to the live two-way and in ways which tend to be more complex than the transitions from news kernel to news report, as can be seen in the following examples:

Ex. 3.6.1
1 PRESENTER: ... our Ireland correspondent Dennis Murray
2   has been following the campaign trail
3   and he's in Belfast now

Ex. 3.6.2
1 PRESENTER: well our correspondent Stephen Sachar
2   was at that court hearing this afternoon
3   we can talk to him now in Sweden

Ex. 3.6.3
1 PRESENTER: well I'm joined now from Sedgefield
2   by our political editor Andrew Marr
3   and from the world summit in Johannesburg
4   by our world affairs editor John Simpson

In each of these cases the news presenter performs three kinds of work. First they establish or project verbal co-presence with the intended but distant interlocutor: "Let's talk to ..."; "we can talk to him now"; "I'm joined now by ..." Second, the distant interlocutor is identified by both first and last name ("Matt Frei"; "Dennis Murray"; "Andrew Marr" ...) and also by institutional role ("our Ireland correspondent"; "our world affairs editor").

And finally some characterisation of their (distant) location is provided: for example, "... who's at the White House"; "... from Sedgefield"; "Richard Bilton is in Northumberland"; "from the world summit in Johannesburg"; "he's in Belfast now"; "our chief political correspondent Mark Mardell is at Westminster".

Identifying the next speaker and their location is performed primarily for the viewing or overhearing audience, though it also may be seen as providing an anticipatory cue for the correspondent waiting on a live feed. Once this introduction has been accomplished, there follows a distinct shift of footing – in Goffman's terms – with the presenter switching from addressing the broadcast audience to addressing directly the correspondent on first name terms.

In the following examples the first line is to the broadcast audience and the subsequent discourse is addressed to the reporter/correspondent.

Ex. 3.6.4

| 1 PRESENTER: | Richard Bilton is in Northumberland | INTRODUCTION |
| 2 | Richard / what (h)ave people there been saying? | ONSET OF 2-WAY |

Ex. 3.6.5

1 PRESENTER:	and our world affairs editor John Simpson is at the summit	INTRO
2	uh / John /	ONSET OF 2-WAY
3	Mugabe first /	

Ex. 3.6.6

1 PRESENTER:	let's talk to Matt Frei who's at the White House	INTRO
2	Matt / a week ago we heard that	ONSET OF 2-WAY
3	Mr Blair wasn't on the inside track with America	
4	now he's flying to Camp David for this summit	
5	just how involved is he?	

Ex. 3.6.7

1 PRESENTER:	well our correspondent Stephen Sachar was at that court hearing	
2	this afternoon we can talk to him now in Sweden	INTRO
3	so . Stephen uh	ONSET OF 2-WAY
4	as well as being in court you conducted your own investigations	
5	what have you been able to find out?	

There are, of course, quite distinct postural shifts associated with these changes of footing, accompanied by use of graphics and changes of visual frame. Often the remote interlocutor will be displayed on video screen in the news studio and the news presenter will turn to face the screen as part of the transition (Figures 3.5 to 3.7).

In addition to changes in visual frame, the style of delivery will – quite typically – change from the tighter script of the news kernel to the looser,

Figure 3.5 Transition from news presentation to live two-way. Presenter still addressing the broadcast audience: **"but first Matt Frei is in Washington ..."**

Figure 3.6 Transition from news presentation to live two-way continued. Presenter now turned to face studio image of Matt Frei: "... **Matt / this was already an unpopular war in America ...**"

more relaxed, if formulaic, utterances of the transition. In these ways – posturally, paralinguistically and verbally – news presenters register the switch from monologic news presentation to dialogic interaction with the news reporter/correspondent. As Goffman's description of footing describes it – "they switch the alignment they adopt to themselves and to others

Figure 3.7 Presenter continuing to frame question to Matt Frei but now in voice-over to full image of him looking to camera listening to question unfold: "... but there are a lot of people who are not sure that the President's strategy will work ..."

as expressed in the way they manage the production of their utterances" (Goffman, 1981, p. 128).

but first Matt Frei is in Washington ... ...

... .Matt / this was already an unpopular war in America ... .

... .but there are a lot of people who are not sure that the President's strategy will work ...

3.7 Closing a live interview with a reporter/correspondent

If the management of the transition from news presentation to interview is relatively complex, then closings are at face value relatively simple. The following examples are typical.

Ex. 3.7.1
I CORRESPONDENT: ... we're not in a position
2   where this country can go to war alone against Iraq
3 PRESENTER: Matt / thank you very much indeed

Ex. 3.7.2
1 CORRESPONDENT: ... there are many questions . and not many answers
2 PRESENTER: uh Stephen / thanks very much

Ex. 3.7.3
1 REPORTER: ... is expected by the end of the year / Fiona
2 PRESENTER: thanks Richard

Ex. 3.7.4
1 WORLD AFFAIRS EDITOR: ... that is I suppose except for the environmentalists
2 PRESENTER   John Simpson / thank you

Ex. 3.7.5
1 REPORTER: ... but more research into the potentially long term effects
2   that this drug could have / Fiona
3 PRESENTER: Richard / thanks very much

Ex. 3.7.6
1 REPORTER: ... will be refunded and will be looked after in Zeebrugge / Fiona
2 PRESENTER: Catherine in Hull / John in Zeebrugge /
3   thank you both very much

However straightforward these may seem, it is worth noting that closing is an act collaboratively signalled and achieved by both parties to the interview. In several examples, the *reporter* or *correspondent* names the *presenter* (by first name) at the conclusion of their final interview turn. In each case the first name is produced as a separate tone-unit with a prominent syllable and falling tone. First-naming in this fashion is more than simply a mode of address to the *presenter*. It carries the force of termination to the interview, passing the discourse back from the space of the news field to the space of the studio. Conversely, the use of reciprocal first name in return by the *presenter* acknowledges the nature of this act, and concurs with it, for literally speaking there is no need for the *presenter* to first-name the interviewee in turn-initial position. (Identification is not an issue since this was already done at the beginning of the interview. And nominating the next speaker is not at stake since the interviewee does not normally speak again after this turn.) In most cases it is only then that the two-way is finally terminated by use of the formulaic "thanks"; "thank you"; "thanks very much".

Occasionally, of course, time and scheduling constraints force an untimely and unilateral closure by the *presenter*; but these are marked when they occur, and recognised as such – "I'm sorry, I'm going to have to stop you there". Otherwise closure is a collaborative accomplishment by both parties. Indeed, though difficult to formalise, there is a sense of a reasonable length for a two-way interview that both parties (and the audience) collectively orient to, which amount to a 'natural completion' point for the two-way interview, a shared assessment of what counts as the interview having run its course.

It should be noted, in any case, that the issue of relative length applies even at the level of the individual turn within the interview itself. A satisfactory response turn within an interview in the broadcast mode requires more than minimal replies. A question from a *presenter* such as "John / on this issue does the US have any friends in the world besides the UK?" is not going to be answered with a minimal one word answer even though in terms of pure logical form the question may require no more than simply "yes" or "no". In certain adversarial genres such as court-room cross-examination there may well be overt attempts to restrict the answer to a simple yes or no (Atkinson and Drew, 1979). In the broadcast context, however, and indeed in interviews in general, such minimal responses would be seen as aberrant. It is difficult to specify exactly what length of reply would be seen as sufficient/adequate, or indeed what length of reply might count as interminable. But it is most rare, for instance, for presenters, **when interviewing reporter/correspondents**, to cut short or interrupt them – reflecting (amongst other things) a professional capacity on the part of broadcast journalists for 'speaking to length (or time)'. There is most likely, for interactants within these situations, an intuitive sense of length something like 15–20 seconds for a reply and 40 seconds to a minute and a half for an interview.

Even though both interactants in the live two-way will not necessarily have the other in vision, turn transitions typically take place with the minimum of either pause or overlap, relying on a range of syntactic and intonational signals of where turn transition is relevant. If a clause or sentence ends with a slowing down of speech rate and a stepping down of pitch height it will be heard as a relevant point for turn transition. And if two or three interview replies have already been elicited then it is not just turn transition that is relevant but termination of the interview. Experienced correspondents are also capable of crafting the well-rounded phrase at the end of a turn to produce a satisfactory conclusion to their side of the interview. Thus, stylistic patterning using syntactic parallelism, coupled with the end of a pitch sequence, can provide a strong cue for closing. The BBC's world affairs editor ended his side of one interview slowing down with a neat syntactic pair (ll. 2–3), separated by a pause, to round it off:

Ex. 3.7.7

1	WORLD AFFAIRS EDITOR:	because quite frankly now
2		there are many questions (.)
3		and not many answers

3.8 'Open' versus 'closed' discourse structures in broadcast news

This description of the structure of broadcast news discourse has so far been grounded in examples drawn from bulletin news programmes occurring as part of mixed programming schedules on what might be called 'general interest' channels, such as BBC1 or ITV1 on British television. News bulletin programmes, as suggested in Chapter 1, are still the main conduit for news as well as the prototypical form of broadcast news. They occupy fixed weekday slots (in terms of both time and duration) in the programme schedule, where they are surrounded by contrasting kinds of broadcast material from which they need to be distinguished. In addition, editorial decisions on news items have to be made against a background of tight temporal constraints: however variable the scale of significance of events on a specific day, there will still be only a fixed slot – usually of 30–60 minutes – to present them.

The last three decades, however, have seen the launch of dedicated, news-only channels such as CNN (1980), Sky News (1989), Al-Jazeera (1996), and BBC News 24 (1997), with a special commitment to covering 'breaking' and 'running' news, which they broadcast continuously around the clock. These dedicated news channels may still preserve a rudimentary schedule – switching, for instance, between background and current material, between finance, politics and sport, between world news and regional news; but the slots that comprise the schedule are both more extended and more flexible, producing more fluid discourse structures than those of bulletin news. In principle, dedicated news channels are poised to open up their schedule to a breaking story and to run with it as long as it remains of significant interest.

The similarities between news on a dedicated channel and news programmes on multi-purpose channels still tend to outweigh the differences. The former have, nonetheless, had a far-reaching effect on the general ecology of news forms so that these now span between what might be called 'open', loosely-framed, news structures and 'closed', tightly-framed, news structures. In open news structures on a dedicated news channel, the news unfolds more as a continuous thread of 'updates', which are constantly iterated and re-iterated. The boundaries between items are less punctuated and less clear-cut. The temporal balance between presenter/anchor and correspondent/reporter shifts in favour of the latter to the extent that news unfolds more from the field, 'there', than from the studio, 'here'. This leads to some flattening of the hierarchy familiar from the traditional (closed structure) news programme. The news is more de-centred, with the studio presenter deferring to the current knowledge of the reporter in the field. Indeed the role of the presenter is subtly re-defined. In a closed structure news programme, the presenter not only orchestrates the role of other speakers and the transitions to filmed reports but provides the scripted, authoritative, summative thread that runs through the programme. By contrast, the role of the presenter/anchor on the dedicated news channel depends more upon unfolding the news through interview with correspondents, commentators and 'news-makers'. Their role is less scripted, more improvised, and more a question of blending together, in the real-time flow of broadcasting, the voices that are drawn upon to make up the news.

An ideal-typical representation of closed and open structure news discourse, accentuating the differences between them, may be given schematically as follows:

CLOSED STRUCTURE NEWS DISCOURSE	v	OPEN STRUCTURE NEWS DISCOURSE
Fixed timing		Fluid timing
Tight framing		Loose framing
Terse		Prolix
Retrospectively summative of event		Unfolding simultaneously with event
Presentational/monologic		Interpersonal/dialogic
Single-voiced		Multi-voiced
Studio-centred discourse hierarchy		Flattening of hierarchy in favour of non-studio voice
Punctuative/Completitive		Flow

These are tendencies. It is possible to find features of open news discourse in mixed channel news programmes and vice versa. For instance, BBC Radio 4's *Today* programme is on the air for 3 hours from 6 a.m. to 9 a.m. daily. The medley of news summaries, background interviews and discussion is markedly more fluid in its format than the 6 p.m. half-hour news programme later in the day on the same channel – closer, indeed, to the output of a dedicated news channel.

3.9   Open structure news discourse

Some characteristics of open discourse structure may be seen at work in *News from CNN* broadcast daily from 10.00 to 11.00 a.m. (ET). This is how the programme opens on 16th February 2005 after the assassination, two days previously, of Lebanese statesman Rafik Hariri:

Ext. 3.9.1:

1 PRESENTER:	Unfolding this hour on *News from CNN*
2	focusing on Syria
3	its hold on Lebanon
4	its ties to Iran
5	the friction between Damascus and Washington
6	we'll examine the impact on the Middle East
7	part of that pulses right through the streets of Beirut
8	mourning for a native son
9	the death of Rafik Hariri and the anger it's generated.

This is quite different from the declarative sentences used to open the kind of bulletin news programme discussed in section 3.3 above. Here, for instance, is a classic single-sentence, BBC bulletin headline

Ex. 3.9.1
1 PRESENTER: Russia investigates
2   whether terrorists caused two passenger jets to crash

By comparison the structure of the sentence or sentences in Extract 3.9.1 from CNN is looser. Many of the verb forms are non-finite ('unfolding', 'focusing', 'mourning') and the whole is more like a succession of groups paratactically linked together as an associated chain of topics rather than discrete one-sentence headlines for discrete news items. And although *News from CNN* does employ headlines after the introduction, they take a much fuller form here than those one-sentence headlines considered in section 3.3. Thus, even though the CNN presenter/anchor refers to 'headlines' in his preface below, they sometimes take the form of summaries that are several sentences long (in contrast to those of bulletin news).

Ext. 3.9.2
1 PRESENTER: First some other headlines now in the news.
2   A call to take action on Social Security from the Fed chairman,
3   Alan Greenspan.
4   In testimony today Greenspan said
5   benefits promised to ageing Baby Boomers
6   will eventually strain the working population.
7   In his prepared remarks he made no comment on the partial privatisation
8   proposed by President Bush.
9   Have we reached hockey's meltdown?
10   No official word yet.
11   But we could find out one hour from now
12   when the National Hockey League is scheduled
13   to hold a news conference
14   on the current lockout.
15   The league and the players union are at odds over
16   a proposed salary cap
17   and the season may be scrapped ...
[two more similar summaries follow]

Individual news items themselves have a less clear-cut structure. Here is the lead item from CNN's programme that day. Note that it takes the form of a relatively short news presentation from the anchor/presenter, Wolf Blitzer, serving as much as anything to contextualise an extended live two-way interview with the reporter/correspondent in the field, Ben Wedeman. In other words, the news item itself unfolds not so much in news presentation as such, or as scripted and edited news report, but as reported within a live two-way interview.

```
 I PRESENTER:  Up first this hour on News from CNN        [FIRST NEWS ITEM]
 2            the plummeting relations between the United States and Syria.
 3            Ambassador to Syria Margaret Scoby is due back here in Washington
 4            two days after that enormous attack in Beirut
 5            that killed Lebanese statesman Rafik Hariri
 6            and about a dozen others.
 7            Stopping short of blaming Syria
 8            United States officials are saying
 9            the assassination was the final straw in a series of disagreements
10            that also involve Iraq.
11            Our coverage begins in Beirut with our Middle East correspondent
12            Ben Wedeman
13            Ben / what's the latest news there?              [OPEN LIVE 2-WAY]
14 CORRESPONDENT:  Well today Wolf
15            we saw a massive funeral here in Beirut
16            I'm in Martyr's Square
17            the heart of the Lebanese capital
18            where we saw
19            at least one hundred thousand Lebanese converge on this area
20            to attend the funeral for the assassinated Lebanese Prime Minister
21            former Prime Minister Raki Hariri
22            they came from predominantly Muslim West Beirut
23            as well as Christian east Beirut
24            Lebanese joined for the first time in many years
25            in a massive show of support for a man they respected
26            they saw as the leader
27            during the major reconstruction of this city
28            after fifteen years of brutal civil war
29            we also heard many people here
30            pointing the finger of blame towards Syria
31            many believe that Syria was in some way
32            behind the the killing of Rafik Hariri
33            now here in Beirut today is ... .
   [turn continues for a further 7 lines, resumes]
40            now the Americans are not at this point
41            accusing Syria of involvement in the assassination of Rafik Hariri
42            but relations it appears between Damascus and Washington
43            are at a very low level
44            and according to our sources will continue to go down / Wolf
45 PRESENTER:  Ben is there any progress on who actually killed Rafik Hariri
46            and the others
47            any DNA evidence from the scene
```

48   any hard evidence directly implicating Syria or anyone else
49 CORRESPONDENT: no there is no hard evidence implicating Syria
50   and we heard for instance
51   that the chief investigating judge met today with the heads
52   or rather yesterday afternoon
53   with the heads of all Lebanon's security services
54   trying to get all the information together
55   that they have got so far
[turn continues for a further 14 lines, resumes]
69   so no real progress at this point to the investigation
70   we have to keep in mind Wolf
71   that there have been a series of high-profile assassinations
72   here in Lebanon going back to the mid 1970's
73   many in most cases the belief is that
74   an outside power was involved
75   but no-one was able to come up with a final definitive decision
76   on who was behind these murders
77   and the fear here in Beirut is
78   that may be the case regarding Rafik Haririr / Wolf
79 PRESENTER: Ben Wedeman in Beirut
80   Ben / thanks very much   [CLOSE LIVE 2WAY]
81   on the Iranian front   [SECOND NEWS ITEM]
82   tensions rose briefly today ... .

The logic of this item is dictated by the exigencies of the live two-way format. Coherence is set up by the questions from the studio which drive the twin news values[4] of topicality – "Ben, what's the latest there" (l. 13) – and facticity – "Ben,.. any hard evidence directly implicating Syria or anyone else" (ll. 45–48). The topicality question provides for a loose chaining of themes based upon their currency either at the present moment or just prior to it. Thus, "well *today* Wolf we saw (ll. 14–15) ... *now* here in Beirut *today is* (l. 33). *now just a little while ago* he was (l. 36) ... but *earlier today* he met (l. 37) ... *now* the Americans *are not at this point* (l. 40) ... so no real progress *at this point* (l. 69) ...". Facticity is reinforced not merely through insisting on closeness to sources ("according to our sources") but also that the news gathering is close to the sounds and sights of the event: "we *saw* a massive funeral *here*" (l. 15), "we *saw* at least one hundred thousand Lebanese converge on *this area*" (ll. 18–19), "we also *heard* many people *here*" (l. 29) ... "*we heard,* for instance, that the chief investigating judge" (ll. 50–51) ... "we *heard* the interior minister of Lebanon" (l. 67). In addition, the interview dramatises not only 'the now' of the news – the closeness of the programme in time to the time of the event – but also the collapsing of distance: we have both the studio and the field combined within the interaction of the interview taking place between the visually-defined locations of Beirut and Washington. The emphasis here falls on and foregrounds the process of newsgathering itself, to a greater degree than the bulletin news programme.

But one of the paradoxes of the live two-way as a mode of news delivery, which will be discussed at greater length in Chapter 6, is that the foreshortening of distance to the place and time of the news leads to fewer substantive averrals rather than more. The correspondent can provide first-hand witness by reporting sights and sounds from the field in Beirut:

Ext. 3.9.2
15	we saw a massive funeral

Ext. 3.9.2
18	we saw
19	at least one hundred thousand Lebanese converge on this area

Ext. 3.9.2
29	we also heard many people here
30	pointing the finger of blame towards Syria

Ext. 3.9.2
50	and we heard for instance
51	that the chief investigating judge met today with the heads
52	or rather yesterday afternoon
53	with the heads of all Lebanon's security services

In response, however, to this question from the presenter

Ext. 3.9.2
45 PRESENTER:	Ben is there any progress on who actually killed Rafik Hariri
46	and the others
47	any DNA evidence from the scene
48	any hard evidence directly implicating Syria or anyone else

the correspondent has little substantive to offer:

Ext. 3.9.2
49 CORRESPONDENT:	no there is no hard evidence implicating Syria

Ext. 3.9.2
69	so no real progress at this point to the investigation

Ext. 3.9.2
75	but no-one was able to come up with a final definitive decision
76	on who was behind these murders
77	and the fear here in Beirut is
78	that may be the case regarding Rafik Hariri / Wolf

So, although this is the lead item in news from CNN at noon local time and although the first question asks, "Ben, what's the latest there?", the interview recapitulates events from earlier and confirms that otherwise there is little development: "no real progress at this point".

Other items in the hour-long programme include a lengthy live interview with two American politicians – a former US Senator, now president of the UN Foundation, and the current chair of the Senate subcommittee investigating the UN. This interview begins with a video clip quotation of Condaleeza Rice talking to the Foreign Relations Committee about Syrian involvement in the Lebanon: "listen to what she said just a few moments ago …". The programme also includes an interview with a senior Lebanese journalist in the studio and a studio interview with Claire Short, a former member of Blair's government, about the war in Iraq. The burden of the news within this programme is carried by interviews – sometimes with correspondents but just as likely with expert commentators or with those who have an insider's perspective on events. Considerable attention is given to projecting forward to what is to come – "that's coming up next", "we have much more coming up on this issue", "they're coming up next", "that's coming up as well". This is partly prompted by switching out of news into commercials or trailers for other CNN material. And this in turn prompts various ways of reactivating the news thread of the programme. The simplest kind of re-focusing is done through welcoming viewers back to the programme – "welcome back to News from CNN", "I'll be back later today", "and we're back in a moment", "welcome back". In this way CNN unfolds less as an ordered sequence of structurally uniform elements and more as a series of takes on a few topics which are re-cycled from different angles.

3.10   Conclusions

The traditional bulletin news programme continues to occupy a significant fixed place in the daily schedule of broadcasting and remains an important part of a ritual pattern of news consumption in which the news ("Today's top stories") is experienced as a completed summary of what had happened that day. Items follow one another in presentational series within the programme in a well-defined structure that is widely adopted and recognised. Inasmuch as news items deal with events, these are encapsulated within the form as complete up to the broadcast point in time (for instance, as "Today's testimony in the long-running murder trial"). Such programmes reflect a domestic pattern of consumption where the news was most likely to be experienced within the privacy of the household as a distinct temporal landmark within a daily round.

The development of dedicated news channels, however, such as CNN, Sky News, BBC News 24 and Fox, has wrought subtle changes to the discourse structure of news output. The structure of news within the dedicated news channel is now less defined – more topic-driven and circular, than discrete, sequential and episodic. The unfolding of the discourse of the news in these new formats is more closely in step with developments in the news field itself (although sometimes, of course, no new developments do take place). New happenings and events – the piece of testimony, for instance, just given to a house select committee – can be inserted by video-clip or live feed within the flow of the programme at the time of or within minutes of their occurrence.

The emergence of dedicated news channels and other new forms of output suggest a changing habitual framework of attention to the news. Whereas the older programme became itself a habitual event within a daily round, switched on deliberately in the home to chime with other activities such as a meal or the close of day itself, the dedicated news channel suggests a different pattern of attention and different conditions of consumption. CNN or Sky News is as likely to be carried in public spaces as in private. News channels such as these will be found in the pub, on the trading floor, in the hotel lobby or at the airport as continuous backdrop to other activities that occupy the viewer, such as checking in or out, share-dealing or waiting for a flight. Attending to Sky or CNN is likely to be more a kind of intermittent sampling where the news commands only momentary attention – the viewer staying with the flow of the programme as long as curiosity demands. Indeed, it is difficult to watch a dedicated news channel for more than 30 minutes or so without being overwhelmed by cyclic repetition – unless of course a major story/event is breaking of such proportions that its interest is all-consuming and other activities become overwhelmed by it.

Nonetheless, although these two kinds of news discourse – the closed and the open – are rooted in different frameworks of consumption – the relatively focused versus the relatively free-floating, intermittent sampling – the open news structures are emerging as dominant and influential tendencies, ones which have begun to recast the sharpness of the older structures. The emphasis on news from the field and on updates, on constant forward projection through time and to later moments in the programme, seems best understood as a feature of the newer structures now beginning to permeate the whole of broadcast news. On the face of it they might seem no more than the simple elaboration of existing structures rather than the dismantling of old. These changes do, however, imply a different relationship between discourse and the audience and discourse and the event – a tightening of one but a loosening of the other – that cannot help but have profound consequences on the epistemological presuppositions of broadcast news[5] – as we will see in later chapters.

4   News presentation

[I]n the diverse areas in which television seems, fairly evenly and openhandedly, to reproduce the 'real world' to which it refers, the practice of television inevitably intervenes, mobilizing distinctive forms of narration, specific modes of address and types of camera positioning so as to selectively structure the viewer's orientation to the 'real world' it re-presents.

(Bennett *et al.*, 1981, p. 86)

4.0   News presentation: its role and performance

From the perspective of the previous chapter, news presentation refers to the studio-based elements of the news, at the core of which are headlines and the kernels of news items but which also include opening and closing the programme, shifting the plane of the discourse from kernel to subsidiary elements and back again, as well as interviewing correspondents and other figures whose discourse contributes to the overall news broadcast. News presentation encompasses these elements but it is also at the same time a specialised, distinctive and variable kind of speech performance performed by a particular individual. This chapter will first consider some aspects of news presentation as performance (in sections 4.0–4.2) before identifying in further detail in its remaining sections some of the discourse characteristics of main discourse elements of presentation – headlines and kernels.

As noted in Chapter 2, various terms are used to designate the presenter's role: newsreader, newscaster and anchor – as well as presenter itself. A newsreader is a presenter whose role is to read the news; and this term is sometimes distinguished from newscaster, defined as a presenter with some kind of journalistic background who participates in compiling the script as well as reading it. A common term in North America is 'anchor', used to designate someone who presents material prepared for a news programme and who at times will improvise commentary for live presentation. The term adopted here, as the most easily understood superordinate, is 'presenter'; and it is used to encompass all these roles, basically because in bulletin news they are usually combined in one person. Thus, in bulletin news it is common for one person to open and close the programme, read the news, introduce reports and interviews and close them and so in this way handle all the news presentation throughout the programme. Nonetheless, it must be recognised that sometimes roles become bifurcated, with the task of reading scripted news summaries or kernels delegated at points in a programme to a specialist newsreader. This is particularly so in the case of extended news magazine programmes such as UK Channel 4 News or BBC Radio 4's *Today* programme.

The presenter as newsreader occupies a distinctive relationship to the words that are uttered, these being for the most part supplied to the presenter by the editorial team of the broadcast institution to be read aloud (though usually in a manner that calls as little attention to their being read as possible). As noted in Chapter 2, the peculiarities of this relationship are usefully clarified by applying Goffman's three-way distinction between 'author', 'animator' and 'principal' (Goffman, 1981, p. 144). A *principal* carries responsibility for the words spoken. An *author* composes them. An *animator* utters them. Typically in most speech situations in everyday life we do all three things at once: we are simultaneously author, animator and principal of the words we speak. But in some speech situations the stances of author, animator and principal become separated. When President Bush makes his state of the union speech some may doubt that he is really the *author* of the words which he utters even if he is their *animator* and their *principal* (since, whether he composed them or not, they remain his responsibility). By contrast, when Tony Snow as President Bush's Press Secretary addresses the White House Press Corps he may be the *author* and of course the *animator* of the words which he uses, but will not always be the *principal*, who remains the President himself when Snow is speaking for him[1].

When news presenters such as Trevor MacDonald or Natasha Kaplinsky are reading the news they are not taken to be the *author* or the *principal* of the scripts which they read: they are not assumed to have composed the script nor are they held responsible for it. In delivering the news, theirs is the voice not of an individual in their own right but of the institution on whose behalf they read. As such they are *animators*. As animators, however, there are restrictions on the amount of animation that is deemed appropriate. Presenters, when newsreading, do not animate in the fashion of theatre or screen actors, where success depends upon inhabiting the words emotionally so as to bring the script to life. Presenters need to deliver the news in a manner which contrives to be neither dramatic on the one hand nor completely inexpressive on the other. Thus, although they may lighten their delivery for a human interest item, become sombre for the tragic accident and coolly professional for the stock market report, these changes take place within a narrow emotional range. And just as the voice of the newsreading presenter needs to be engaging without being overly emotional, dispassionate rather than passionate, so the range of postural behaviour is limited.

Figure 4.1 Presenter Natasha Kaplinsky reading a Six O'Clock News item: "... should pupils be forced to stay at school until eighteen ... well ministers say they should ...".

Newsreading presenters address us most often from a seated position (often behind a table or desk) observed in a mid-close-up shot of the head and shoulders with the face occupying the upper half of the screen. (See, for example, Figure 4.1 above.) Positioned in this way their posture is static, their hands invisible. Kinesically, there is little scope for the normal 'leakage' of emotion by the speaker through hand movements, postural shifts and so on. They may turn to face a different camera, but they do not raise their eyebrow, nod, scratch their head or even blow their nose. Broadly, the emphasis falls on the words themselves rather than to call attention to the person delivering them. Newsreaders – ideally anyway – are not the news themselves. Nor are they characters in a drama. Their role may be compared to that of the classical chorus: they do not have an individual fate – except to record, dispassionately, the fates of others.

Speech, it is well documented in sociolinguistics, is an act of social identity. Speakers normally signal inescapably their position within the social order in terms of age, gender, class, education and regional provenance in the smallest details of their speech. However, when presenters read the news on major, nationally networked, news programmes, marked features of social identity are typically not in evidence. They appear and sound neither markedly old nor markedly young. It is difficult to identify their regional provenance except only in the broadest terms, not in terms of a well-defined locale. They may be inescapably male or female, but not camp or effeminate. In their speech we detect only the accents of the mainstream of national life so that any visual markers of ethnicity are neutralised by the use of unmarked or prestige forms of pronunciation[2]. In their voices, then, newsreaders do not tend to project the indices of any distinctive social position. Newsreading works best when only so much – and not too much – is revealed by the speaker about herself or himself.

In their broadcast role news presenters are familiar figures. Once publicly accepted and established, they become instantly recognisable. In this way, however, successful news presenters become tied to the role with little room for role discretion. Occasional cameo appearances outside the news studio may be possible but most often in a presenter's role. Trevor MacDonald may front a programme about the English language; Angela Rippon may appear on a Christmas comedy show; Natasha Kaplinsky and Bill Turnbull separately competed in *Come Dancing*. But there are tight limits on other kinds of public performance. It's thought to be inappropriate, for instance, for them to voice-over a TV commercial. As the voice of the news institution (ITN, BBC News, CNN) they come to be identified with the values which the institution wishes to project as a news provider; and for that reason alternative kinds of fame would be incompatible with their news presentational role[3].

Despite formal constraints on the performance of the news presenter's role, newer styles of news presentation are emerging. *Channel 5 News*, launched in 1997, pioneered in the UK the use of a presenter who spoke from a standing position, and who turned and moved within the studio space. This innovation is gradually spreading to other mainstream bulletin news programmes in the UK, transforming the dynamics of the news studio to accentuate the performative character of news presentation so that it now increasingly involves interaction with graphic displays as well as with other presenters (discussed further in Chapter 8). BBC1 News at 6.00 p.m. and at 10 p.m., for instance, now allows the newsreader to stand for some items in order to introduce graphic or video elements displayed within the studio shot on a screen (see Figures 4.4 and 4.5).

In addition, the increasingly common use of dual presenters, particularly upon 24-hour news channels as well as on bulletin news programmes, has opened up a type of news presentation that is more relaxed and informal compared with more traditional newsreading (see Figures 4.2 and 4.3). Breakfast television in the UK features both styles of presentation in the one programme, using a traditional newsreader as well as dual presenters.

These generally are innovations in the realm of the presentation of self as normally managed within the constraints of studio news presentation. They all carry connotations of dynamism as opposed to stasis, informality as opposed to formality.

Figure 4.2 BBC Breakfast presenters Bill Turnbull and Susanna Reid towards the end of a bulletin in more expansive delivery style (12/01/07).

Figure 4.3 BBC Breakfast presenters Bill Turnbull and Susanna Reid towards the end of a bulletin in more expansive delivery style (12/01/07).

Figure 4.4 More flexible use of studio space: after the opening headlines, BBC's Ten O'Clock News leads into the first news item with Fiona Bruce depicted in a zoom shot in standing position away from her console.

Figure 4.5 Beginning of the first news item: "Good evening ... Tony Blair has given a resounding justification ...".

4.1 Television news presentation, news-reading and direct visual address

One of the particular curiosities of television news-reading is its distinctive *mode of address* (Corner, 1995; Tolson, 1996; Allan, 1999/2004). The autocue or teleprompter (widespread from the 1960s onwards) enables the presenter to read the news while gazing directly at the camera[4]. In this way, visually, on the basis of direction of gaze, they adopt a direct relationship with their audience; since neither the autocue nor the camera is visible to the audience, the newsreader seems to look through them directly to the broadcast audience beyond. It is, however, a complex look. As members of the broadcast audience, we see the newsreader looking at us but know (without reflection) that the newsreader is simply looking at a camera while reading a script. In this sense, to describe the mode of address as 'direct' does little justice to its multilayered quality. It is, for instance, qualitatively different from the visual direct address of the mutually present encounter in which each party knows that the other experiences their look. Unlike co-present encounters, the newsreader's visual direct address is not grounded in mutual reciprocity. Admittedly the presenter engages with the audience much more than if depicted reading visibly from a text that forestalls or interrupts the look-to-camera[5]; nonetheless the scripted delivery (even if the script is invisible) and the conditions of mediation ultimately preclude any form of actual reciprocity. In this way, there is a quality of *para-social interaction* (Horton and Wohl, 1956) about the performance in which the visual direct address of a multilayered non-reciprocal kind personalises to a degree the quality of the relationship between the news reader and their audience; and the promise of a personal relationship in the look blends with impersonality in the delivery. Establishing this personal frame through the look is supported at openings and closings of the programme by verbal direct address in the form of greetings ("good evening") or leave-takings:

Ex. 4.1.1
[ITN pm News]
1 PRESENTER: And tha:t is the news tonight.
2 From all of us here: goodbye

Ex. 4.1.2
[BBC Newsround]
1 PRESENTER: I'll be back here tomorrow at five twenty five
2 Bye for now

Indeed, in these moments when verbal direct address and visual address to the audience coincide and when the presenter is freed from the constraints of the script, they become noticeably more expressive – as in Figure 4.6 illustrating Fiona Bruce at the end of a news programme[6].

Figure 4.6 Presenter more expressive than in Figure 4.5, smiling: "... bye for now ..."

And so in television news presentation the two modalities of the verbal and visual run in counterpoint rather than exactly in parallel. The words of the news by and large are presented as if for anyone. The look of the newsreader is as if for someone (Scannell, 2000).

4.2 The space of the news studio versus the space of the news field

The primary space of the news is the news studio. The kernels of TV news items are delivered in direct visual address from the studio, with the presenter most often positioned behind a table or console. The studio space of the news is generally marked as such and in surprisingly similar ways from programme to programme and from channel to channel. A common option, for instance, is to present the organisation's newsroom itself as background to news presentation. Thus, in camera shot behind the news presenter we can apparently observe, if we care to notice, some aspect of news analysis and preparation at work. (See for example Figure 4.7.)

But we can understand 'space' in this context in several overlapping ways. There is the space from which the news is presented. Behind this we can see a place from which the news may be understood as assembled. But frequently there will in addition be visual and verbal references to the geographical position in which the studio is located. UK national news from ITN or the BBC comes from London and this will be signalled iconically by using an image such as Big Ben or the Houses of Parliament or a segment of a map or atlas. (See for example Figures 4.8 and 4.9.)

Figure 4.7 BBC Scotland's newsroom is discernible as background to David Robertson's presentation.

Figure 4.8 Time, space and programme title blended in opening signature graphic for ITN's 'News at Ten'.

The space of the studio is the site from where the news is enunciated in the here and now; in contrast to this is the space of the news field itself from where the news is gathered and reported. These are deictic points, proximate and distal, and are marked as such in the discourses of transition: we now "go", for instance, "to our reporter in Baghdad" from where we are then "handed back to the studio". Television, in particular, accentuates

Figure 4.9 The title of this Scottish news programme, *Reporting Scotland*, has been superimposed on part of a map of Scotland to compose the opening signature graphic.

the distinction between these two different kinds of space. But particular care is taken to articulate and embody visually and verbally the primary space of the studio as the site of enunciation, the deictic zero point, the notional centre of which is the face of the presenter or newsreader looking through the camera to the audience. This is the news enunciated for and to the audience in the voice and person of the newsreader 'from CNN' or 'from ITN' and from a particular taken-for-granted point of primary intelligibility. These two deictic points – the unchanging, stable, familiar, zero point of the studio and the shifting, remote, deixis of the field[7], fluctuating in actuality footage from one report to another – provide two fundamental axes of broadcast news discourse: the axis of reporting, along which the world is brought to the studio – from the field to the deictic zero point; and the axis of presentation – along which the news is presented to the audience. These two axes are the discursive lines of force for rather different kinds of discourse. The discourse of the news report arises on the axis between the studio and the news field. The discourse of news presentation arises on the axis between the studio and the audience. Live feeds and interviews provide ways of bringing these axes together. In Chapter 5 close consideration will be given to the discourse of reports; Chapters 6 and 7 will examine the discourse of interviews. The remainder of this chapter will be devoted to those discourse elements that are particularly crucial to the space of the studio and the discourse of presentation: headlines, and the kernels of news items.

4.3   The discourse of headlines

Headlines constitute a specialised subgenre of discourse within the news. As was noted in Chapter 3, they function, despite their name, in a different fashion from print headlines. Broadcast headlines may be separated by several minutes from the news item to which they refer and so for this reason may be better understood as 'trailers', projecting forward into the programme, providing clues to its overall structure and providing the audience with reasons to keep viewing or listening. Extracts 4.3.1 and 4.3.2 below are two sets of headlines, one set from the opening of a standard evening bulletin programme, ITN's News at Ten, the other set from a lunchtime BBC news programme.

Ext. 4.3.1 [ITN News at Ten 2200/11/04/97: Trevor MacDonald]
1 ANNOUNCER: News at Ten with Trevor MacDonald
2 PRESENTER: Conservative minister at centre of Europe election row
3   IRA's deadliest weapon is found in South Armagh
4   Schoolboy guilty of canal-side gang-rape
5   And a touch of sadness as the Royal Navy leaves Hong Kong
6   Good evening   [GREETING]
7   A row over single currency ... .   [1ST ITEM]

Ext. 4.3.2 [BBCTV1 1300:19/02/04: Anna Ford]
1 PRESENTER: Train disaster in Iran.
2   Nearly two hundred people are killed as a derailed train explodes.
3   An earthquake forced the wagons
4   carrying petrol and chemicals off the track
5   Dentists' crisis.
6   Hundreds queue as bosses warn the system is breaking down.
7   Europe's big three meet
8   as the EU's smaller countries say they are being left out.
9   Essex fire-fighters have voted to strike over spending cuts.
10   And the mobile phone scam
11   that could be costing you a small fortune

Like other kinds of description, news fundamentally deals with persons, events and circumstances. But in order for descriptions to function as headlines they must pass a certain semantic threshold.

4.3.1   The semantics of headlines

4.3.1.1   Persons

Persons in headlines are designated by expressions that refer to them not so much as particular individuals but as members of significant groups or institutions: 'Europe's big three', 'Essex firefighters', 'Conservative minister', 'dentists', 'bosses', 'the Royal Navy' and so on. Occupation and stage of life are common descriptors. If these are difficult to apply then sheer numbers may suffice. "Hundreds queue . . ."; "Nearly two hundred people . . ." Thus, the description of persons proceeds, not so much by individuation (e.g. through the use of a proper name such as 'Angela Brown'), but by 'membership categorisation device' (MCD) (Schegloff, 1972; Hutchby and Woofit, 1998; Housley and Fitzgerald, 2002) (e.g. "Conservative minister"). This is partly a question of significant scale; but it is also a question of relevance. In limited cases where an individual is extraordinarily well-known ('a household name') then no MCD will be necessary. Thus "Diana Dies in Crash" could work as a headline – better perhaps than "Princess Dies in Crash". The semantic rule implicated here is: individuate when the person is already presumed to be famous (for example, "Posh and Becks"); otherwise categorise by membership of the most salient or significant group.

4.3.1.2   *Events/Actions*

An additional semantic rule also applies in the context of headlines. MCDs implicate what are described as 'category-bound activities'. The normal application of the device usually activates a set of (stereotypical) assumptions about appropriate behaviours performed by members of a category. Thus 'mothers' as a membership category are assumed (among other things) to nurture children, 'dentists' (among other things) to fix teeth, and so on. Yet a noticeable feature of the headlines above is that the activities or actions linked with the selected membership are not within the range of normal category-bound activities for that membership. Instead, the actions are discrepant with the MCD. Stereotypically, for instance, dentists do not have a crisis; firefighters do not strike; schoolboys do not rape; and hundreds do not queue. Thus a second semantic rule for headlines suggests that, where possible, select an activity that clashes with those of the MCD.

4.3.1.3   *Circumstances*

Routinely headlines will refer to the location of an event, as for example in

Ext. 4.3.1
5   the Royal Navy leaves Hong Kong
and
Ext. 4.3.2
1   Train disaster in Iran

It is not sufficient to account for this by noting the prescription on journalists that they cover details such as, 'who, where, when, how and why?', when introducing a story. In the context of broadcast news, it also relates to the task of presenting the news as occurring in a spatially dispersed fashion. News for broadcasting does not happen 'just here' but takes place 'out there'. It may be "in your region" or "nationwide" or "around the world"; but it is gathered from 'there' (Iran, Hong Kong, Jakarta, Leeds, Birkenhead) and brought to 'here' in the studio. In this way it is difficult to improve – in purely news terms – on an item that begins "we just have news coming in of an ___[event] ___ in __[location] ___" (for example, "an arrest in Suffolk", "a plane crash in Baltimore").

4.3.2   *The lexicogrammar of headlines*

Headlines often take a specialised grammatical form. Full sentences are uncommon – though they do occur, as for example in:

Ext. 4.3.2
8   Essex fire-fighters have voted to strike over spending cuts.

More frequently, however, headlines employ various kinds of grammatical ellipsis. The most common is verb deletion:

Ext. 4.3.1
4   Schoolboy [0] guilty of canal-side gang-rape
Ext. 4.3.1
2   Conservative minister [0] at centre of Europe election row

The deletion of the definite or indefinite article is also common. The second example above in its more complete form would be:

A Conservative minister **is** at **the** centre of **a** European election row.

And lexical compounding is also noticeable: "canal-side", "gang-rape". Of course, the precedents for these deletions, compounding and ellipses go back historically not only to newspapers, where similar processes can be identified (Fowler, 1991; Van Dijk, 1991; Bell, 1991; Conboy, 2003), but also to the telegraph (Schudson, 2003). In the case of newspapers constraints of space are clearly relevant. In the case of the telegraph, speed (and cost) of transmission counted.

But compression is only part of the picture, for two consequences flow from the deletions. First we find a high proportion of non-finite clauses in headlines and second the semantic slack created by missing verb groups is taken up by nominalisation (Fowler, 1991; Biber, 2003). Take the case of non-finite clauses such as:

Ex. 4.3.1.4 Dentists' crisis.

Or

Ex. 4.3.1.1 Train disaster in Iran.

The absence of a verb group means that some information about the nature of the process being described is simply not encoded. More specifically the 'non-finiteness' of the clause means that no selection of tense takes place and so details of the timing and duration of the event are not stipulated. Instead, grammatically the construction takes on the form of a nominal group with a head ('crisis'/'disaster') and where clauses become assimilated to the role of postmodifiers in the nominal group, as in

Ext. 4.3.2
9   And the mobile phone scam that could be costing you a small fortune

It is not that these nominalised structures pose in context serious difficulties of interpretation. Their meaning seems at first hearing to be clear. All the same, the 'process-character' of events becomes compacted so that under more considered scrutiny the complexity of the original event becomes difficult to recover. What, for instance, has happened in the case of the Conservative minister? Is there an election in which a policy row has taken place or a procedural row about an election? Is the minister at the centre of an election? Or at the centre of a row? Or maybe at the centre of Europe? Has the minister taken up a central position in the row? Or has she found herself placed there involuntarily? These kinds of complexity are unresolved in the headlines as they stand. What we get instead is 'crisis', 'disaster', 'row' and 'scam' as the grammatical node with further details appended through post-modification.

It would, in any case, be misleading to suggest that the grammar of headlines is dominated only by compression. One very common pattern is the following: 'X does Y as P does Q'.
Thus:
Hundreds queue   /   as bosses warn the system is breaking down.
Europe's big three meet / as the EU's smaller countries say they are being left out.
Nearly two hundred people are killed   /   as a derailed train explodes.
And a touch of sadness   /   as the Royal Navy leaves Hong Kong.

All these, bar the last one, involve two-part structures with each part comprising a full clause and both parts in the present tense (a characterisation that might be seen as running apparently counter to the previous observations about the 'non-finiteness' of headlines). In these cases we have fully finite clauses, marked for tense: people are killed, the system is breaking down, a derailed train explodes, the Royal Navy leaves Hong Kong. Each two-part example links one state or action in the present with another action in the present. But the result is a peculiar flattening of temporal perspective. Thus events, even when finite clauses do encode their relation to a time-line, happen in a timeless present with each event treated as somehow continuous with another and with the moment of utterance. Temporal sequence is suppressed; and without a sense of temporal sequence, causal relations – which are often crucial – are lost.

Thus, although headlines constitute a specialised sub-genre within broadcast news, they are noticeably not self-contained as instances of discourse at work. For one thing they draw intimately on public knowledge for their interpretation. In the case, for instance, of the junior conservative minister caught up at the centre of an election row, her name – Angela Brown – would not mean much to any constituency except the political class itself. So the headline begins not with her name but with an appropriate MCD – 'Conservative minister'. The reference, on the other hand, to 'Europe election row' was immediately explicable when broadcast at the beginning of a news programme during a British general election.

For another thing, however, opening headlines occupy a specialised anticipatory position within the sequence of the programme. Their role is not simply to frame the news, nor even to surprise the listener. Nor is compression the only – or even the crucial – determinant. Headlines function in their particular position to offer the audience metaphorically 'bait on a hook'. A tactical incompleteness is in this respect part of their design, providing audiences with reasons for listening or viewing further. Indeed, this is a feature of their design even at the local level of the headlines themselves where structures such as the following depend upon a heading followed by a supplement.

Ext. 4.3.2
1	PRESENTER:	**Train disaster in Iran.**
2		Nearly two hundred people are killed as a derailed train explodes.
3		An earthquake forced the wagons
4		carrying petrol and chemicals off the track.
5		**Dentists' crisis.**
6		Hundreds queue as bosses warn the system is breaking down.

"Train disaster" and "Dentists' crisis" function as cataphoric headings, projecting forward to the immediately following discourse, which then provides further material to supplement their meaning.

Projecting forward in the discourse to hold the audience can work within the headlines themselves, between heading and supplement, but is broadly the function of headlines in relation to the succeeding items of the programme, not merely to the first or second item in the news, but right down the running order. For a story occurring late down the running order, the following was probably a most effective headline:

Ext. 4.3.2
| 9 | And the mobile phone scam that could be costing you a small fortune |

Anyone with a mobile phone (a fairly substantial component of the audience) would most likely want to discover how they might be losing 'a small fortune'.

4.4 News items and news kernels

As was developed in Chapter 3, broadcast news items consist of an obligatory component – the news presentation embodying the news kernel – and one or more of several optional subsidiary[8] components. Sometimes news items may consist solely of the obligatory element – the newsreader's scripted delivery of the news kernel. This is the minimal form. Not every news item, for instance, will contain a report featuring actuality footage from the field, even though – for television news at least – video footage is clearly, whenever possible, a preferred dimension to news. Nor, for that matter, do live two-ways take place in relation to every report.

More complex news items feature elaborations from the minimal form by, for example, including footage from the field in the later section of the presentation with the newsreader's scripted kernel as voiceover to the footage. Another kind of elaboration uses the newsreader's presentation as an introduction to a report from the field. And a yet further elaboration is to attach or embed a live element from the reporter/correspondent/editor in the field within or after the report. This last might be considered the most fully elaborated version of a news item.

Recapitulating the diagram from Chapter 3, we can present the structure as follows:

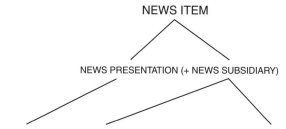

NEWS ITEM

NEWS PRESENTATION (+ NEWS SUBSIDIARY)

NEWS KERNEL (+ NEWS REPORT) (+ LIVE INTERVIEW WITH REPORTER/CORRESPONDENT)

Or as re-write rules:

1. NEWS ITEM   ➡   NEWS PRESENTATION (+ NEWS SUBSIDIARY)
2. NEWS PRESENTATION   ➡   NEWS KERNEL
3a. NEWS SUBSIDIARY   ➡   NEWS REPORT (+ LIVE 2WAY)
or
3b. NEWS SUBSIDIARY   ➡   LIVE 2WAY < NEWS REPORT > (where the report is embedded within a live 2-way)
or (very occasionally)
3c. NEWS SUBSIDIARY   ➡   LIVE 2WAY

In extended news programmes such as Channel 4 News even further elaborations may occur which use studio interviews for comment, for expert explanations, or to question the behaviour or the views of protagonists. The news kernel delivered by a presenter, however, is the essential element of broadcast news and it is this element that is the basic – sometimes the only – element in routine news programmes.

4.5   Features of news kernels

The news kernel is a condensed summary of the key facts of a news item, as in the following example.

Ext. 4.5.1

1 PRESENTER:	Israel's tanks and troops moved further	KERNEL
2	into the Palestinians' main West Bank city of Ramala today.	
3	There were more gun battles	
4	but the loss of life was not on the scale of yesterday.	
5	Tomorrow, America's peace negotiator arrives	
6	to try to put a stop to any killing.	
7	John Irvine reports …	REPORT

As a description this kernel is built around material involving typical news values of scale, recency, elite news and negativity. In addition, however, there are certain prevailing formal characteristics at work. The news event (or events) is encoded as text without incorporating any obvious modality or signalling the presence of a manifest narrator[9]. It is instead rendered by a simple sequence of precise, but un-sourced, averrals that locate what has happened in a time and place ("today", "yesterday", "tomorrow", "Israel", "West Bank", "Ramala"). The choice of tense is simple past ("tanks and troops **moved** further") or present ("… America's peace negotiator **arrives** …") and these choices carry a factual certainty unmodified by expressions, such as "appear to", "may have", "perhaps", that would indicate the role of an observer or news gatherer. Where alternation of tense takes place, it is usually from the past tense to the present tense, from a completed occurrence to an unfolding present ("tanks **moved** further today … tomorrow America's peace negotiator **arrives**"). The tense choices project a sense of factual certainty – an uncontroversial version of events is being offered, as if unlikely to be prone to dispute or contest. The discourse of a news kernel does not carry marks of the need to persuade an audience of an argument or a position. It establishes or presents the facts of the case as if generally uncontested. The function of these averrals is simply to describe what can be taken as the generally understood facts of the case.

This is not to say, of course, that these really are 'simply the facts', unadorned by any shaping rhetoric. Many news kernels conform to a straightforward rhetoric of contrast. In Extract 4.5.1 the contrasts are built around Israelis and Palestinians, yesterday and today, large scale versus small scale, today versus tomorrow and war versus peace. Other kinds of common news contrast are event or proposal versus reaction, capital versus labour, expectation versus reality and so on. Extract 4.5.2 below is a fairly typical case based on a contrasting two-part parallelism between outside and inside, between demonstrators ("**they**") and the Prime Minister, between dissent and agreement:

Ext. 4.5.2

I	PRESENTER: Outside Parliament they said
2	the Home Secretary's plans were demoralising the force.
3	Inside Parliament the Prime Minister said
4	most officers agreed with most of the changes.
5	Julie Ghosie reports …

The function of this contrastive rhetoric is to imbue the news with a sense of significance over and beyond what can be achieved through the projection of 'facticity' (Tuchman, 1978). News values (as discussed in Chapter 1) admittedly provide one kind of guarantee of interest through the notion of being 'up to the minute' (recency) and dealing with 'issues that matter' (scale and relevance). But another kind of guarantee of interest lies in the kind of aesthetic structuring built on a contrast of oppositions evidenced in Extracts 4.5.1 and 4.5.2.

Of course, the discourse of the news kernel is only one of the discourses that comprise the news. Accordingly, it functions as part of repertoire of discourses each with its own particular role to play alongside the others. As such, it operates differently from the discourse of headlines and it also operates differently, as we shall see, from the discourse of reports and the other kinds of subsidiary news discourses. Indeed, where subsidiary discourses follow the kernel, the role of the latter is not just to sum up the news but also to set the scene for the succeeding discourse. In this case, as described in Chapter 3, we find instances of discursive management at the end of the kernel where the transition from kernel presentation to subsidiary is managed by introductory prefaces such as:

Ex. 4.5.3

I	PRESENTER: Our Africa correspondent Tim Ewart
2	is one of the few television journalists
3	who've been covering the elections from inside Zimbabwe … .

Or

Ex. 4.5.4

PRESENTER: Here's our business editor Caroline Kerr …

Or

Ex. 4.5.5

PRESENTER: Here's Helen Wright …

In this way the transition is managed from presenting the *news kernel* to the *subsidiary discourse* of the report from the field of news. The institutional voice of the newsreader is replaced by that of the reporter, correspondent or editor. Although the latter speak from a position much closer to the event itself (e.g. "inside Zimbabwe"), for the purpose of the discourse at this point in time they are "here". In effecting transitions of this kind, the news presenter invariably identifies the next speaker not only by name but also by institutionally defined role, "our business editor", "our Africa correspondent". Indeed, all transitions from one speaker to another in broadcast news are handled by the news presenter and it is noticeable that this never happens without the presenter providing a first-time identification in terms of name and credentials-to-speak for a speaker within a news programme. In doing so, a clear line is drawn between those affiliated to the institution (in formulations such as "**our** ... editor", "**our** ... correspondent", "**our** reporter") and those not.

In considering features of the discourse of news kernels, it is natural to regard them as primarily concerned with encoding events, as well as with introducing other speakers with rights and/or obligations to speak from a site close to or identified with such events. Much news, however, does not deal with events as such – unless these are most broadly construed perhaps in terms of 'change of state'. Instead, broadcast news is commonly focused not so much on the/an event itself but on reactions to, on verbalisations about, and on the implications of the/an event, which is in itself simply presupposed. Here, for instance, are two typical news kernels:

Ext. 4.5.6
1 PRESENTER: The British mother arrested for kidnapping her own son in Dubai
2   has told ITV news
3   that it had been a last desperate effort to have some contact with him.
4   Sara Fotheringham was charged today but given bail.
5   Here's Helen Wright ... .

Ext. 4.5.7
1 PRESENTER: Here a one million pound pay-rise for the boss of BP
2   has been criticised tonight by union leaders.
3   Lord Browne's salary is going up to just over three million pounds.
4   The timing is embarrassing as petrol prices start to rise again.
5   The head of one union said the increase made him the fattest of fat cats.
6   Here's our business editor Caroline Kerr ...

The news event in this latter kernel is not so much the pay-rise itself (which is simply presupposed). It is rather that the pay-rise has been criticised: "The head of one union said the increase made him one of the fattest of fat cats" (Extract 4.5.7, l. 5). Similarly, it is not so much the kidnapping or the arrest that is the news event but what the mother has told ITV news.

Much of what counts as broadcast news is – perhaps surprisingly – verbal comment by parties to events: "detectives said …" … "President Mugabe was duly **declared the winner** of the elections in Zimbabwe. **The arguments** about whether they were fair **continued.**"

There are good reasons for this, which have been well-documented by sociologists of the media (Allan, 1999/2004; Gans, 1979/2004; Schlesinger, 1978/1992; Tuchman, 1978). Individual staff journalists tend to be assigned a specialist beat – for example, the courts and judiciary, local government, parliamentary politics, police, home affairs, business, celebrities – in the course of which, as gatherers of news, they receive circulars, press releases, statements, and other kinds of documentation, as well as briefings, announcements, confidences, and non-attributable gossip. They also attend regular press conferences associated with their beat. Much of what constitutes raw material for a news item starts life as text – ready-to-be-quoted. Sometimes the text is a reaction to an event. But equally often the news event is the text itself or a juxtaposition of texts.

The facticity of news kernels can be related to their use of unmarked modality and the absence of the speaker's point of view in the utterance: averrals that take the form of categorical assertion without obvious modal features or sharply evaluative lexis accrue to themselves the value of objectivity. However, a further way of 'doing objectivity', or impartiality, is by harvesting quotations from a range of representative viewpoints while aligning with none of them (as in Extracts 4.5.2 and 4.5.7). In addition, the contrastive structure of many kernels helps maintain a neutral equipoise in which neither side of an opposition is singled out for approval or blame. In Extract 4.5.7, for instance, the news that the 'boss of BP' has gained a pay increase is structured in terms of a simple opposition of employers versus unions, action versus reaction; but the account does not particularly take sides. In conclusion, therefore, it is possible to understand neutrality or impartiality as a produced consequence of the text's structure. And both objectivity and impartiality are most at stake when the institutional voice of the news provider is most dominant – especially in the kernel elements of the news.

4.6   Conclusions

The established and pervasive discursive default mode for communicating television news consists of a news presenter reading a scripted news kernel in direct visual address (through the camera) to the viewer as a representative of a news organisation such as CNN, or Fox or the BBC, rather than as individuals in their own right. The mode of presentation adopted with its institutional voice and associated forms of discourse projects a synoptic account of reality in which it is hard to discern a consistently identifiable evaluative position. This voice dominates broadcast news. But in most broadcast news the discourse supplied by the institutional voice is supplemented and elaborated by a range of other voices – some, such as correspondents and reporters, affiliated to the institution, some, such as politicians, bystanders, experts and witnesses, not. The presenter sets the discursive base-line of the news in the news kernel; but throughout the news programme they effectively orchestrate and integrate the other voices of the programme by introducing them, managing links between them and interviewing them. In their person presenters set the tone of the programme, define the quality of its relationship with the audience and constitute the discursive frame or aura that dominates the other kinds of subsidiary news discourses that may be drawn upon to constitute or elaborate the news. It is to these other voices and the discourses that they produce that we now turn.

5   The discourse of television news reports
Narrative or commentary?

5.0   Introduction

In Chapter 4 two main sites of broadcast news were distinguished: the constant space of the studio, from which presentation takes place, and the visually marked, fluctuating and dynamic site of the news itself. News is presented to us from the studio but television takes us to the news field as the discourse of the programme gathers in reports by video- or audio-clip or live feed from location after location. These are contrasting deictic points, proximate and distal, and are marked as such, for instance, in the discursive practices of transition: we now '**go to** our reporter **in Baghdad**' from where we are then 'handed **back to** the studio'.

Television, in particular, accentuates the distinction between these two different kinds of space. And these spaces in turn underpin two fundamental axes of the news programme: the axis of presentation – along which the news is presented from the deictic zero point to the audience; and the axis of reporting, along which the world is brought to the studio – from the field to the deictic zero point. As pointed out in Chapter 4, these two axes are the discursive lines of force for rather different kinds of discourse. If the discourse of news presentation arises on the axis from the studio to the audience in direct visual address, the discourse of the news report arises on the axis between the news field and the studio primarily as voice over. The use of actuality footage or video clips from the news field in conjunction with the discourse of the reporter, occasionally seen in direct visual address from the field, but mostly in unseen voice-over, is a major way of emphasising the difference between the studio and the field. And the use of voice-over to deliver words to pictures is one of the reasons that TV news reports are often cited as a form of narrative.

5.1   TV news and narrative

Indeed, it is something of a truism that news is a narrative form. For one thing, this view chimes with our common-sense description of news in terms of 'news stories' – a way of thinking shared alike by analysts, producers and consumers of the news. As Bell (1994) writes at the beginning of his article on press journalism – significantly entitled *Telling stories* – "Journalists do not write articles. They write stories" (p. 100). And certainly his analysis of press journalism as narrative is illuminating, demonstrating not only how narrative forms of the news have changed but also how professional pressures (sub-editing to meet the constraints of space, etc.) have helped to mould and re-mould those particular versions of narrative that dominate the press. In this he shares common ground with Caldas-Coulthard (1997) and Van Dijk (1988a,b), who in specifying the discourse structure of news stories draw upon schemata as well as, in Caldas-Coulthard's case, Labov's work on 'natural narrative' (Labov, 1972; Labov and Waletsky, 1967) to account for the coherence that news discourse displays[1].

Although the discourse of television news has received much less attention than that of print journalism, the well-established sense of news as narrative still provides a dominant model (see, for example, Hartley, 1982; Fiske, 1987; Graddol, 1994). Here, for instance, is Graddol:

> TV news tells stories about the world and the dominant narrative technique for such storytelling is what is called *realism*. Realism of the kind I am referring to here first arose as literary convention (p. 140) . . .

> The cinema adopted and adapted the realist narrative techniques of the novel (p. 141) . . . Realism thus provides a powerful visual technology for cueing narrative modalities. The regime of camera work and editing is so naturalized that we rarely stop to think about its artifice. (p. 142) . . . Indeed, the realist technique is so naturalized that TV news cannot avoid drawing on its resources when telling its own narratives (p. 142).

This is a very strong claim about the way pre-existing cinematic codes have determined a narrative tendency in TV news discourse[2].

Despite the confidence with which such perspectives are advanced, several problems arise when notions of narrative are applied to television news. Firstly, on closer inspection it is not at all clear – despite what Graddol says – that TV news footage bears much (or, indeed, any) resemblance to the narrative forms of fiction cinema. At a very obvious level the pervasive and habitual mode of address of TV news, involving direct visual address to camera, is hardly ever seen in fiction film. More fundamentally, perhaps, the guiding principle of mainstream narrative cinema is to unfold an action in which identifiable protagonists are engaged, so that the task of continuity editing, as evidenced in classic Hollywood cinema, is to develop character and action in a narrative trajectory that leads to a resolution (Kuhn, 1985; Bordwell and Thompson, 1979; Bordwell, 1985).

Television narrative, however, as Ellis (1982) persuasively claims, is more diffuse, more fragmentary, more episodic and iterative than cinema.

This is particularly true of news. Even in an area where comparisons are often made – the depiction of war – television news coverage conspicuously lacks the narrative coherence of the Hollywood war movie – even of those films where '(documentary) realism' is a much declared production value (such as, for example, the opening scenes of *Saving Private Ryan*). For, unlike cinema, where the structure of editing is devoted to following the fate of a character (or characters) to some kind of closure, television news presents actions which are often incomplete and where no identifiable character or protagonist is offered to help structure the subjective identification of the viewer[3].

A second and more serious difficulty is that much television news in its textual particulars quite simply fails to exhibit story-telling characteristics. On the contrary, the core principle of intelligibility in television news reports might be summed up as the convincing deployment of pictures – and, in this respect, narrative is only an occasional discursive resource even when the notion of an event or happening provides an important background element in news coverage.

Indeed, as many have noted, news as a system is uncomfortable for various reasons with the unfolding complexities of abstract social and historical processes such as economic change or international diplomacy. These become foreshortened in routine news coverage to the most recent action/event and its consequences. Examples abound: labour unrest becomes condensed to a strike, visualised as picket lines, and its consequences for the public. The democratic process becomes condensed to the election campaign. Parliamentary policy-making becomes condensed to a crucial vote, or Prime Minister's Question Time. The invasion of Iraq by a Western coalition takes place as bombing raids, firefights and overturned statues. Television news coverage, in the face of complexity, seeks out the iconic and emblematic incident.

In this foreshortening, however, even those events that are reported may lack a narratable structure. More crucially, perhaps, many news reports – although they may take the background of events for granted – set out to tell no story but to do some other kind of discursive work. Indeed, attempts to conceptualise television news primarily in terms of narrative distort our understanding of the prevalent characteristics of journalism as a textual system – especially in its televised manifestations.

Instead of assuming from the outset, therefore, that the intelligibility of television news is grounded in narrative, it is arguably more revealing to identify some pervasive characteristics of the texts of television news and then to elaborate from these characteristics some core principles of their discursive intelligibility. In what follows, therefore, I will lay out some recurring elements of the verbal texts of television news reports in order to suggest some crucial principles of non-narrative coherence that the discourse of TV news reports relies upon, before returning to the question of narrative in TV news.

5.2   Some textual features and principles of intelligibility of television news reports: tense and reference

Despite variations depending on the time of day and the 'house style' of the broadcaster, television news reports often rely heavily on the present tense. In particular, daytime (rather than evening) television reports and the BBC (as opposed, for example, to ITN) tend to favour the present tense. (Lettering at the beginning of examples – ASRA, RCF, SETI, WIC, ES, PCCD – refer to transcribed television reports reproduced at the end of the chapter. Vertical lines in the reports are used to designate shot boundaries.)

[ASRA]
8   REPORTER: | Bad weather *cloaks* the mountains above Kaprun
9 | *bringing* yet more warnings of avalanches. |

[ASRA]
10 REPORTER: | Heavy snowfalls *are* only *adding* to the risks.
11   Warmer temperatures at |
12   this time of the year *make* the fresh snow unstable
13   – more liable to move. |

[ASRA]
14 REPORTER: | For now, most of the ski slopes here *are* shut.
15   The authorities | *aren't taking* any chances. |

[RCF]
15 REPORTER: | The friendly society which commissioned the survey *says*
16   grieving | relatives rarely *get* a | true picture of the funeral costs
17 | before committing themselves.
18   Its spokesman *says* funeral directors *are giving* them cheap initial quotes
19   which typically *double* before the funeral's over,
20   an issue *being investigated* by the Office of Fair Trading. |

[SETI]
11 REPORTER: | No-one *knows* how many stars are in our universe.
12   And so far no-one *knows*
13   if | – like our sun – they can support life on nearby planets.
14   But by *using* the | Araseevo radio telescope at Puerto Rico –
15   the largest of its kind | in the world –
16   astronomers *are trying* to find out
17   if there is intelligent alien life outside our solar system. |

[WIC]
52 REPORTER: The wounded *are* brought here to a bar ...
53   Hygiene *is* minimal. Standards low.
54   This *is* how they sterilise surgical instruments.
55   But what they *lack* in perfection,
56   the medical team *makes up for* in determination,
57   desperately trying to save the life of yet another comrade-in-arms

This is not the historic (or conversational historic) present – the use of the present to describe past events – noted by analysts of narrative (see, for example, Woolfson, 1979, 1982) ("She reached into her bag. She *feels* for her mobile phone. *Realises* with a shock it's missing ...). In examples of the historic present, sequence is recoverable as well as a sense of the events having been completed in time before the moment of telling. This is not the case with the present tense of news, for which various uses may be distinguished.

First of all, the action may be projected as contemporaneous with and projecting beyond the moment of utterance. Thus, examples such as "most of the ski slopes are shut" (ASRA), or "heavy snowfalls are adding to the risks" (ASRA), refer to an ongoing state of affairs at the time of broadcast utterance. Second, a version of the customary present may be used to refer to an action that is routinely repeated or a state of affairs that endures: for example, "The wounded are brought here to a bar" (WIC), "Funeral directors are giving them cheap quotes" (RCF), "Astronomers are trying to find out ..." (SETI) or "No-one knows how many stars are in the universe" (SETI). Third, the present tense is used to refer to an action that could still apply even though it is completed: thus, "the friendly society says grieving relatives ..." (RCF) refers to an action that has been completed but since the proposition that it governs ("grieving relatives rarely get a true picture of funeral costs") is taken as continuing to apply after the moment of utterance, then the act of saying can be taken as reiterated as long as the proposition still applies.

In part this salience of the present tense is driven by the news value of 'recency' (Galtung and Ruge, 1965a and b; Golding and Elliott, 1979). The news has to be new – dealing with *The Day Today*, as the satirical parody of a news programme was called. But the common use of the present tense in news reports does more than project the news as right up to date and dealing with 'the now'; it also helps to create a sense of referring to a present reality. The frequent selection of the present tense helps to collapse the distance between the news field and its report in such a way that undermines chronology. In addition, the present tense, inasmuch as it is unmarked for modality, contributes to the routine 'facticity' (Tuchman, 1978) of televisual news discourse.

5.3   Textual cohesion in television news reports: the interplay of the visual with the verbal

If the choice of tense emphasises the 'present-ness' of the reality depicted in the report, images of that reality serve as a visual back-up to the words. The presence of these images ensures that the way textual cohesion works in the verbal track of a news report is somewhat different from the way it works in standard written text. Consider the following extract from the verbal text of a news report.

PCDD

I	REPORTER:	Another motorist is pulled over by the police
2		as part of their crackdown on drink-driving.
3	POLICEMAN:	"A good strong blow please an ah'll tell ye when to stop.
4		Keep blowin'. Keep blowin'. Keep blowin'" [fade out]
5	REPORTER:	This man hadn't been drinking. He was simply lost.
6		But last year one in six deaths on our roads were drink-related.
7		And across the UK the figures are edging upward.
8		A new survey suggests half of Britain's drivers admit
9		drinking before getting behind the wheel.
10		And many have little idea about the potency of alcohol.
11		Anything over two units will put you over the limit.
12		Each of these drinks represents one unit of alcohol:
13		that's a glass of wine, a half-pint of beer and a measure of spirit.
14		But what happens if your wine comes in a large glass
15		or the lager you're drinking happens to be a strong continental type.
16		Each of these on their own will put you over the limit
17		and merely adds to the confusion.
18	PUB CUST'ER:	"This a Stella Artois which ah know is quite strong.
19		It's heading towards a whole one and a half to two units.
20		So again it's probably a pint is as much.
21		But the best thing is not to do it."

If this were standard written text the reader would be puzzled in the first instance by who/what is the referent for "this man", "each of these drinks" "each of these on their own" and so on. But this text, of course, is part of a package assembled from video and audio material gathered on location, at the roadside, or in a pub. The visual and verbal elements are edited together along with the reporter's 'voice-over'. So the passage in quotation marks, transcribed above, for instance, is not introduced by reporting clauses such as 'The Strathclyde Police Officer said: ...'. The package merely shows the police officer, the drinker in the pub, the reporter – and simply uses the visual depiction (sometimes supported by caption) to identify them. Indeed, there are several points in the transcription of the verbal track where the verbal text makes sense by reference to what is visible in the visual track.

I	Another motorist is pulled over ...
5	This man hadn't been drinking ...
16	Each of these drinks represents one unit of alcohol ...
18	This is a Stella Artois ...

Broadly what is at stake in this, and most TV news reports, is a presumption of shared reference between the verbal track and the visual track so that for any single report there will be at least some overlap for some of the time between word and image. This is reinforced verbally by a specialised use of spatial deixis:

[SETI]
19 REPORTER: | If you're hoping for proof of an alien civilisation
20   then the best place to be in the UK is *here* at the Jodrell Bank Observatory
21   *here* in Cheshire.
22   Because its radio telescope is so sensitive
23   it could detect *one* | *of these* from 220 million | miles away. |

[RCF]
21 REPORTER: | Few of the people buried *here* in Highgate Cemetery have endured a |

[ASRA]
20 REPORTER: | Not *everyone here* seems aware of the danger. |

[ASRA]
14 REPORTER: | For now, most of the ski slopes *here* are shut. |

[ASRA]
29 REPORTER: | Relatives of those who died in the accident
30   have also been arriving *here* |

[ASRA]
31 REPORTER: | The number of avalanches *here* has increased sharply
32   during the last few years.

In addition to this kind of deixis there are related patterns of usage of demonstrative reference:

[PCDD]
This man hadn't been drinking ...

[RCF]
In *this* demonstration of a typical funeral ...

[SETI]
It could detect one of *these*

[PCDD]
Each of these drinks

[PCDD]
Each of these on their own

[WIC]
This is as far as Russian patrols dare go

[WIC]
This is one section of the front line

[WIC]
This is how they sterilise surgical instruments

In these examples, and commonly elsewhere in TV news reports, deixis and demonstrative reference is proximate rather than distal and, in some cases at least, it seems to refer not simply to 'near' rather than 'far' but to what is visible in the visual track of the report. These sentences cue a close connection between what is being said in the verbal track and what can be seen in the visual track of the report.

Indeed, there is a general sense in TV news reports of co-reference along the two tracks so that what the verbal dimension of the text refers to is also seen to be referred to in the visual track. So a clause such as

[ASRA]
| Flashing lights tell skiers and snowboarders there's a serious possibility of avalanches.

is accompanied by a shot of a flashing light.

[ASRA]
| Bad weather cloaks the mountains above Kaprun |

is accompanied by a long shot of a snow grooming vehicle obscured by wind-driven snow. And a clause such as

[ASRA]
| For now, most of the ski slopes here are shut.

is accompanied by a shot of an empty set of ski-lift chairs swinging in the wind.

Thus, whilst expressions such as "one of these" or "most of the ski slopes here" function to cue a connection between the verbal and visual tracks, there is a more generalised sense of co-reference at work. It is important to note, however, that identifying a visual correlate of a verbal referring expression is the outcome of sometimes complex and cumulative inferential work: in other words, although it may seem transparent on casual viewing that the visual track refers to same things as the verbal track, the connections depend upon an inferential accomplishment. Thus, a group of three adults huddled together is seen as a group of mourners precisely because – against the background of a presumption of a connection between word and image – the verbal track tells us in voice-over to the shot:

[ASRA]
29 REPORTER: | *Relatives of those who died* in the accident
30   have also been arriving here | mourning their sudden loss. |

5.4 Principles of intelligibility in TV news reports

Thus, the supposition of co-reference between the verbal and visual tracks is an effect of the discourse in which sentences including proximate deixis and demonstratives ("here", "this", "these") cue us to find an overarching relationship between word and image. In practice, of course, the relationship between the verbal and visual components of a news report proves to be uneven and erratic. Meinhof (1994), for instance, notes three main kinds of interrelationship, which she describes as 'overlap', 'displacement' and 'dichotomy'. Overlap is where the visual footage and the verbal text share the same action component. Displacement is where the footage and the text represent different action components (e.g. the effect of a disaster depicted in image, with its cause described in words). Dichotomy is where footage and text represent action components of different, if related, events. There is obviously a cline or gradient between extremes and it is important to note that different economies of exchange between word and image can obtain at different moments within the same news report. Nonetheless, despite the potential for shift and variation, a primary principle of intelligibility of the televisual discourse of news reports may be formulated as follows:

RULE 1:
FOR ANY REFERRING EXPRESSION IN THE VERBAL TRACK,
SEARCH FOR A RELEVANT REFERENT IN THE IMAGE TRACK.

Conversely, however, a secondary and complementary principle might be formulated thus:

RULE 2:
TREAT ANY ELEMENT DEPICTED IN A SHOT IN THE VISUAL TRACK
AS A POTENTIAL REFERENT FOR A REFERRING EXPRESSION
IN THE VERBAL TRACK.

It is the operation of these twin rules of interpretation (or principles of intelligibility) that achieves a closure between what we can see and what we can hear represented in televisual news discourse. This might be called 'the effect of simultaneous (verbal and visual) reference'. It is this effect that explains a problem noted by Meinhof (1994). She observed that the same shot of a man with a container on the back of his bike included in both a German news programme and a British news programme was interpreted by viewers respectively as transporting water or petrol. The variable reading of the image was prompted by alternative wordings in the two reports: the German programme referred to food shortages whereas the British programme referred to petrol shortages (Meinhof, 1994, pp. 217–221). Underlying the discrepant interpretations are the twin rules of interpretation, noted above: viewers were predisposed to find the container on the back of the bike as either petrol or water on the basis of the presumption of simultaneous overlapping reference.

The presumption of overlapping reference is reinforced not just by cueing sentences (for example, "the best place to be in the UK is *here at the Jodrell Bank Observatory here* in Cheshire. Because its *radio telescope* is so sensitive it could detect *one* | *of these* from 220 million | miles away. |") where proximate deixis and demonstratives reinforce the relationship between word and image. It is also reinforced by synchronised editing in which the transition from one shot to the next coincides with clause and sentence boundaries, though the degree of synchronisation varies. In cases of close synchronisation as many as two-thirds of the cuts between one shot and the next within the body of the report will occur at clause and sentence boundaries. And it is rare to find less than one-third correspondence between shot boundaries and the boundaries of clause and sentence. On average there is close to a 50 per cent correspondence between shot boundaries and those of clause or sentence[4]. In the following example of a short news report on endangered species (see 1–10, pages 99–104 below), the correspondence of shot transitions with major clause boundaries is very tight at 80 per cent. (Each shot is numbered and its onset in the transcribed verbal track is marked by the symbol ▶. The shot itself may be held and it may track or pan to follow an object or zoom to close in on it. But each cut to a new shot is marked by ▶. The transcribed verbal track is divided into clauses marked by the symbol '/'. The two symbols coincide eight out of ten times.)

(1) ► // meet the red panda / it's a bit like a racoon / a bit like a bear / and it's just one of a group of unusual animals that are genetically unique and threatened with extinction /

(2) ► // scientists say too many of the world's most extraordinary animals are being ignored / "An(d) these species are really the crown jewels er er in in biodiversity /

(3) ▶ / there's nothing out there like them / they're unique in the way that they live in the way that they behave and the way that they look / and not only that / they're threatened as well / so it's important that we act now to conserve them" /

▶   // some would say it's often the smaller members of

(4) ► / the animal world that are neglected // most species of lima

(5) ► / are in danger and they don't have many close relatives

(6) ▶ / so if these disappear it's a big loss

(7) ▶ // also at risk is the elephant shrew named because of its long flexible
    trunk / it's found only in Kenya / but it's now threatened by hunting /
    and its habitat is being destroyed /

(8) ► // more familiar is the camel / but this is the two humped version or baktrian camel /

(9) ► // they're critically endangered with less than a thousand remaining the wilds of Mongolia and China /

(10) ▶ // scientists are calling for more research into unique creatures like these before its too late / Christine McGourty / BBC News /

It can be seen that the onset of most shots here corresponds with a major clause boundary[5]. This form of visual editing which is closely synchronised with the verbal syntax helps to reinforce a sense of mutual assembly of the words and images and hence of their reciprocal relevance: the words seem to be driving the pictures at the same time as the pictures seem to be driving the words.

Finally, the presumption of overlapping reference is supported by the notion that the words and the pictures in news reports emanate or issue from a defined and visualised space. In each of the reports cited below (see appendices) the speakers deliver their wording for the most part as unseen voice-over; but at some point in the report this same speaker will be featured in direct address to camera – even if only momentarily – and thereby situated in the space from which the report (in part, at least) is projected. And routinely, of course, the voice of the report 'signs off' with some kind of locational formulation: "Brent Sadler, CNN, Grozny"; "Andrew Verity, BBC News in Highgate Cemetery"; "Jonathan Charles, BBC News, Kaprun". Thus the speaker in voice-over not only identifies him or herself by name but simultaneously situates him or herself in the space of the broadcast.

In summary, therefore, prevalent characteristics of television news reports include:

- Common use of the present tense to refer to an ongoing reality, parts of which may be interpreted as visible in the visual track.
- Frequent use of proximate deixis to refer to items in the visual field presented in the news package, so that the verbal track 'cues' attention to items represented in the visual track.

- Synchronised editing that helps establish parallelism between verbal and visual tracks: not only does the verbal track refer us to the visual track, but the visual track has been edited to match the verbal track (and/or vice versa) so that the boundaries of formal units from the separate tracks coincide.
- Locating the voice of the reporter as coming from (or at least associated with) the scene depicted visually – this being done both visually (through the inserted piece to camera) and verbally (through the routine of 'signing off' from the apparent location).

These features combine to underpin an overarching principle governing TV news reports – the presumption of overlapping or complementary reference between the verbal and the visual. No-one assumes, watching a news report, that the pictures have been selected randomly and that they have little bearing on the words being spoken.

5.5   The intelligibility of television news reports: an example

Most of these processes can be illustrated in more detail by considering a fuller version of an example referred to in 5.3 above, but now with a shot analysis added.

[PCDDD]

1a   {Long shot from interior of one stationary car – a police car – towards two police officers on either side of stationary car ahead.}

1 REPORTER: | Another motorist is pulled over by the police

2   as part of their crackdown on drink-driving. |

3a   {Close up shot of man blowing into instrument}

3 POLICE OFFICER: | "A good strong blow please an ah'll tell ye when to stop.

4   Keep blowin'. Keep blowin'. Keep blowin'"

[fade out of voice of policeman and diegetic sound, replaced with voice-over of reporter]

5 REPORTER: | This man hadn't been drinking. He was simply lost. |

6a   {Mid shot of same man flanked by two police officers}

6 | But last year one in six deaths on our roads were drink-related. |

7a   {Shot of police-car roof with flashing lights from rear}

7 | And across the UK the figures are edging upward. |

8a   {Panoramic shot of (pub) interior}

8 | A new survey suggests half of Britain's drivers |

9a   {Close up of Christmas decorations}

9 | admit drinking before getting behind the wheel. |

10a   {Low angle close up profile shot of male drinking from a pint glass labelled Guinness}

10 | And many have little idea about the potency of alcohol. |

11a   {Close up profile shot of man drinking from pint glass}
11 | Anything over two units will put you over the limit. |

....

12a   {Close up of man A speaking in profile}
12 PUB CUST'ER: | "This a Stella Artois which ah know is quite strong.
13   It's heading towards a whole one and half to two units.
14   So again it's probably a pint is as much.
15   But the best thing is not to do it." |
16a   {Close up of man B speaking in profile}
16 PUB CUST'ER: | "Everybody is different innit they? (....)
17   It's what ye limitations are, I suppose,
18   or what ye think are yer limitations." |
19a   {Close up of reporter speaking to camera in visual direct address}
19 REPORTER: | Every year government sponsored adverts
20   ram home the dangers of drink driving.
21a   {Reporter speaks over a sequence of seven shots from a
         Government sponsored advert}
21 | It works for many motorists but for others the police are the deterrent. |
22a   {Mid shot of police officer in front of damaged car}
22 POLICE OFFICER: | "The core message is 'don't drink and drive'.
23   You can see the results behind me.
24   If ye are gonna drink and drive, we're gonna do our damned nest
to catch ye." |
25a   {Panning shot up and zoom close on front of damaged car}
25 REPORTER: | The results of ignoring the warning, say the police,
26   are more wrecked cars and wrecked |
27a   {Close up from beside car on some kind of cloth material draped
         over front seat and steering wheel}
27 | lives. Andrew Cassell. BBC News. Glasgow |

The material – as with most edited news reports – seems on casual viewing to be discursively coherent and intelligible. Thus, at the beginning of
the report, when the verbal track tells us about a motorist being stopped
by police, the visual track shows us police on either side of a stationary
car. And we likewise interpret images of a man blowing into some instrument as exemplifying the police crackdown on drink-driving. At the end of
the report we see a damaged car again as exemplary – as fitting the verbal
reference to a 'wrecked car' – one that comes from 'ignoring the warning'
about drink-driving. There is a high degree of correspondence between clause
boundaries and shot transitions. The middle section of the report includes
a piece to camera by the reporter. The report signs off with the routine
reference to the identity of the reporter and a specification of where the
report is from.
    It is crucial to stress, however, that the presumption of simultaneous
reference is an effect of the text and of the inferences which it prompts.

If we consider the opening of the news report, transcribed in its entirety above, most viewers will make several perfectly routine and commonplace assumptions about what they can see. They will assume, for instance, that:

- The two men in uniform wearing yellow jackets and peaked hats visible on either side of a stationary car are police officers.
- The two men (police officers) have stopped the car that is stationary.
- The driver of the stationary car is suspected of drink-driving.
- The man seen blowing into an instrument in the second shot is the driver of the stationary car in the first shot.
- He has been asked to blow into the instrument because he is suspected of drink-driving.
- The instrument into which he blows is for measuring quantities of alcohol on breath (a breathalyser)
- We see part of this from the vantage point of a police car.

It would be difficult to account for these inferences on the basis of the pictures alone. Without the verbal track to guide and prompt them, other conclusions could be drawn. Indeed, as the report itself subsequently reveals "This man hadn't been drinking. He was simply lost". Elsewhere, for example, the report asserts "| And many have little idea about the potency of alcohol. |". This assertion is accompanied by a shot consisting of a {low angle close up profile shot of male drinking from a pint glass labelled Guinness}. A routine assumption will link these elements by means of the inference that the man drinking Guinness (an assumption in itself) is one of the many who have little idea about the potency of alcohol. These assumptions arise in a matter-of-fact way (reinforced by the reporter pointing up the confusions surrounding units). They are little disturbed by the ensuing shot of 'an ordinary drinker' at a bar giving a very precise estimate of the units at stake in the Stella Artois which he's drinking.

This is not to claim that some kind of deception or *trompe-l'œil* is being perpetrated in news reports – only that such packages invite routine assumptions dependent upon co-referencing between word and image. And two kinds of assumption are present in this routine co-referencing:

- that there is a reciprocal connection between word and image of the kind stipulated in Rules 1 and 2 above;
- that what is visible in the image has a kind of documentary status.

Unless marked to the contrary, the image depicts an element found in reality, not staged for the camera. The image may be 'illustrative' or 'representative' but it is 'real', not 'faked' or 'staged'[6].

Indeed, the processes at stake support exactly Tolson's observation that the "illustrative use of the image is one way in which the news gives the impression of 'fact' – that is to say, factuality is a produced consequence of this text's particular structure" (Tolson, 1996, p. 18). The news field – the world depicted in the pictures of television news – is constituted for us as indexically real – as a reality which is presumed in every act of reference to be pre-existing it and enduring beyond it. It is not summoned into existence for the purpose of the news (like the mimetic or diegetic worlds of drama or fictional cinema). It requires no willing suspension of disbelief or act or willed credulity to believe in it. Rather the news constantly seems to index a reality to be taken for granted in its existence (even though what we see and hear from there may intrigue, appal, dismay, hearten or entertain). Television news reports what is there, linking word and image in routine acts of reference which require reciprocally routine acts of inference to be intelligible, marking out the contours of the news field in a continuously re-asserted compact between reporter and audience.

5.6 Conclusions: narrative or commentary in TV news reports?

Considering news as a system in its entirety ('*the* sense-making practice of modernity' as Hartley describes it: 1996, pp. 32–33) one can of course find examples of narrative, just as one can reveal the narrative elements implicated in therapy, drama, gossip, fine art, cinema, historiography, conversation, court-room cross-examination, or jury deliberation. But news on television only intermittently relies on narrative. It nearly always, however, relies on pictures. And in doing so it has evolved a quite distinctive discursive practice and posture within the overall order of discourse of the news. Although news as a whole admittedly does bring us a world of happenings, television news is not so much about telling the structure of events as about showing where incidents are located. It is a curious kind of mimesis as much as it is diegesis. It is about referencing the familiar parameters of a world taken-for-granted but which most of us rarely see at first hand. Indeed, it defines the significant parameters of that very world which it makes familiar and goes on to inhabit it with scenes or settings or faces or types which become iconic and immediately intelligible: Trafalgar Square and demonstrators/supporters, the House of Commons and the Prime Minister or the Leader of the Opposition, Cardiff Arms Park and football supporters, traders gesticulating on the New York stock exchange, lawyers arriving at the Old Bailey. Even where the spaces, the people and the incidents are highly particular, television news invests them with a representative status. Individuals and settings cannot be shown without them becoming emblematic typifications. A portly man in glasses blowing into a breathalyser at the roadside becomes 'the motorist (who may have drunk too much)'. A tall thin man sipping a pint of Guinness becomes 'one of the many (of us) who don't understand units of alcohol'.

Only occasionally are these reports 'history in the making'. Often they cover broadly what might be called 'public information': a toll motorway is opening parallel to a busy section of the M6 – motorists will be able to pay to avoid congestion; using a mobile phone while driving will become illegal from tonight; the police will crack down this Christmas on drink-driving; a new scientific assessment casts fresh doubt on the possible link between the MMR vaccine and autism; the government is proposing an 'honesty box' to make credit agreements more transparent; house prices are still rising in most parts of the country; obesity is on the increase in young people. These announcements ratify or produce a world held in common with particular structures, not so much of narrative but of concern – with health, with property, with life-style, with transport, with the law. Those who watch the news, it is implied, are concerned about our children, take package holidays, want to observe the law, enter into credit agreements, have mortgages and so on. The news in its iterative fashion refers us repeatedly to this world which it produces and reproduces as a normative order. For this reason, it would seem fair to say that much of what is spoken by news reporters as voice-over to news reports is better described as "commentary", or maybe as a species of public announcement, rather than narration. And while some news events and some genres of news give rise to storyable forms, television news generally is best understood in other terms. In television news, word is to image as commentary is to illustration. That, rather than narrative, is its core principle of intelligibility.

Appendices

The data on which this chapter is based are drawn mostly from news reports broadcast by BBC television either at 1.00 p.m. or during the late evening (usually 10 p.m.) news programme. One report is from CNN. They were selected at random from the main body of their respective news programmes. In other words none of them was broadcast as part of the lead or the closing news item. As such they would seem to be fairly typical of routine, unmarked news items. They were transcribed and punctuated as if they were written text (except where, as in APP1, there is strong presence of vernacular forms). In addition some transcripts include information about shot transition, indicated by | ▶.

Information about the nature of the accompanying shot has been included in the first transcript within curly brackets thus: {Mid shot of same man flanked by two police officers}.

A sample of transcripts drawn on in this chapter is given below.

Ext. I: Police crackdown on drink-driving [PCDD]
Ia   {Long shot from interior of one stationary car – a police car – towards two police officers on either side of stationary car ahead.}

1	REPORTER:		Another motorist is pulled over by the police
2			as part of their crackdown on drink-driving.
3a		{Close up shot of man blowing into instrument}
3	POLICE OFFICER:		"A good strong blow please an ah'll tell ye when to stop.
4			Keep blowin'. Keep blowin'. Keep blowin'"

[fade out of voice of policeman and diegetic sound, replaced with voice-over of reporter]

5	REPORTER:		This man hadn't been drinking. He was simply lost.
6a		{Mid shot of same man flanked by two police officers}
6			But last year one in six deaths on our roads were drink-related.
7a		{Shot of police-car roof with flashing lights from rear}
7			And across the UK the figures are edging upward.
8a		{Panoramic shot of (pub) interior}
8			A new survey suggests half of Britain's drivers
9a		{Close up of Christmas decorations}
9			admit drinking before getting behind the wheel.
10a		{Low angle close up profile shot of male drinking from a pint glass labelled Guinness}
10			And many have little idea about the potency of alcohol.
11a		{Close up profile shot of man drinking from pint glass}
11			Anything over two units will put you over the limit.

....

12a		{Close up of man A speaking in profile}
12	PUB CUST'ER:		"This a Stella Artois which ah know is quite strong.
13		It's heading towards a whole one and half to two units.
14		So again it's probably a pint is as much.
15		But the best thing is not to do it."
16a		{Close up of man B speaking in profile}
16	PUB CUST'ER:		"Everybody is different innit they? (....)
17		It's what ye limitations are, I suppose,
18		or what ye think are yer limitations."
19a		{Close up of reporter speaking to camera in visual direct address}
19	REPORTER:		Every year government sponsored adverts
20		ram home the dangers of drink driving.
21a		{Reporter speaks over a sequence of seven shots from a Government sponsored advert}
21			It works for many motorists but for others the police are the deterrent.
22a		{Mid shot of police officer in front of damaged car}
22	POLICE OFFICER:		"The core message is 'don't drink and drive'.
23		You can see the results behind me.
24		If ye are gonna drink and drive, we're gonna do our damned nest
to catch ye."
25a		{Panning shot up and zoom close on front of damaged car}
25	REPORTER:		The results of ignoring the warning, say the police,
26		are more wrecked cars and wrecked

27a   {Close up from beside car on some kind of cloth material draped
       over front seat and steering wheel}
27 | lives. Andrew Cassell. BBC News. Glasgow |

Ext. 2: Endangered Species [ES]

I REPORTER: ▶ // meet the red panda /
2   it's a bit like a racoon a bit like a bear /
3   and it's just one of a group of unusual animals
4   that are genetically unique / and threatened with extinction /
5   ▶ // scientists say
6   too many of the world's most extraordinary animals are being ignored //
7 ZOOLOGIST: "An(d) these species are really the crown jewels er in in biodiversity /
8   ▶ / there's nothing out there like them /
9   they're unique in the way that they live /
10   in the way that they behave and in the way they look /
11   and not only that / they're threatened as well /
12   so it's important that we act now to conserve them" /
13 REPORTER: ▶ // some would say
14   that it's often the smaller members of the animal world that are neglected
15   / most species of lima
16   ▶ are in danger and they don't have many close relatives /
17   ▶ / so if these disappear it's a big loss /
18   ▶ // also at risk is the elephant shrew
19   named because of its long flexible trunk /
20   it's found only in Kenya / but it's now threatened by hunting /
21   and its habitat is being destroyed /
22   ▶ // more familiar is the camel /
23   but this is the two humped version or baktrian camel /
24   ▶ / they're critically endangered
25   with less than a thousand remaining in the wilds of Mongolia and China /
26   ▶ // scientists are calling
27   For more research into unique creatures like these before its too late /
28   Christine McGourty / BBC News /

Ext. 3: Austrian Ski Resort Avalanche [ASRA]

I PRESENTER: Rescuers have abandoned
2   the search for two snow-boarders
3   missing after yesterday's avalanche in Austria
4   because of dense fog and the risk of further slides.
5   Eleven people died near the ski resort of Kaprun
6   and as our correspondent Jonathan Charles reports
7   this morning most of the ski runs were closed.
8 REPORTER: ▶ *Bad weather cloaks* the mountains above Kaprun |
9   ▶ bringing yet more warnings of avalanches. |
10   ▶ Heavy *snowfalls* are only adding to the risks.

11   Warmer temperatures at |
12   ▶ this time of the year make the fresh snow unstable –
13   more liable to move. |
14   ▶ For now, most of the ski slopes here *are shut.*
15   The authorities | ▶ aren't taking any chances. |
16   ▶ | Flashing lights tell
16   skiers and snowboarders there's a serious possibility of avalanches.
17   Yesterday's tragedy appears to have been triggered
18   by a group that were skiing | ▶ away from marked paths
19   right in front of a massive wall of snow. |
20   ▶ | Not everyone here seems aware of the danger.

.... INTERVIEW CLIP ....

21   ▶ | Few of the skiers appear to have been deterred by the avalanche though |
22   ▶ | *One British group* told us the risks are minimal
23   as long as you stick to slopes which are properly prepared and monitored. |

.... INTERVIEW CLIP ....

24   ▶ | *Military helicopters* were called in earlier today
25   to help in the search for two snowboarders
26   ▶ | who are still missing after the avalanche. |
27   But the operation ▶ | is now being abandoned
28   because visibility at the top of the ▶ mountain is too poor. |
29   ▶ | *Relatives of those who died* in the accident have also been arriving here
30   ▶ | mourning their sudden loss. |
31   Reporter [to camera] ▶ | The number of avalanches *here*
32   has increased sharply during the last few years.
33   That's not just dangerous.
34   It's also bad for the tourist industry.
35   The Austrian authorities are now trying to persuade people
36   that it's still safe to ski.
37   Jonathan Charles, BBC News, Kaprun |

Ext. 4: The Rising Costs of Funerals [RCF]

1 PRESENTER: The cost of a burial has risen by a quarter since 1998
2   and has more than doubled since 1990.
3   The annual survey of funeral costs in Britain shows
4   a large increase in bills for both burials and cremations.
5   The average burial service now costs more than £2000.
6 REPORTER: ▶ | *Funerals* are a distressing time for a family
7   even without ▶ | the fear of excessive costs.
8   In this demonstration of a typical funeral the real life cost
9   ▶ | would be two thousand and fifty pounds

10   up twenty five per cent from two years ago. |

11   ► | According to today's survey the price of an average cremation

12   went up by a tenth to one thousand, two hundred and fifteen pounds.

13   ► | Funeral directors say

14   they shouldn't be held to blame for the rising prices.

.... INTERVIEW CLIP ....

15   ► | The friendly society which commissioned the survey says

16   grieving ► | relatives rarely get a | ► true picture of the funeral costs |

17   ► before committing themselves.

18   Its spokesman says funeral directors are giving them cheap initial quotes

19   which typically double before the funeral's over,

20   an issue being investigated by the Office of Fair Trading. |

.... INTERVIEW CLIP ....

21 REPORTER: ► | Few of the people buried here in Highgate Cemetery

22   have endured a | ► pauper's funeral.

23   But the fear is that,

24   if burial and cremation costs continue to rise more and more,

25   relatives | ► of the dead will find it hard to give their loved ones

26   a dignified send-off.

27   Andrew Verity, BBC News in Highgate Cemetery |

Ext. 5: The Search for Extra-Terrestrial Intelligence [SETI]

1 PRESENTER 1:   Now, one of mankind's greatest questions must be:

2   "Are we alone in the universe?".

3   And for the last four decades scientists around the world

4   have been trying to find out the answer.

5 PRESENTER 2:   Well, so far, human beings appear to be unique.

6   But, who knows? E-T could already be out there.

7   It's just that we haven't picked up his call.

8   But for forty years now scientists working for SETI,

9   "The Search for Extra-Terrestrial Intelligence",

10   have been listening out for his number.

11 REPORTER: ► | No-one knows how many *stars* are in our universe.

12   And so far no-one knows if | ► – like our *sun* –

13   they can support life on nearby planets.

14   But by using the | ► *Araseevo radio telescope* at Puerto Rico –

15   the largest of its kind | ► in the world –

16   astronomers are trying to find out

17   if there is intelligent alien life outside our solar system.

18 | REPORTER TO CAMERA

19   ► | If you're hoping for proof of an alien civilisation

20   then the best place to be in the UK is
21   here at the Jodrell Bank Observatory here in Cheshire.
22   Because its *radio telescope* is so sensitive
23   it could detect *one* | ▶ *of these* from 220 million | ▶ miles away. |
24   ▶ | This 76 metre radio telescope is used
25   in conjunction with the dish at Araseevo.
26   They're conducting the most sensitive and comprehensive search
27   ever undertaken | ▶ for extra-terrestrial radio signals. |
28   ▶ | It's part of Project Phoenix –
29   a privately funded research programme with the SETI Institute.

.... INTERVIEW CLIP ....

EXTRACT FROM BT ET ADVERT

30   ▶ Astronomers have spent forty years looking for *ET*. |
31   ▶ | For the last eleven months | ▶ people with home computers
32   have joined in the search using *a SETI 'at-home* | ▶ *screen-saver'*
33   to help analyse all the signals | ▶ received from the sky. |
34   ▶ | But *one woman* takes the amateur approach more | ▶ seriously.
35   *Jenny Bailey* is a computer consultant | ▶ specialising in radio systems
36   ▶ | and a member of the SETI league.
37   Her search for extra-terrestrial intelligence
38   incorporates a two metre dish in her Cambridge back-garden,
39   ▶ | with equipment in the kitchen for processing the signals |

.... INTERVIEW CLIP ....

RADIO SIGNAL NOISE

40   ▶ | And if E-T ever | ▶ does phone home, Jenny will be | ▶ waiting. |
41   ▶ Sue Nelson, BBC News.

Ext. 6: War in Chechnya [WIC][7]
The Russians were supposed to conquer Grozny in one day – a simple   [1]
operation lasting a few hours.

But now – a month after launching one of the most devastating attacks on
a city since the Second World War – their troops are bogged down.

The capture of the Presidential Palace – now a skeletal ruin – failed to
break the resistance.

This is as far as Russian patrols dare go.

A few more yards beyond the palace and they'll be targeted by rebel rockets
or gunfire.

The civilian catastrophe engulfed the population of 400,000 in just a few weeks.

This is the heart of the capital – torn apart.

It looks as if civilisation died here decades ago.

There are too many bodies to count: Chechen fighters entombed in a car;
a soldier incinerated beyond recognition.

The survivors barely notice the corpses or the smell anymore.

Living conditions are subhuman.

Carrying a chunk of ice an old woman said sarcastically:

"This is the kind of water we have. Not bad is it?"

Those who are fit enough to escape plead with soldiers to take them
out – any way they can.   [20]

Too few places for too many people.

Moscow's troops were presented with a mission impossible – take Grozny
and kill few, if any, civilians in the process.

Unless there is a ceasefire and a mass evacuation of civilians, Russian forces
may in the end have no choice but to storm the city regardless of the
appalling consequences.

So far the military has been neither able to do its job quickly nor
quietly.

In the old Red Army days it would have been different – a free hand to crack
down in dissent; no international scrutiny, and no open condemnation of   [30]
their own side.

"One of our planes – a MIG – dropped two bombs on us in a house",
said a soldier. "Thirteen of us died".

At Grozny's command headquarters – marked by a graveyard of destroyed
armour – the Russians are supposed to be on the verge of completing
military operations.

This is one section of their front line.

Soldiers don't believe what Moscow claims and condemn their own officers
for incompetence.

"We shoot at each other", said this Russian.   [40]

"It's a mess. There are no commanders: they're drunk every day".

Chechen fighters are slowing down their advance.

Here an anti-sniper squad uses old tricks to locate a source of
incoming fire.

The Russians have convinced themselves that women sharpshooters like this – with experience in the Yugoslav War – are fighting as mercenaries in Chechnya.

"The snipers are doing most of the killing", said this Captain. "They're very hard to see, and even harder to eliminate".

They work at night, striking fear into Russian ranks, inflicting many casualties.   [50]

The wounded are brought here to a bar converted into a makeshift field hospital.

Hygiene is minimal.

Standards low.

This is how they sterilise surgical instruments.

But what they lack in perfection, the medical team makes up for in determination, desperately trying to save the life of yet another comrade-in-arms.

Moscow's official account of the numbers of troops killed in action is less than a thousand.

Those on the ground who say they know better believe their losses are much higher – at least two, maybe three thousand and rising – a high price to pay for a war which Moscow promised would be over before it started.

Brent Sadler.
CNN.
Grozny.

6 The discourse of live, two-way affiliated interviews

> It was a mistake. It was the kind of mistake that does arise in live broadcasting. . . . but it was a live broadcast and once the words are out of your mouth, the – you know, I did not go back and look at the transcripts.
>
> (Andrew Gilligan, in evidence to the Hutton Inquiry)

6.0 Introduction

In previous chapters it was suggested that the discourse of reporting may be seen as arising on the axis from the news field to the studio, whereas the discourse of news presentation arises on the axis from the studio to the audience. These two kinds of discourse are broadly different in their modes of address, in their setting and in their relation to the moment of broadcasting. News presentation is primarily studio-based, while reporting is from the news field. News presentation is in direct visual address while news reporting is mostly in voice-over. And news presentation is live-to-air, while news reporting is primarily pre-recorded in a 'news package'. Thus, it is possible to discern two rather different strands of discourse running through any bulletin news programme. Although different in many respects, however, there are occasional points of overlap or cross-over between discourse on the two axes. Reports, for instance, will routinely include a segment in direct address; while presentation will sometimes include a segment of voice-over to pictures. More significantly, a substantial and increasing component of broadcast news involves now the use of a live feed between the studio and the news field, between the presenter and the reporter. Indeed, the technological possibilities of the live feed (MacGregor, 1997) have provided 'a communicative affordance' (Hutchby, 2001) for articulating together the contrasting axes and contrasting discourses. By means of the live two-way interview between a representative of the broadcast institution in the field and the presenter in the studio it is possible to bridge the gap between the moment of the pre-recorded report and the moment of the broadcast and between the space of the studio and the site of the news. In this chapter, therefore, we will consider some aspects of the discourse of the live two-way interview.

Because this particular kind of interview is often with a member of the news institution known as a correspondent, an obvious way to describe this kind of interview would be as 'a live two-way with a correspondent'. But terminology within and between broadcast institutions varies and includes other terms such as 'reporter' and 'editor', depending on factors such as seniority within the institution and degrees of specialism. For this reason, the term 'affiliated interview' will be adopted to cover any of these eventualities when the presenter is in communication on air with an accredited journalist of the same institution – whether this be reporter, correspondent or editor – concerning an item in the news.

6.1   Live discourse, scripted discourse and the news

There is much debate about 'liveness' and broadcasting. While some argue that 'liveness' is a quintessential property of television as a medium, others maintain that it always remains an ideological effect (see Auslander, 1999; Feuer, 1983; Altman, 1986). For the purposes of this chapter I wish simply to maintain that in broadcast news the 'liveness' of an item signals not so much a particular ontological status for the material on view but rather a distinctive condition under which discourse can be produced. Thus, when what is being spoken by reporters or correspondents is coincident with its moment of reception by the broadcast audience, it is marked as such in various ways both to indicate and determine a particular kind of verbal performance. An obvious marker of this condition is the use of a caption "LIVE" in the corner of the screen. It is also routinely oriented to verbally in phrases such as "we now go live to John Simpson in Baghdad". Curiously enough news presenters such as Katie Couric, Brian Williams or Natasha Kaplinski do not read the news in the studio with a red caption, "LIVE", on screen even though one assumes that they too are speaking contemporaneously with the moment of reception. Indeed, we assume that the studio presentation of broadcast news is **not** pre-recorded even while we routinely assume that a report from the field by a reporter-correspondent **has** been pre-recorded, unless marked to the contrary. So when liveness is invoked as a category within news it indicates more than simple contemporaneousness. It signals more than anything the lack of a precise script. It is not just the person or the scene that is presented to us live. It is the discourse from the scene or in which the scene is embedded that is live.

The increasing use of live discourse on the news overlaps with another tendency that several researchers (Fairclough, 1992; Cameron, 2000; Scannell, 1996; Pearce, 2002) have noted and commented upon – the increasing adoption in public and institutionalised forms of discourse of conversational or dialogic modes. Broadcast news is no exception: increasingly it is delivered through interactional exchanges – from dual presenters on early morning news in the UK to the increasing use of pundits, experts and correspondents interviewed in or from the studio. A range of different formats are implicated in these changes, blending the tendency to conversationalise the news with an increasing emphasis on live, unscripted talk.

The focus in what follows is upon one particular format – the live, 'two-way' exchange. A standard sequential position for a live 'two-way' comes at the end of a major or significant news item in a broadcast news programme. As was noted in Chapter 2, news items in bulletin news programmes commonly display the following structure.

NEWS ITEM

NEWS PRESENTATION (+ NEWS SUBSIDIARY)

NEWS KERNEL (+ NEWS REPORT) (+ LIVE AFFILIATED INTERVIEW WITH REPORTER/CORRESPONDENT)

The news presenter/reader provides the kernel details on the item. On television there routinely follows an edited news report from a reporter/correspondent featuring footage from the site of the news event which adds information visually and verbally to that already supplied by the presenter. On the completion of the report, the news presenter may either move to the next item or conduct a short exchange live from the studio with a correspondent at the scene. Practitioners – news editors, journalists – call these latter inserts simply 'two-ways', with the title hinting at some of the technical demands of integrating live material from 'on location' into the studio-regulated flow of the news. The link with location has to be established; the reporter/correspondent placed on stand-by; then the link at a distance has to be activated at a precise point in the programme. Until fairly recently the technical demands of such a link must have been forbidding. But the rapid development of electronic and digitalised methods of transmission (MacGregor, 1997) has greatly simplified the process.

Although these conversational exchanges could be seen as driven by the more general shift in public discourse to informality, in the case of news there is a widely held opinion that its role is closely tied to issues of 'reality', 'actuality', 'immediacy'. Implicitly they seem to carry connotations of 'an update', and occasionally they will even be referred to as such. In a related way, they can be seen as dramatising the important spatial distinction in television news noted earlier. The inclusion of the live two-way in the format of television news promotes a constant counterpoint between these two kinds of space – the site of enunciation and the site of action. In this way news provides a fundamental illustration of what is taken by some to be a core property of the modern media of communication, 'time-space distanciation' (see, for example, J.B. Thompson, 1995.) Prior to the modern era there was (roughly) a proportional relationship between time and space: the further away an event, the longer it took for news of it to arrive. The modern media have eradicated this proportional relationship. Information crosses the globe instantaneously. The time it takes for news to travel is no longer a function of distance, and 'the news' makes great play of this quality, insisting absolutely on the recency of what it chooses to report. In this respect 'the news' is the mediated genre that makes the most of a central property of the modern mass media. And within the genre of 'the news', the live 'two-way' is that sub-genre that most emphasises the capacity to collapse the deictic spaces of the news between the 'there-then' of action and the here-now of its enunciation.

6.2   The discourse of the live two-way compared with the discourse of news presentation

This way of understanding the role of the live two-way clearly has much to commend it. But other properties than immediacy come into play if we look closely at the particulars of its performance – properties as much to do with 'naturalness' and 'spontaneity' as with 'facticity' and 'truth'. Indeed, there are some quite marked differences between the discourse of the 'two-way' exchange and the discourses of news presentation and reportage. These differences may be illustrated by considering a fairly typical example of news presentation alongside an example of the live two-way. Here first is a short piece of news presentation read by Anna Ford as an entire news item within a BBC news programme.

Ext. 6.2.1

I	PRESENTER:	International observers have questioned
2		the fairness of the weekend Parliamentary elections in Russia.
3		The United Russia Party which was created last year
4		to support President Putin won a convincing victory.
5		Hardline Russian Nationalist parties also did well.
6		But it was a disappointing result for the Communist Party
7		and for pro-Western liberal groups.

Every indication on the recording suggests that the piece is read to camera by Ford. There are no disfluencies: no hesitations, no fillers, false starts or self-corrections. The delivery is measured, with no signs of extempore performance. The item does contain some evaluative expressions – for example, 'convincing victory', 'disappointing result' – but overall it carries no sense of being the personal point of view of an individual or group. Instead, the simple set of categorical assertions or averrals are projected in the 'institutional voice' (Lerman, 1983) of the news organisation – impersonal, authoritative. Propositions are not qualified by marked modality choices. ("International observers have questioned", not – for example – "International observers have *apparently* questioned".)

Students of ideology might want to point out that it offers a less than ringing endorsement of the election result: the item leads, for instance, not on the victory of Putin but on possible irregularities in the election; and the remainder of it is rhetorically structured around an opposition between victory versus disappointment and between the United Russia Party and hardline Nationalist parties on the one hand and communist and pro-Western parties on the other. Nonetheless, whatever the ideological baggage being carried around the edges of the piece, it projects a kind of facticity at its base – as if the facts which it reports are unlikely to be questioned or even questionable. Compare this with the following example of a live two-way from a similar BBC news programme in which the presenter/newscaster, Peter Sissons, interacts with BBC world affairs editor, John Simpson, and political editor, Andrew Marr.

Ext. 6.2.2

I	PRESENTER:	well I'm joined now from Sedgefield
2		by our political editor Andrew Marr
3		and from the world summit in Johannesburg
4		by our world affairs editor John Simpson
5		John / on this issue
6		does the US have any friends in the world besides the UK
7	SIMPSON:	well you wouldn't think so Peter
8		if you go the rounds of the diplomats and the politicians here
9		uh you'd think that they're all solidly against it .
10		but . hh you get the feeling actually that
11		that's partly because they . know .
12		the folks back home want them . to be against it
13		want them . to be talking ag_about it
14		er there's a lot of worries about
15		what might happen to the western alliance
16		for instance . er . if the bombing starts .
17		but . the Americans certainly believe that
18		once the thing starts to get into place
19		then quite a lot of the governments
20		that seem to be opposed to it at the moment will be . in favour
21		what . you hear . sometimes wistful British er diplomats
22		and uh erm more importantly politicians saying
23		is that it's so extraordinary
24		that probably the world's worst dictator
25		with the world's worst record should . be .
26		one of the most popular people here
27		if Saddam Hussein had turned up here today
28		he'd have got a rr rip-roaring reception
29		and er that is er uh slight problem for the Americans
30		and the way they've been handling the whole thing ...

[Interview continues]
31 PRESENTER: John Simpson thank you
32   Andrew Marr in Sedgefield
33   there are very few ifs and buts now
34   about Tony Blair's position on Iraq
35   but he has left himself this small UN get-out clause
36   will he push Washington for one more UN try
37 MARR: yes I think that's one of the messages here today
38   erm he has a real problem
39   as the person who always claims that he can bridge the Atlantic
40   on these matters .
41   everybody in Europe
42   erm everybody around the world
43   is insisting that the United Nations must matter
44   whereas the Americans just simply see this
45   as another way of putting it off
46   another form of delay and faffing around
47   giving Saddam Hussein more time
48   and Tony Blair's answer to that appears to be
49   the United Nations will matter does matter
50   so long as it is part of the solution
51   so long as they're gonna try
52   and enforce international law
53   and their own resolutions quickly and clearly
54   and this is not just another excuse for delay
55   so that will be the message to the United Nations I think
56   one last throw ...
[Interview continues]
57 PRESENTER: Andrew Marr John Simpson thank you

Broadly, what distinguishes the discourse of the live two-way from the surrounding discourse of a news programme is the intrusion of 'authorial stance' as well as features of what linguists are referring to as 'evaluation' (see Hunston and Thompson, 2000). These include **Markers of Propositional Attitude/Personal Point of View**, exemplified by the following:

Ex. 6.2.2, l. 37
I think [that's one of the messages here today]

Ex. 6.2.2, l. 55
[that will be the message to the United Nations] **I think**

Ex. 6.2.2
my instinct is that [he will do what he thinks is right in the circumstances]

as well as by phrases/expressions such as "quite honestly". Note for example how unlikely such formulations would be in standard news presentation from Ford

*Ex. la
PRESENTER: **Quite frankly** hardline Russian Nationalist parties
also did well, **I think**.

Another important characteristic of the live two-way that distinguishes it from studio news presentation may be found in marked **Modality** choices[1]. The simple averrals of standard news presentation use unmarked modality (e.g. "Tony Blair visited Iraq today"). Live two-ways by contrast are rich in marked modality choices signalling variations in the speaker's "degree of commitment to the factuality of statements" (Saeed, 1997, p. 125). In the live two-way these are carried by **Adverbial expressions** (actually, certainly, probably, possibly, perhaps ....) rather than auxiliary verbs (might, may):

Ex. 6.2.2, ll. 10–12
you get the feeling **actually** that [[that's **partly** because
[they.know .the folks back home want them . to be against it]]]

Ex. 6.2.2, ll. 21–26
what . you hear . **sometimes** wistful British er diplomats and uh
erm more importantly politicians saying is that [it's so
extraordinary that **probably** the world's worst dictator with the
world's worst record should . be . one of the most popular people
here]

Ex. 6.2.2
perhaps the most interesting conversation I've had in the last
twenty four hours

Again, it is important to note that these formulations would be out of place in routine news presentation. It would be unusual for Anna Ford's account of the Russian election to include the following:

*Ex. lb
PRESENTER: And **certainly** hardline Russian Nationalist parties
also did well.

Another way of 'modalising' propositions within the live two-way is to advance them as part of **Hypothetical Conditionals** which sketch the circumstances in which a proposition might apply.

Ex. 6.2.2, ll. 27–28
if Saddam Hussein had turned up here today he'd have got a rr
rip-roaring reception

Ex. 6.2.2, ll. 7–8
well you wouldn't think so Peter [that America has any friends]
if you go the rounds of the diplomats and the politicians here

In any case the live two-way often handles material in a more speculative, conjectural fashion than in newscasting. Propositions, for instance, may be presented as part of a general ongoing universe of discourse – as 'what people are saying/thinking'. Effectively the correspondent puts forward a proposition but attributes it to someone else's speech or thought in a kind of propositional ventriloquism. Here is the BBC's John Simpson:

Ex. 6.2.2, ll. 21–22
what . you hear . sometimes wistful British er diplomats and uh
erm more importantly politicians saying is that [...

And here is Andrew Marr:

Ex. 6.2.2, ll. 48–54
and Tony Blair's answer to that appears to be
[the United Nations will matter does matter so long as it is part
of the solution
so long as they're gonna try and enforce international law
and their own resolutions quickly and clearly
and this is not just another excuse for delay]

Ex. 6.2.2 ll.
we were all sitting there today looking for any sign of a flinch
or a hesitation or
[hey you know it's a little bit more than I uh expected
and I'm gonna give it a bit more time]

Finally, in the live two-way we find a greater degree of colloquial and idiomatic speech than in studio presentation, as exemplified by the following phrases from Ex. 6.2.2, hardly any of which are likely to found in studio presentation.

go the rounds of
  . the folks back home
they'll . do anything and open any door
Tariq Aziz for instance has been er schmoozing people
another form of delay and faffing around

Thus, the differences between news presentation and the live two-way may be summed up as follows. Even though the use of autocue may have reduced the visibility of the script so that the news presenter seems to speak directly to camera, news presentation axiomatically is scripted: it is clear for the most part that this is not an 'off-the-cuff' or even memorised performance. In a live two-way, by contrast, correspondents are relatively 'unbuttoned'. They speak as if they are licensed to project a particular point of view as personal observers of a scene. And whereas news presentation offers a series of apparently established 'facts', the live two-way can afford to explore possibility and to indulge in conjecture[2]. The differences can be displayed schematically as follows.

LIVE TWO-WAY v. NEWS PRESENTATION & REPORT

Unscripted	Scripted
Informality	Formality
Marked modality	Unmarked modality
Statements of possibility	Statements of fact
Interpretative (Reaction/comment)	Descriptive
Personal Voice	Institutional Voice

6.3 Further discursive properties of the live two-way and the question of truth values

Inasmuch as the live 'two-way' is a distinct subgenre of discourse, different not only from the 'news presentation' of the studio (iconically the site of news assembly) but also from news reports – scripted, pre-recorded, edited – it performs a different role in relation to the news. It is not just that two styles of discourse surface in broadcast news, depending on whether material is delivered live and extempore or scripted for reading aloud. The complementary distribution of features relating to modality signal different kinds of truth-conditional status for the two kinds of discourse. Since routinely 'the facts' have already been supplied in news presentation and news report, the role of the two-way is to offer something else – to provide an element of 'mild spice' in the form of "what if ...", "maybe", some vague rumour, unattributed gossip, displaced or imagined sentiments. And the different 'truth-conditional status' of the live two-way is very much evident in the modality choices themselves.

These repay close attention because they oscillate in a distinctive fashion on a moment-by-moment basis from strong to weak and back again. Whenever a strong assertion takes place it is usually matched by some kind of 'hedge' (Stubbs, 1996; Lakoff, 1972). Thus a strong concluding assertion, such as "so **that will be the** message to the United Nations", is followed by a personal point-of-view marker: "**I think**" amounting to a kind of counterpoint between 'pushing' a claim and 'pulling' it[3].

Ex. 6.3.1
so **that will be** the message to the United Nations {push} I **think** {pull}

A similar alternation may be seen in the following example

Ex. 6.3.2
it's **gonna happen** {*push*} **quite** {*pull*} quickly

The wider context for Ex. 6.3.2 is complex. The claim by the BBC's political editor, Andrew Marr, is taken from a programme which pre-dates the invasion of Iraq and is prefaced by a passage of indirect speech reporting Blair's view about 'regime-change' in Iraq.

Ex. 6.3.3
he (Blair) could not have been more unequivocal or absolutely clear
that Saddam Hussein's regime has got to go
and it's **gonna happen** {*push*} **quite** {*pull*} quickly
something {*pull*} **pretty** {*pull*} substantial and serious
is gonna happen {*push*} this winter

The precise way in which modality is operating here may be elucidated by contrasting the utterance with what seem to be[4] its underlying propositions:

An invasion will happen
An invasion will happen quickly
A substantial and serious invasion will take place this winter

Presented in this fashion, stripped of most of the modal modifications of real-time utterance, the bare propositions carry the force of categorical assertions. Indeed, sequenced in this way, it is as if they operate by moving up a scale of increasing rhetorical intensity. By contrast, in the form they take in Example 6.3.3, the force of the assertions are modulated by the 'hedging' (Lakoff, 1972; Stubbs, 1996) that takes place – the use of indefinite reference (something, it) and 'de-intensifiers' (pretty, quite). It is difficult to be precise about the overall effect; but what seems to be at issue is a blend of **both** assertiveness and tentativeness in which a strong assertion will be 'pushed' or promoted only to be almost immediately downgraded or 'pulled'; alternatively 'hedging' will be upgraded with a 'push'. Other examples of this type are as follows:

Ex. 6.3.4
but . the Americans **certainly** believe {*push*}
that **once the thing starts to get into place** {*pull*}
then **quite a lot of** {*pull*} the governments

that **seem to be** {*pull*} opposed to it at the moment
will be . in favour {*push*}

Ex. 6.3.5
that's a **kind of** awesome list **when you er put it out like that**
{*push + pull*}

Ex. 6.3.6
and Tony Blair's answer to that {*push*}
appears to be {*pull*} the United Nations **will matter does matter** {*push*}
so long as it is part of the solution {*pull*}

Ex. 6.3.7
uh **you'd think that** {*pull*} they're **all** solidly against it {*push*}.

6.4   The use of scalar expressions to support *Push* versus *Pull*

The alternation between 'pushing' an averral and 'pulling' it is paralleled by use of scalar expressions and quantifiers (all, some, any, none) to state something either forcefully or guardedly. Here is a forceful statement

Ex. 6.4.1
we were **all** sitting there today looking for **any** sign of a flinch
or a hesitation
and there was **none** of that (=equivocation)

Interestingly, these cannot count as literal or precise descriptions of states of affairs. Who, it might be asked, is meant by 'all'? And was there absolutely not the slightest sign of hesitation? Instead, the adoption of expressions such as 'all' or 'none' that come from the extreme end of scales of size, number, or frequency underscores the strength of the averral: they help to make the point in as strong a fashion as possible.

A similar use of the extreme ends of a scale may be seen in the following:

Ex. 6.4.2
everybody in Europe erm **everybody around the world** is insisting
that the United Nations must matter

Again, as a matter of literal fact, this overstates the case but helps to make the point emphatically. Thus, at the extreme ends of scales we have expressions such as:

Ex. 6.4.3
Tariq Aziz has been er schmoozing people **ever since** he's arrived

Ex. 6.4.4
everybody in Europe erm **everybody** around the world is insisting
that the United Nations must matter

Ex. 6.4.5
we were **all** sitting there today looking for **any** sign of a flinch
or a hesitation and there was **none** of that

Ex. 6.4.6
they're perfectly happy to have **anybody** in there
and they'll . do **anything** and open **any** door .

Thus, the use of 'all', 'none', 'everybody', 'always' helps to increase the force of averrals. Conversely, however, averrals can be weakened or downgraded by drawing upon expressions from the middle ranges of quantifying scales. Weaker expressions – because they are less determinate and do not occupy the extreme ends of quantifying scales – are:

Ex. 6.4.7   **quite a lot** of the governments

Ex. 6.4.8   you hear . **sometimes** wistful British er diplomats

Ex. 6.4.9   **a little bit more** than I uh expected

As with the patterning of modal 'push' versus 'pull', it is important to stress that there is no mechanical alternation between the choice of a full versus an intermediate scalar expression. Equally, however, the discourse of the live two-way eschews an even plane of certainty or forcefulness. Instead it rings the changes from moment to moment. And in doing so it foregrounds or dramatises the relationship of the correspondent to the topic and the shifting relationship of the discourse to the world. Overall, if the discourse of the news-reader is shaped and delivered under the constraint of 'doing facticity' (sounding objective and unbiased), the discourse of the live two-way is about 'doing being interesting' (sounding lively and engaging) in relation to a facticity already established.

6.5   Issues of identity in the live two-way

In this respect the institutional position of 'editor-correspondents' such as John Simpson or Andrew Marr is significant. Routinely they speak, as we noted above, from where the news is happening rather than from the studio (where the news is enunciated). This is always reinforced iconically by careful choice of background image and ambient sound. The framing of their position underscores both a literal and a metaphorical distance from the news institution itself; and this gives them an ambiguous status. Does the correspondent-editor belong to the institution or not? As 'world affairs' or 'political' editor they are clearly not simple reporter-journalists. Indeed, there is a trace of deference on the part of presenters in references to their veteran status. They are invoked as figures in their own right, speaking almost separately from the institution, embodying in their voice and person an independent insight and authority. They are interviewed on air, invited to explain, to conjecture and to comment; and they are then thanked for their contribution – as if the institution had no idea in advance what they might have been thinking.

Thus, the live interaction between the institution in the person of the presenter and these semi-independent, free-floating individuals licenses in the accounts of the latter a different relationship to the material of the news and to its truth value. Consider, for instance, the little re-duplication 'surprise surprise' in the example below:

Ex. 6.5.1 [ANDREW MARR]
erm my instinct is that
he will do what he thinks is right in the circumstances
which is
surprise surprise
to stand alongside the Americans

Andrew Marr could have said, 'Tony Blair is standing and will stand alongside the Americans'. He could have said, 'Tony Blair will do what he thinks is right – stand alongside the Americans'. Instead he says:

erm my instinct is that
[Tony Blair will do what he thinks is right – stand alongside the Americans]

In other words he projects the key proposition embedded inside a truth-conditional health warning – 'this is only my judgement'.

But he also adds 'surprise surprise', which means by convention the opposite of what it says: although I (Andrew Marr) projected the proposition as a revelation of my own distinctive point of view ("my instinct is that . .") (after all, that's the warrant for my having highly expensive air-time), I know that you (Peter Sissons) think the same thing too. I'm not telling you anything new; we share the same view. So it's a little act of truth-conditional solidarity. And although this remark is manifestly for Peter Sissons in the first instance, there's no doubt that it is an interpolated aside not just for Sissons but for a wider (knowing) audience beyond. Thus we can see that the point of the live discourse is not necessarily to be scrupulously factual and informative. Its role is to extemporise and to improvise on the factual basis already supplied and to move from what we know already to what might be the case as the events of the news unfold. The discourse of the two-way and the discourse of news presentation are of two quite different kinds. In this respect, note, of course, that it would be grossly inappropriate for a news presenter to slip an interpolation such as "surprise, surprise" into standard news presentation. For example:

* Ex. Ic
AF: The United Russia Party which was created last year to support
President Putin won a convincing victory, **surprise surprise**.

Equally, however, it tends to be those correspondents with a certain degree of achieved status ("our world affairs editor", "our political editor") who have won the rights to the kinds of licence that the two-way affords, especially when the live two-way occupies the particular sequential position within a news item of allowing the speaker not just the latest but the last word.

6.6   The live two-way, the Gilligan affair and the Hutton inquiry

The discourse of the live two-way is thus very different from the discourses of presenting and reporting. Indeed, in articulating the axis of presentation with the axis of reporting the discourse of the live two-way raises important issues about the truth-conditional status of different discourses. In their informality and improvisational brio, live two-ways bring an important extra dimension to the changing discourses of broadcast news. But they also can have profound consequences for individuals and institutions caught up in the real-time pressures of its assembly and delivery. We can see these clearly in the case of the BBC, and one of its defence correspondents, Andrew Gilligan.

On 29th May 2003 at 6.07 a.m., immediately following the opening news headlines on BBC Radio 4's Today programme (a news and current affairs programme), in the course of an interview with presenter John Humphrys, Andrew Gilligan claimed:

Ext. 6.6.I
1 REPORTER: what we've been told
2   by erm one of th::e . senior officials in charge of . erm
3   drawing up that dossier
4   was that erm . actually the government probably . knew
5   that that forty five figure was . wrong
6   even before it decided to put it in

The background to this claim was as follows. In September 2002, amidst wide concern about impending war with Iraq, the British government, in an effort to inform public debate, published a dossier summarising the available intelligence and included within it a claim that not only did Iraq possess weapons of mass destruction but that some of these were deployable within 45 minutes. On 18th March 2003, the government won a debate in Parliament authorising the use of British forces in the military invasion of Iraq – a debate in which some members, it seemed, were influenced by the 45 minutes claim. Two days later British and American forces invaded Iraq. The moral, legal and strategic arguments, however, did not stop with the invasion, not least because the coalition forces subsequently failed to find any weapons of mass destruction whose supposed existence had buttressed the case for war. Some commentators asked, indeed, in the weeks which followed whether war had been prosecuted on the basis of a false prospectus. It was against this background that Gilligan declared on radio that he had been told by one of the senior officials in charge of drawing up the dossier that the government probably knew that the 45 minute figure was wrong "even before it decided to put it in". Downing Street, in short, had ordered the dossier "to be sexed up".

Britain was by then, as a member of the US-led coalition, a nation uneasily at war; and relations between the BBC and the government had begun to deteriorate as they typically do under the pressure of war-time hostilities. The BBC's distinctive position as a national public service broadcaster is designed to insulate it equally from market pressures and from state control. It is established by Royal Charter, periodically renewed, which provides it with revenue raised through a public levy, thus insulating it from the direct pressures of the market. The Charter also provides a mechanism for insulating the BBC from direct state control. The Director General of the BBC, for instance, was appointed and overseen by a Board of Governors (now a Board of Trustees) not by a government minister. In news programming, its commitment to balance and impartiality is incorporated in the Charter. And its independence is a cherished part if its commitment to broadcast quality programmes 'in the public interest'. Thus, by fiscal and institutional arrangement, as well as by ethos and tradition, the BBC is provided with a complicated set of buffers between itself and the raw exigencies of state control or brute commercial pressure.

In time of war, however, its commitment to the public interest is subject to a range of interpretations. At one end of a spectrum, the public interest can be interpreted in partisan national terms and at the other end by reference to some transcendent commitment to truth. Governments of the day tend to interpret the public interest in patriotic terms and tend to want the BBC to do likewise. The BBC in contrast has tended to espouse a transcendent commitment to truth, as long as this does not too blatantly undermine the national interest ("The British Voice of Truth" as one Director General described it)[5]. The resultant contradictions provide an enduring recipe for conflict. During the Falklands War, for example, the BBC was criticised for even-handedly balancing information from the Ministry of Defence with reports from America and Argentina. ("Totally offensive and almost treasonable", complained a Conservative MP.) Margaret Thatcher, who made her displeasure clear on several occasions, declared in Parliament: "I know how strongly many people feel that the case for our country is not being put with sufficient vigour on certain – I do not say all – BBC programmes". Her interpretation of the public interest identified it very much in patriotic terms. As Harris (1994, p. 86) comments:

> The BBC is rarely popular with Prime Ministers, especially Prime Ministers in time of war. As long ago as the Second World War, Winston Churchill ... described the Corporation as "an enemy within the gates doing more harm than good". At the time of the Suez crisis, Anthony Eden was incensed by what he saw as the BBC's unpatriotic behaviour.

It was hardly unusual, therefore, that relations between the Blair government and the BBC deteriorated during the build-up to war in Iraq, and even more thereafter. Alastair Campbell, Downing Street's then Director of Strategy and Communications, frequently criticised the BBC's coverage, believing that the organisation was dominated editorially by those sympathetic to the anti-war movement and that its coverage in consequence was less than fair to the government's case. But relations became particularly acrimonious when the BBC broadcasted Andrew Gilligan's claim about the dossier.

BBC Radio 4's *Today* programme – a prestigious news magazine programme which is broadcast daily from 6 a.m. to 9 a.m. – features a mix of news summaries, reports, features and mostly serious interviews. The presenters of *Today* are experienced and respected journalists; and leading politicians are commonly interviewed on the programme. It has some claims to set the hard-news agenda for the day. When Gilligan declared in the broadcast at 6.07 a.m on 29th May "that erm . actually the government probably . knew that that forty five figure was . wrong even before it decided to put it in" there was an immediate and forceful response from Downing Street. Alastair Campbell issued an immediate rebuttal of Gilligan's claim; and within the space of little more than an hour the *Today* programme acknowledged this in the following way: "we've had a statement from 10 Downing Street that says it's not true ..: 'Not one word of the dossier was not entirely the work of the intelligence services' ". From this point forward the positions of the BBC and the government became entrenched. The government insisted that there had been no reason to doubt the intelligence claim about a 45 minutes capability when it was included in the dossier; the BBC insisted that the essential core of Gilligan's story – that the intelligence community was uneasy about the 45 minute claim – was true. The government treated Gilligan's statement as an accusation of lies and distortion. The BBC backed the broadcast as an important contribution to the public debate about the justification for war. Alastair Campbell demanded a retraction from the BBC. The BBC refused to rescind Gilligan's claim.

These acute tensions provoked a search for the source of Gilligan's statement. A respected government weapons scientist, Dr David Kelly, reported to his superiors that he had met Gilligan on more than one occasion and that he may, therefore, be the source of the claim. He was interviewed by his superiors at the Ministry of Defence; and by 9th July his name had become public knowledge. Following these revelations, he was interviewed on 15th July by a Parliamentary Foreign Affairs Committee. With public pressure mounting on David Kelly he left his Oxfordshire home on 17th July and failed to return. His body was found the next day. The Blair government responded to widespread concern at the apparent suicide of Dr Kelly by rapidly establishing an independent inquiry under a senior judge, Lord Hutton, who on 21st July defined his remit as 'urgently to conduct an investigation into the circumstances surrounding the death of Dr David Kelly'. The inquiry took evidence in open session from many figures and examined in close detail the roles of the government and the BBC in Kelly's death.

Hutton's report, published at the end of January 2004, confirmed that Dr Kelly took his own life but found little fault with the government. Hutton did, however, find much to question in the editorial practices and policy decisions of the BBC as they relate to Gilligan's broadcast at 6.07 on 29th May. He found that Gilligan's allegation was unfounded, that the BBC failed to ensure proper editorial control over the crucial broadcast, that the BBC failed properly to investigate the background to Alastair Campbell's complaints, failed to check Gilligan's notes – which did not support the wording of his broadcast – and so on. Following publication of the report, both the Director General of the BBC and the Chair of the Board of Governors resigned. Alastair Campbell also resigned from his government post in order to spend more time on personal projects but made it abundantly clear in a televised and much-quoted statement that he considered himself and the government to be completely vindicated by Hutton. The report itself had a mixed press. *The Independent* newspaper for instance regarded it as a 'whitewash' because it found no fault with the government. *The Financial Times*, on the other hand, regarded its criticisms of the BBC to be justified.

The affair and its aftermath had enormous consequences for the BBC, for public perceptions of its role and for relations between the BBC and the government[6]. In all of the debates, however, little attention was paid to the role of a subsidiary player in the cycle of events – and that is the changing discourse of the news itself. Hutton in his report does allow the question of wording some limited space – a small walk-on role.

> Where a reporter is intending to broadcast or publish information impugning the integrity of others the management of his broadcasting company or newspaper should ensure that a system is in place whereby his editor or editors give careful consideration to the wording of the report and to whether it is right in all circumstances to broadcast or

publish it... I consider that the editorial system which the BBC permitted was defective in that Mr Gilligan was allowed to broadcast his report at 6.07 a.m. without editors having a seen a script of what he was going to say and having considered whether it should be approved.

(Hutton, 2004, p. 181)

Hutton's approach, however, rests upon the notion that the news generally is a carefully scripted discourse. On the occasion of Gilligan's broadcast, however, as evidence presented to the enquiry seemed to establish, there **was** no script. Gilligan himself admitted under cross-examination in respect of his specific allegation about the government:

It was a mistake. It was the kind of mistake that does arise in live broadcasting .... it was a live broadcast and once the words are out of your mouth, the – you know, I did not go back and look at the transcripts.

To some it might seem surprising that, despite the premium on the accuracy of news discourse, Gilligan should be broadcasting live without a script. However, as the previous discussion in this chapter shows, there is a considerable amount of live, unscripted material in news programmes – and this from presenters, reporters and correspondents, not to mention interviewees and eyewitnesses. Indeed, issues of the 'scriptedness' of news discourse are much more complex than Hutton allowed for. They interact, as we have seen, with questions of 'liveness' and the general exigencies of delivering the news; they interact with topic, with variable validity requirements and the greater need for certainty, for instance, if making a serious allegation; and they interact with the differences of status and role-identity amongst accessed voices on the news. (Senior correspondents – 'editors', for example – are more likely than reporters to speak unscripted.)

Even now, after exhaustive investigation and more than one inquiry, there is some confusion about what actually occurred in relation to the script on the morning of 29th May 2003. The BBC, for instance, conducted their own internal review into the implications of the Hutton inquiry. Although their report remains confidential they issued a press release (10th May 2004) stating:

In relation to the broadcast on the Today programme, on 29th May 2003, we are satisfied that a core script was properly prepared and cleared in line with normal production practices in place at the time, but was then not followed by Andrew Gilligan. We consider the BBC's evidence to the Hutton Inquiry could have been clearer in this respect.

(BBC Online: 'BBC Hutton inquiry clears editors', 10/05/04)

This is starkly at variance with Gilligan's own evidence to the Hutton inquiry. Having emphasised under cross-examination by his own counsel that he considered his broadcast to be an allegation of spin, of exaggeration, rather than dishonesty, he is asked: "if you had seen it as an allegation of out and out dishonesty, would you have done anything different in preparing the story?" He answers:

> Yes. There is a process, a BBC process. Everything has to be scripted. The scripts have to be approved by the lawyers and everyone, including the presenters, has to stick to the scripts and that is for every appearance on the programme .... The reason this was not done in this case was it was simply perceived as a different beast. This is a political charge essentially.

It is difficult to reconcile this answer with the outcome of the BBC's own, post-Hutton, internal review.

Clearly, then, not only what was said, but how it was said, and with what degree of preparedness, continue to trouble discussions in the aftermath of Hutton. It is possible to show, however, that if there was a script it was hardly Gilligan's fault if he departed from it. Gilligan's questionable allegation was produced in interview as part of a live two-way, the general purpose of which, as we have seen, is to avoid 'scriptedness'. Let us return to the utterance by Gilligan quoted earlier, but this time situated in the overall context of the complete live two-way:

Ext. 6.6.1

```
 1 HUMPHRYS:  The government's facing more questions this morning
 2                 over its claims about weapons of mass destruction in Iraq
 3                 our defence correspondent is Andrew Gilligan
 4                 this in particular Andy is Tony Blair
 5                 saying they'd be ready to go within forty five minutes
 6 GILLIGAN:  that's right
 7                 that was the central claim in his dossier
 8                 which he published in September
 9                 the main erm case if you like against er against Iraq
10                 and what we've been told erm by one of the: . senior officials
11                 in charge of . drawing up that dossier
12                 was that erm . actually the government probably . knew
13                 that that forty five figure was wrong
14                 even before it decided to put it in
15                 what this person says
16                 is that a week before the publication date of the dossier
17                 it was actually rather a bland production
18                 it didn't the the draft didn't say
19                 very much more than was public knowledge already
20                 and erm Downing Street our source says
21                 ordered a week before publication ordered it to be sexed up
```

22   to be made more exciting erm
23   and erm and ordered more facts to be er to be discovered
24 HUMPHRYS: when you say 'more facts to be discovered'
25   does that suggest that they may not have been facts
26 GILLIGAN: well erm our source says
27   that the dossier as it was finally published
28   made the Intelligence Services unhappy
29   erm because to quote erm the source
30   he said there was basically
31   that there was there was there was unhappiness
32   because it didn't reflect the considered view
33   they were putting forward
34   that's a quote from our source
35   and essentially erm the forty-five minute point er
36   was was probably the most important thing that was added
37   erm and the reason it hadn't been in the original draft was that
38   it was it was only erm it only came from one source
39   and most of the claims were from two
40   and the intelligence agencies say
41   they don't really believe it was necessarily true
42   because they thought the person making the claim
43   had actually made a mistake
44   it got had got mixed up
45 HUMPHRYS: does any of this matter now all this all these months later
46   the war's been fought and won
47 GILLIGAN: well the forty-five minutes isn't just a detail
48   it did go to the heart of the government's case
49   that Saddam was an imminent threat
50   and it was repeated four times in the dossier
51   including by the Prime Minister himself in the forward
52   so I think it probably does matter
53   clearly you know if erm if it if it was if it was wrong
54   things do things are got wrong in good faith
55   but if they knew it was wrong
56   before they actually made the claim
57   that's perhaps a bit more serious
58 HUMPHRYS: Andrew
59   many thanks
60   more about that later

The hallmarks of the live two-way are evident not only in the central claims
but throughout the exchange. There are many of the disfluencies of extempore speech, including **pause fillers** and **repetitions** ("the main erm case if you
like against er against Iraq", "well erm our source says", "clearly you know if erm if
it if it was if it was wrong", "erm and the reason it hadn't been in the original draft

was that it was it was only erm it only came from one source", "and essentially erm the forty five minute point er was was", "erm because to quote erm the source"). We also find **pseudo-cleft constructions** ("what this person says is that . . ."), **colloquial idiom** ("it got had got mixed up", "what it thought Iraq was up to"), **markers of propositional attitude**, such as "so **I think** it probably does matter", and **hypothetical conditionals** ("but **if** they knew it was wrong before they actually made the claim that's perhaps a bit more serious").

In addition there is the use of marked modality choices exhibiting the kinds of '**push**' + '**pull**' alternations identified above:

Ex. 6.6.1, l. 9
the main erm case {*push*} **if you like** {*pull*} against er against Iraq

Ex. 6.6.1, l. 15–17
what this person says is that a week before the publication date of
the dossier it was **actually** {*push*} **rather** {*pull*} a bland production

Ex. 6.6.1, l. 52
so **I think** {*pull*} it **probably** {*pull*} does matter

Ex. 6.6.1, l. 57–60
clearly {*push*} you know if erm if it if it was if it was wrong
things do things are got wrong in good faith
but if they knew it was wrong before they **actually** {*push*} made the claim
that's **perhaps** {*pull*} **a bit more** {*pull*} serious

Ex. 6.6.1, l. 12–13
was that **actually** {*push*} the government **probably** {*pull*} erm knew
that that forty five figure was wrong

The *Today* programme comes on the air at 6 a.m. and runs without interruption until 9 a.m. In this respect it is different from many UK broadcast
news programmes. It includes extensive interviews with people 'in the news',
particularly politicians, and has some claims to set the (hard) news agenda
for the day. Nonetheless its verbal formats for news overlap considerably
with television news, in particular in distinctions between the live two-way
and news presentation and report. Here, for example, are the opening news
headlines from 6 a.m.

Ext. 6.6.2
1 NEWSREADER: Tony Blair will set foot on Iraq soil today –
2   just seven weeks after Saddam Hussein was swept from power.
3   His visit comes amid continuing controversy about
4   the likelihood of weapons of mass destruction being found.
5   The US Defence Secretary, Donald Rumsfeld, has suggested

6	that the weapons might have been destroyed
7	before the fighting began.
8	This report is from our political correspondent John Pienaar,
9	who's travelling with the Prime Minister … .

And here, for example, is a news report broadcast by Gilligan soon after 7 a.m. later that same morning after a headline and following short introduction by the newsreader, Corrie Corfield

Ext. 6.6.3

1 NEWSREADER:	A senior official involved in preparing
2	the Government's dossier
3	on Iraqi weapons of mass destruction
4	has told this programme that the document was rewritten
5	just before publication – to make it more exciting.
6	The official claimed that the intelligence services
7	were unhappy with the changes.
8	Andrew Gilligan reports:
9 GILLIGAN:	The dossier published in September last year
10	was launched in the Commons by the prime minister himself.
11	It received saturation coverage.
12	In the preface, Mr Blair stated explicitly
13	that some of some of Saddam's weapons of mass destruction
14	could be ready within 45 minutes of an order to use them.
15	One senior British official has now told us
16	that the original version of the dossier
17	produced by the intelligence services
18	added little to what was publicly known.
19	But one week before publication, said this official,
20	the dossier was transformed on Downing Street's orders.
21	The 45 minute assertion was one of several claims added
22	against the wishes of the intelligence agencies,
23	who said it was from a single source
24	which they didn't necessarily believe.
25	The official told the BBC
26	that most people in intelligence
27	were unhappy with the dossier
28	because it did not reflect
29	the considered view they were putting forward.

This is a much tighter piece covering broadly the same ground but in less than half the number of words of the earlier 6.07 broadcast. There, by comparison, Gilligan reproduces the common patterning of live two-ways: he adopts a looser, less formal, more speculative, unbuttoned approach to the material, displaying many of the characteristics of the live two-way that we have already described – the same displacement of claims onto unattributed sources, a kind of spicey rehearsal of hearsay and uncertain oscillations through fluctuating modality choices in its truth-conditional status. The comparison between the later scripted item and the earlier unscripted one highlights two kinds of problem with the 6.07 broadcast. Indeed, Gilligan's live two-way at 6.07 was doubly problematic. First of all, in status and identity terms, live two-ways, as we have seen, tend to be associated with senior journalists – those entitled 'editors', rather than 'reporters' or 'correspondents'. If we consider the two-way exchanges at Ex. 6.2.2 we can see that Marr is introduced as 'our political editor' and Simpson has the even loftier title of 'world affairs editor'. Their senior status warrants the kinds of speculative questions that are addressed to them: "as a Baghdad veteran John how do you read Iraq's various statements about UN inspectors; do they ever intend that they should return?" or to Marr "will [Blair] push Washington for one more UN try?" It is rare for reporters or correspondents to be asked to perform in this speculative mode. Second, it is rare for this speculative mode of discourse to occur without a preceding report establishing the 'facts of the case' on which to hook it. In general, live two-ways typically **follow** a scripted report. Admittedly, they may on occasion be used to introduce a scripted report but it is most unusual for them to occur **without** a scripted report. In the case of the Gilligan's 6.07 item, however, this, unaccountably, is what happened. In effect, the 6.07 two-way encouraged the discourse of opinionated improvisation in the position normally occupied by a tighter news report. (It is noticeable that all Gilligan's later pieces that day on the topic begin in scripted form.) In short, there was a misalignment of discourse to situation. For whatever reason, Gilligan slipped into or was positioned into the wrong sub-genre of news discourse for what was at stake: basically, he found himself using a soft discourse for a hard topic. As he himself admitted to the Hutton inquiry, with hindsight, it would have been better to have scripted the 6.07 item. Into the space between two kinds of discourse Gilligan's allegation fell, with serious consequences for him, for the BBC and, of course, for Dr David Kelly.

6.7 The aftermath of the Gilligan–Humphrys two-way

In the event, of course, the 6.07 two-way was treated in terms of uptake exactly as if it were a report. The government (in the person of Alastair Campbell) and government counsel to the Hutton inquiry treated what Gilligan had said as part of a veridical discourse of truth and facticity. Within minutes of the live two-way the *Today* programme had received an instant rebuttal from Downing Street which was noted by *Today* when they returned to the item at 7.32. Much later its factual inaccuracies were to be painfully unravelled under extended cross-examination by government counsel to the Hutton inquiry. In fine detail and contrary to the wording of the broadcast, Dr Kelly did not work for the Intelligence Services; Dr Kelly did not use the words "sexed up" (except in response to their use by Gilligan); Downing Street did not order changes to the dossier; the 45 minute warning was a late addition not because it was 'single-sourced' but because the intelligence only became available late. Just to give the flavour:

Mr Sumption QC:	Why did you describe him {Dr Kelly} as your Intelligence Service source?
Andrew Gilligan:	I do not know. It was a mistake. It was the kind of mistake that does arise in live broadcasting.
Mr Sumption QC:	Is that right?
Andrew Gilligan:	It is extempore. That was the only time in all my broadcasts, and there were 19 of them on this subject, that I described him in this way. That is a mistake that I have already admitted to.
	.....
Mr Sumption QC:	That statement (a press release) that none of the reports had ever described him as a member of the Intelligence Services was wrong, was it not?
Andrew Gilligan:	Yes, it was. One of 19 had described him as such, but it was a live broadcast and once the words are out of your mouth, the – you know, I did not go back and look at the transcripts.

Gilligan's defence – that it was a live broadcast – provokes some sympathy when the routine licences of other live broadcasts are examined. At another point in cross-examination, however, he uses an alternative defence. As we noted earlier, he maintains that it was not intended as an allegation of dishonesty. If it had been intended as such it would have been managed very differently as an item:

> There is a process, a BBC process. Everything has to be scripted. The scripts have to be approved by the lawyers and everyone, including the presenters, has to stick to the scripts and that is for every appearance on the programme.

"The reason this was not done in this case" claimed Gilligan "was it was simply perceived as a different beast." It was not considered as an allegation of dishonesty. "This was a political charge essentially." This is how he elaborated its status under cross-examination by his own counsel:

> This was an allegation of spin, of exaggeration. Politics is an arena in which such allegations are the stock in trade. And this came as part of a continuing debate over the authenticity of some of the information

in the dossier. And even on the morning of the broadcast for instance, there were two or three articles in the newspapers, before I had said a single word, explicitly accusing the government and the Prime Minister of lying over the dossier. So there was a continuing and lively political debate. This did not start it and did not set it off. This was regarded by all of us as a contribution to that debate.

There is some tension here between the two lines of defence. It is not the normal function of broadcast news reports to take up sides in a debate in the way that an article (say, an 'op ed' piece) in a newspaper might. If Gilligan thought to make an implicit comparison between what might be done in a newspaper article and what might be done in a BBC news item then it is one that elides the discursive differences between the two and their quite contrasting truth-conditional statuses. (Just as also there are important differences between a politician alleging dishonesty of another politician and a journalist doing so[7].)

Other news professionals were not slow to reinforce this point. The reaction of the Deputy Editor of ITV News, Deborah Turness, is instructive (even allowing for ITV's competitive relation to the BBC).

> I can't possibly conceive of a case in which we would commit the same errors as the BBC ... If we have an exclusive and the journalist hasn't checked with the person we are accusing, or approached the government or the department, for a statement, then the ITN lawyer will ask why ... Because our lawyers legal everything that goes out on the programme, things tend not to slip through the net ... The lawyer is in the newsroom, looking at scripts and he's also in the edit room looking at packages.
>
> (*UK Press Gazette* 03.10.03, p. 13)

Clearly, therefore, some quarters of the public sphere (and not just Alastair Campbell) chose to treat the original 6.07 item as a veridical, scripted discourse of truth. And it is difficult – despite Gilligan's protestations – to fault them in this.

Indeed, if in the heat of the inquiry there was some confusion in Gilligan's lines of defence there remained long after some residual confusion in the BBC's own account. In May 2004 they completed their own confidential internal inquiry. Their short public statement asserted, in defence of their editorial processes, that there had after all been a script which "was properly prepared and cleared in line with normal production practices at the time, but was then not followed by Andrew Gilligan". Not only is this claim clearly at variance with significant sections of Gilligan's evidence to the inquiry (which the BBC did not question at the time), it is also at variance with the transcribed discourse of the programme. Scripted reports are introduced in the following manner: "This report is from our political correspondent John Pienaar who is travelling with the Prime Minister ..."; or, after the 7.0 a.m. news summary, "Andrew Gilligan reports ...". When the 6.07 item involving Gilligan is first introduced by the presenter John Humphrys, it is not as if a report is expected. Instead it is introduced as follows:

Ext. 6.6.1
1 HUMPHRYS: The government's facing more questions this morning
2   over its claims about weapons of mass destruction in Iraq
3   our defence correspondent is Andrew Gilligan
4   this in particular Andy
5   is Tony Blair saying they'd be ready to go within forty five minutes

In view of this conversational opening it seems disingenuous for the BBC to claim that Gilligan departed from a script when none at this stage was being introduced. Indeed, Humphrys proceeded directly into a live interview as if that was all that was expected.

6.8   Conclusion

Some would see the Gilligan allegation, as did Hutton, as a straight-forward failure of journalistic practice analogous to the subsequent mistakes at the *Daily Mirror* newspaper[8]: Gilligan's notes, after all, did not fully confirm his story and there were important errors of fact. But while it is crucial to uphold core journalistic values and practices (such, for instance, as cross-checking and double-checking sources to ensure accuracy), an additional and very real complication in this case is engendered by widespread and far-reaching changes in the forms of public discourse and by the pervasive pressures towards informality, dialogue rather than monologue, improvisation rather than script (see, for example, Montgomery, 1999; Cameron, 2000; Fairclough, 1995). The discourses of the news are neither homogeneous nor static. They amount to an evolving system of discourses in the process of change. And the kinds of change in process amount, for instance, to subtle alterations in the alignments of discourse around the validity claims of truth, sincerity, sociability and personality. As Scannell demonstrates conclusively in *Radio Television and Modern Life*, in the broadcasting of talk the media have aspired as much to entertainment and sociability as to truth and the correspondence to fact (Scannell, 1996). In its increasing emphasis on the person, on dialogue and on conversation as a mode of delivery, news discourse has registered and projected those changes discernible in many areas of public life. In the live two-way we can see a quite particular instance of those broader changes at work. But like all change it produces uncertainty about its status and most particularly about what kinds of validity claims most properly apply to it.

Of course, the BBC's procedures were overhauled in the wake of its own internal inquiry following the Hutton report[9]. It is likely that there were specific recommendations about the use of the live 'two-way' (which have seemed less improvisational since then). There may have been some temporary reduction in its use. But in an age where considerable resources are devoted to the production of news at the same time as audiences for specific outlets are increasingly difficult to attract and to hold, dialogue and unscripted, live informality – with all its attendant risks (and precisely because of them) – will continue to surface. Gilligan (and the BBC) have paid a price for journalistic mistakes. Just like the tango, however, it takes two for a two-way. Not only the two-way but a much broader context of improvisation and informality made Gilligan's mistakes possible – one far too pervasive easily to be brought to book.

7 The broadcast news interview

[I]nterviews can then be seen as part of a larger cycle of reflexivity, in which viewers turn to broadcast representations for material to understand their own responses, watching TV to watch themselves, and the people on TV represent themselves in terms of others observing them.

(Myers, 2000, p. 167)

Among the ways you go about doing 'being an ordinary person' is spending your time in usual ways, having usual thoughts, having usual interests, etc.; so that all that you have to do, to be 'an ordinary person' in the evening, is turn on the TV set.

(Sacks, 1992, Vol. II, p. 216)

7.0 The notion of interview: a short social history

From the sixteenth to the nineteenth centuries the notion of interview referred to "a meeting of persons face to face especially for the purpose of formal conference on some point" (OED) and so was somewhat different to its current usage. The term had an institutional provenance – it was usually people of high rank who met "for the purpose of formal conference" – but unlike today there was apparent symmetry of purpose and role between parties to the encounter. Over the last 150 years, however, the term has become particularly inflected to refer to encounters with a bifurcation of roles – questioning and answering – with these allocated in advance to one or other participant who have become known respectively as the interviewer and the interviewee. In its present guise the interview operates in a variety of institutional domains as, for instance, a research technique (the focused or unstructured interview), as a diagnostic tool (the medical or even psychiatric interview), as a mode of selection (the job interview) or as a forensic instrument (the police interview). All of these types of interview share the notion of an interviewer (or interviewers) who ask(s) questions and an interviewee who answers them and in this way the notion of interview has evolved from designating a symmetrical encounter between relative equals into referring most commonly to an institutional procedure for eliciting, selecting and evaluating information by question and answer.

Overall, interviews in contemporary society most typically elicit commensurable pieces of information in a reasonably standardised fashion. As such they operate at the interface between individual members of the public and organisations or institutions such as health care, education or employment. In the moment of the interview encounter individuals – unsorted members of a population, and the information which they provide – become assimilated to an institutional framework. Furthermore, interviews not only extract and sort information. They are also used to evaluate, select and reject persons. It is this characteristic that leads Fairclough to characterise them as a discursive technology (Fairclough, 1992), one whose fundamental purpose is now most particularly to do with surveillance and control[1].

Thus, despite the use of interviews across a range of institutional domains, there has been undoubtedly some specialisation of purpose. And in this historical evolution from 'a meeting of persons for the purpose of formal conference on some point' to the contemporary practice of interview, journalism has played a vital role. For it is in the journalistic domain that the first specialisation of the term began. Around the 1860s, if not earlier[2], we find 'interview' emerging quite particularly as a word for "a meeting between a representative of the press and someone from whom he seeks to obtain statements for publication". The American nineteenth-century poet Longfellow, for instance (author of a famous epic poem *The Song of Hiawatha*), notes his contact with a newspaper "in which I have been 'interviewed', and private conversation reported to the public". It is also around the middle of the nineteenth century that the bifurcation of interview roles becomes more obvious, with interviewer emerging as the term for one who interviews, especially "a journalist who interviews a person with the object of obtaining matter for publication".

7.1 The media interview and the news interview

Since then, particularly over the last half of the twentieth century, interviews have become common – not just in news settings – but across the range of media output, frequently being used in entertainment and confessional formats (see Bell and Van Leeuwen, 1994). The chat show interview, as one salient type, has been subject to much study (Tolson, 1991; Bell and van Leeuwen, 1994) and is pervasive enough as a form to be the subject of parody (see Tolson, 1991; Montgomery, 1999). Perhaps the most important characteristic of the media interviews in general is that they are talk for an overhearing audience. This distinguishes them from everyday talk in canonical speech situations where the prime protagonists are speaker and hearer and where turns at talk alternate between a pair (or members of a group of people) who constitute the immediate participants to the event[3]. Mediated interviews are designed for public consumption, as is evident in many details of their construction – from references to the audience, from the visible and audible reactions of a studio audience, and from particulars of utterance design. Indeed, it is a central and generally understood condition of this talk that a potentially endless number of people may overlook or overhear it – not as active interlocutors but as an indefinitely large audience. Interviewers and interviewees know, therefore, that what they say will be appraised not just by their immediate interlocutor but by who-knows-how-many beyond. This is not merely a matter of pressure towards increased circumspection in one's choice of words, though that must undoubtedly exist. It is also a matter of the public performance of talk – of talking adequately for the public purposes of the encounter and of acquitting oneself well in public.

In addition, they are characterised by the previously mentioned differentiation or pre-allocation of roles: one speaker asks questions and the other answers them. The speaker who asks questions does so from an institutionally defined position – one in which they hold some responsibility for setting the agenda, the terms or the topic of the discourse. Nor is it a case of simply asking questions; the media interviewer also controls the length, shape and even the style of the encounter. Conversely, of course, the interviewee has not achieved that role by accident. In some way or other they have earned, by virtue of a distinctive attribute, their 'communicative entitlement' as material for a documentary case study, as witness, as celebrity. And always the nature of the entitlement is 'evidenced' or constituted in practice within the interview: in other words, witnessing, 'celebrity-ness', or 'documentary-ness' (Corner, 1995) is an outcome of the kinds of interrogation pursued within the interview. The interviewee 'does witnessing' in the interview in response to questions designed to display it.

The news interview itself, therefore, is simply one manifestation of a widely available mediated public genre, but one that offers journalists a crucial device for supplying quotable material to underpin the news. In practice, of course, broadcast news interviews are themselves not all of a single type. We may distinguish four principal sub-genres: (1) interviews with correspondents (reporting and commenting); (2) interviews with ordinary people affected by, or caught up in, the news (witnessing, reacting and expressing opinion); (3) interviews with experts (informing and explaining); and (4) interviews with 'principals' – public figures with some kind of responsible role in relation to the news event (accounting). These four sub-genres may be defined – as here – by characterising the social identity and role of the person being interviewed and their characteristic contribution to the interview; but they could equally have been described in terms of the kinds of lead-in that set the agenda of the interview or the kinds of question that form its spine. For instance, a prototypical question to a correspondent is "Can you tell us more about what is going on?" (see Haarman, 2004). A prototypical question to an ordinary witness or bystander is "What could you see ...?", or "What did/does it feel like ...?". And the question to an expert explores the implications of a situation: "Given X, can you explain its implications?".

This repertoire of different types of news interview provides multiple threads out of which the web or tapestry of the news programme is woven. In *bulletin news programmes*, for instance, they are routinely used in edited fragments rather than in their entirety, providing perspectival sound-bites for an item (see Ekström, 2001). And so, by the use of interviews, the news becomes a thing of many voices – even if they are ultimately orchestrated in performance by the voice of the presenter. One highly significant aspect, which is mostly overlooked in studies of broadcast news interview, is their quite specifically occasioned character. They arise out of the need to cover journalistically an event or issue and they are inserted into an item or programme to cast light on or fill out an item or report. For this reason their relevance is routinely provided for at or near the beginning of the interview or extract.

Amongst the main sub-genres of news interview, the broadcast encounter with a public, often political, figure has received by far the greatest attention (Harris, 1991; Clayman, 1991, 1992; Clayman and Heritage, 2002; Hutchby, 2005, 2006; Blum-Kulka, 1983; Fetzer, 2002; Fetzer and Weizman, 2006; Lauerbach, 2006) – in part because they are seen as instances of the classic public sphere in action. The focus of discussion in treatments of interviews of this type is on topics such as bias/neutrality, adversarialness, 'holding to account' and evasion. Indeed, the amount of attention devoted to political interviews might be seen as disproportionate, especially since it leads to this one sub-type coming to define the genre and practice of the news interview as a whole (see, for instance, Hutchby, 2005, and Clayman and Heritage, 2002) even though they are in practice extremely rare within the context of the standard *bulletin news programme*. On the contrary, they are the rather exclusive preserve of those extended news programmes that aim to offer in-depth coverage of current affairs, such as ABC's *Nightline*, BBC 2's *Newsnight*, BBC Radio 4's *Today*, Channel 4 *News, Frost on Sunday* or NBC's *Nightly News*. Accordingly, to focus on the political interview as if it were typical of news interviewing in general is neither supported by the history of the journalistic interview nor justified by a survey of current broadcasting practice.

In what follows, therefore, *we* set out to characterise the news interview in general, situating the political interview as merely one type amongst the major kinds of interview that make up the news and offering a typology that distinguishes between them. The four main types of interview are termed the *accountability interview*, the *experiential interview,* the *expert interview* and the news interview with a correspondent, reporter, editor which *we* term the *affiliated interview*. Since *affiliated interviews* have already been discussed in Chapter 6, little more will be said about them here. To help define the position of an interview within a typology of news interview types it is useful to distinguish between four broad parameters or axes. The first parameter defines the interviewee as affiliated with the news institution or not. The second parameter defines the interviewee as involved with the news event as an actor or responsible agent. The third parameter defines the interviewee as having first-hand knowledge of the event or holding knowledge about it. And the fourth stipulates the nature of their presumed alignment with the audience set up by the interview – whether with the interviewee or not.

On this basis, the following matrix can be constructed.

	Affiliation	Knowledge	Agency	Audience alignment
Accountability interview	–	(of)	+	+	–
Experiential interview	–	(of)	–	+	+
Expert interview	–	(about)	–	+	–
Affiliated interview	+	(of/about)	–	–	–
				with Int'er/with Int'ee

Although this matrix generates a set of ideal-typical classifications to which many actual broadcast news interviews unproblematically correspond, there are in practice some instances of mixed or undecidable cases, or instances where an interview starts out as one type and shifts into another. Nonetheless, such typifications are associated with recognisable differences in interview in terms of both broad purpose (within the overall discursive economy of the news) and particular discursive practice (for instance, type of lead-in or question), even though it must be accepted that part of the difficulty in defining the sub-generic types is that the roles of participants may on occasion be re-defined through shifts of discursive practice.

7.2   *The accountability interview* with a public figure (− affiliation; + participant; + knowledge of)

In news interviews of this type the emphasis falls upon calling a public figure to account in relation to an issue or event of the moment either for their own deeds or words or for the actions/statements of the institution with which they are associated. While the interviewer seeks to query the basis of a statement or action, typically the interviewee seeks to justify it. Interviewees are public figures in the sense that they hold institutional positions and by their official status are treated as 'having some locus' on the matter at hand. Heads of publicly listed companies, office-holders in trades unions or professional associations are the kinds of public figure who get called upon for interview. However, perhaps the clearest examples of this kind of interview involve politicians being interviewed in relation to a relevant current news event or topic. The example cited below is from a *news item* broadcast on UK C4 the day before a scheduled meeting between Prime Minister Blair and Colonel Gaddafi in Libya. Relations between Libya and the UK had been strained for over a decade by events such as the shooting of a police officer (WPC Yvonne Fletcher) outside the Libyan Embassy in London, the bombing of Tripoli by US planes flying from bases in Britain and the destruction of a transatlantic flight over Lockerbie, Scotland. The suitcase bomb which destroyed the Pan Am flight was believed to have been planted by Libyan agents, one of whom had been jailed by a Scottish court. Latterly, however, relations between Libya and the West (e.g. Italy, France, UK, USA) had improved following the curtailment of her nuclear weapons programme and the payment of financial compensation for the victims of the Lockerbie bombing. In Extract 7.2.1 Baroness Symons, 'the foreign office minister responsible for the Middle East', is being interviewed by the *presenter* (or programme anchor), Jon Snow.

Ext. 7.2.1

```
 1 SNOW:    in Westminster now the foreign office minister responsible
 2          for the Middle East (.) Baroness(t) Symon (2.0) hh
 3          Minister (1.0) er the Prime Minister is is is gonna go ahead
 4          and do the: (.) the handshake (.)
 5          do we not need more time (.) to:: (.) check Gaddaffi out
 6 SYMONS:  (.) hhh (1.0) I think you know there's been a great deal of time
 7          I think that was very clear from (.) what Mr Mosey was just telling us
 8          in what I thought was er uh a very hh (.) moving er piece
 9          that he did just now
10          (.) the fact is that this has been a process (.)
11          there have bee:n (.) many things (.) asked (.) of the Libyans
12          in relation to what happened in Lockerbie (.) hh
13          and they have met (.) those points that have been raised (0.5)
14          now of course there is the outstanding issue stil:l (.)
15          of er the criminality: in relation to (.) WPC Fletcher
16          and we are (.) pursuing those issues still hhh. (1.0)
17          [but the huge issue
18 SNOW:    [can I just ask you about that (.) specific issue because (.)
19          er I the (.) er Foreign Minister was here (.) a few weeks back
20 SYMONS:                                     [yes Mister (Shargern)
21 SNOW:                                          [we we hadda bit
22          of time with him (0.5) has anything changed since then
23          any evidence of movement on:: the WPC Fletcher front
24 SYMONS: well as was indicated in one of your earlier clips (.)
25          uhm we hope that (.) er with the Prime Minister's visit
26          that what we asked of Mr (Shargern)
27          which was er real co-operation
28          the Met police actually going to Libya
29          talking to those (.) who were in the bureau
30          on the day when WPC Fletcher was shot (.)
31          that we will find that we have er some real agreement forthcoming
32          so I think we've gotto wait over the next twenty-four hours
33          to see what the Libyans are able to say to us about that
34 SNOW:                                          [but do you have any any
35          signal that they're going to
36 SYMONS: well er as I say I think we've gotto wait for the Prime Minister's visit
```

37   we are hopeful er we were hopeful Mr (Shargern) told the
38   Foreign Secretary he certainly told me (.) that he wanted to cooperate
39   and he would do what he could now the Prime Minister is going there (.)
40   so let us see what emerges
41   but but the enormous thing of course has been Libya's willingness
42   to deal with their weapons of mass destruction programme
43   and that has been (.) the big breakthrough (.) hhh
44   and of course it is er that that has been the major building block
45   for taking the relationship forward
46 SNOW: put in the most crude terms
47   I mean it is an extraordinary state of affairs isn't it
48   that that a er er er a sponsor of terrorism (.)
49   who: probably killed more Brits than Saddam Hussein did
50   we're going to go and shake the hand of
51   but (.) Saddam Hussein we went to war with and (.) arrested
52 SYMONS: well you know I think if Mr Mosey (.)
53   can er say that he would shake the hand
54   then probably it isn't for the rest of us to turn round and say no
55   we're not going to do this you don't (.) make breakthroughs (.)
56   in foreign relationships by only talking to your friends (.)
57   it's by talking to those with whom you disagree that you manage
58   to make some some real progress
59   and [my point about this is that only ( ) if I could just make the point
60 SNOW: [er in a sense that was exactly the point I was asking you whether
61   why we didn't do that with Saddam Hussein
62 SYMONS: hhh hhh Saddam Hussein was
63   over eighteen years refused all cooperation
64   that was er that was asked of him
65   from the er from the United Nations
66   he deliberately er turned his face away
67   from all those mandatory United Nations Security Council Resolutions
68   and refused all cooperation
69   here we have the exact reverse of that
70   that is the whole point (.)
71   because Colonel Gaddaffi has cooperated
72   Colonel Gaddaffi has come forward
73   and offered up his weapons of mass destruction
74   he has had the International Atomic Energy Authority in there
75   verifying dismantling those weapons of mass destruction
76   if we had seen that sort of action er from Saddam Hussein
77   things might have been very different
78 SNOW: [Baroness Symons
79 SYMONS: [but in fact of course
80   it is the positive action of Colonel Gaddaffi
81   that has led us to this position

82 SNOW: thank you very much for joining us
83 SYMONS: thank you

There are various markers of this as an *accountability interview*. In programmes where the whole news interview is broadcast, interviewees are always introduced at or just prior to the onset of the interview. This is not just by proper name (**Baroness Symons**) but also by an *identifier* – a specification of the grounds on which they speak for the purposes of the interview at hand. She could have been introduced using any or all of the following *identifiers*:

of Vernham Dean
of the British-American Project
a government spokeswoman
a junior foreign office minister
Deputy Leader of the House of Lords
Minister of State for the Middle East, International Security, Consular and Personal Affairs in the Foreign and Commonwealth Office

The *identifier* adopted, however, is as "the foreign office minister responsible for the Middle East" and this establishes the relevance of her contributions for the interview at hand, which occurs within the context of a news item about the UK government re-establishing links with Libya and will be about the wisdom of an imminent visit to Libya by Prime Minister Blair. Identification in this way also grants a specific kind of communicative entitlement (see Myers, 2000) as part of setting up the accountability interview: her contributions are elicited on the grounds that she by implication shares responsibility for the actions of the government and is accountable to the public on whose behalf she – like the Prime Minister – holds office. Jon Snow's frequent references to *we* (do **we** not need more time; **we**'re going to go and shake the hand of but (.) Saddam Hussein **we** went to war with) invoke not only the UK government but also the audience/public on whose behalf the government acts and on whose behalf Jon Snow presents himself as speaking. In this respect his questions have the force of 'request justification of a statement, decision, policy or course of action'.

Indeed, the questions which he asks are built around propositions that are disputable ('D-events' in Labov and Fanshel's terms; see Labov and Fanshel, 1977; and also Blum-Kulka, 1983). For example,

Ext. 7.2.1
47   I mean it is an extraordinary state of affairs isn't it
48   that that a er er er a sponsor of terrorism (.)
49   who: probably killed more Brits than Saddam Hussein did
50   we're going to go and shake the hand of
51   but (.) Saddam Hussein we went to war with and (.) arrested

Or

60   that was exactly the point I was asking you whether
61   why we didn't do that with Saddam Hussein

[where "that" = you don't (.) make breakthroughs (.) in foreign relationships by only talking to your friends (.) it's by talking to those with whom you disagree that you manage to make some some real progress]

The questions also have an inbuilt preference and may therefore be considered coercive: for example –

Ext. 7.2.1: ll. 47 and 5
47   I mean it is an extraordinary state of affairs isn't it
5   do we not need more time (.) to:: (.) check Gaddaffi out

Answers are treated as if they are evasive by reformulating questions: thus

34/35 but do you have any any signal that they're going to
(cooperate over WPC Fletcher)

takes place as a follow-up to

22/23 has anything changed since then any evidence of movement on:: the WPC Fletcher front

Furthermore, there are two distinctive features of turn-by-turn talk in a public *accountability interview*. One of them is the absence of in-turn vocalisations by the interviewer such as *mmhum, yeh, oh, I see* (sometimes described as *receipt tokens*; Atkinson, 1992; Clayman and Heritage, 2002) that routinely occur as indications of attention in non-status-marked, co-present encounters. (They are particularly noticeable in ordinary telephone encounters when visual feedback such as nodding or smiling is not possible.) Broadly these *receipt tokens* signal acknowledgement by the hearer of what the speaker is saying. One reason that the interviewer withholds them is that they may be interpreted as affiliative: in other words, they may be heard as indications of agreement by the hearer with the speaker's position. In withholding such behaviour the interviewer maintains a neutral position (Atkinson, 1992) with respect to what the speaker is saying. This in part, then, is a way of performing that official impartiality that the broadcasting of current affairs as a public service requires.

There is, however, another interactional dimension to this particular aspect of interviewer behaviour. It is part of the way in which this kind of talk is conducted not only by the interlocutors for the immediate contextual purposes at hand but also as a public act for an overhearing, viewing audience. The production of receipt tokens is nothing but intrusive and distracting for an overhearing audience. Withholding them is a deliberate concession on the part of the interviewer to the silent, invisible broadcast audience for whom the talk is partially designed.

If, however, *receipt tokens* are withheld by interviewers, this does not mean that turns by the interviewee are met with silence by the interviewer. On the contrary, here, as elsewhere among *accountability interviews* we note even in this short interview a high incidence of overlap at the boundaries of turns. Indeed, Baroness Symons hardly finishes a turn before Jon Snow begins his. Since, in these cases, he is producing a new (or a re-phrased) question which runs across what is from her a yet unfinished answer, he gives the impression that she has not provided an adequate response to what has gone before. Or, alternatively, that there is a conflict about agendas – that he, for instance, considers that she should be talking about something else. Certainly, the following exchange registers a difference of view about what is the main point at issue:

Ext. 7.2.1
57 SYMONS: it's by talking to those with whom you disagree that you manage
58   to make some some real progress
59   and [my point about this is that only ( ) if I could just make the point
60 SNOW: [er in a sense that was exactly the point I was asking you whether
61   why we didn't do that with Saddam Hussein

As with other news interviews, *accountability interviews* are cued or occasioned by *news items.* In other words, they occur 'on the back of' a *news kernel,* which provides for the relevance of the interview and shapes its topical scope. It is noticeable, for instance, in this interview how both participants orient at points to previous news discourse on the issue at hand.

More so, perhaps, than other news interviews, however, accountability interviews can also prime the news. In other words they not only develop out of a news item but also have the potential to feed into subsequent coverage – particularly by providing a topical resource in the form of quotation for a later news item (see Ekström, 2001). This may be exemplified by the following exchange on Al-Jazeera's *Frost over the World* between David Frost as interviewer and Prime Minister Blair.

Ext. 7.2.2
1 FROST: in terms of (1.0) Iraq (1.5) prime minister . erm .
2   in the . in the light of the:: . latest figures
3   not just of lawlessness and so on
4   but the the latest figures from the:: er from the:: Iraqi er
5   health ministry that the number of er Iraqis who've died
6   er is between 100,000 and 150,000 and so on (1.0)
7   with those scale of figures .
8   if you had known that that was the scale of bloodshed .
9   would you have sti::ll . gone to war .
10 BLAIR: well the alternative . was leaving Saddam in charge of Iraq .
11   where hundreds of thousands of people died

12   there were a million casualties in the Iran–Iraq war .
13   er Kuwait was invaded erm .
14   a::nd four million people went into exile .
15   so the idea that Iraqis should be faced with the situation
16   where they either have (0.5) a brutal (0.5) dictator . in Saddam
17   or alternatively . a sectarian religious conflict .
18   why can't they have in Iraq what their people want .
19   which is a non-sectarian government .
20   a government that is elected by the people
21   and the same opportunities and the same rights
22   that we:: enjoy in countries such as this .
23 FROST: but but . so far it's been (1.5) you know . pretty much of a disaster
24 BLAIR: [it   it   it   it
25   HAS but you see what I say to people is .
26   why is it difficult in Iraq
27   it's not difficult because of some . accident in planning .
28   it's difficult because . there is a deliberate strategy (0.5)
29   al-Qaeda with Sunni insurgents on the one hand .
30   erm . Iranian-backed . elements with Shia militia on the other
31   to create a situation in which the will of the majority of Iraqis
32   which is for peace .
33   is displaced by the will of the minority for war

This interview was broadcast on 17th November 2006 and formed the basis for widespread reports that Blair had admitted that Iraq was/had been a disaster. By the next day newspapers in the UK carried headlines such as "Iraq is a 'disaster' admits Blair" (*Mail*) or "Iraq invasion a disaster, Blair admits" (*Telegraph*) with CNN on 18th November subsequently commenting that: "Blair's 'Iraq disaster' interview provokes storm". BBC Online used the headline: "Blair accepts 'disaster' in Iraq". Al-Jazeera subsequently ran the recorded interview with the caption "Blair admits Iraq 'a disaster' ". (See Figure 7.1.)

Blair's own words themselves were hardly salient at the time. And it hardly matters that Blair does not in any case say exactly: "Iraq has been a disaster". As lines 23–25 of the transcript show, what actually happens is that Blair agrees elliptically with Frost's utterance: "so far it's been (1.5) you know . pretty much of a disaster" where the reference for Frost's "it" has to be recovered from some way back in the discourse (and Frost's turn itself is full of hesitancy, including the hedge "pretty much", which is omitted from all subsequent quotation). It is also worth noting that Blair's own turn-initial component, "it has" ('the admission'), begins even before Frost's turn had concluded with "disaster". Nonetheless, as long as the subsequent loose quotations (often in headlines, which by convention allow a degree of imprecision) are difficult to refute, this *accountability interview* has done substantive work in priming subsequent news coverage. This, accordingly,

Figure 7.1 Al-Jazeera: Blair admits Iraq 'a disaster'.

is the rubric under which the *accountability interview* runs: not only may the interviewee be held to account within the interview for actions and words prior to it; but it is also the case that the interview may generate material that can be used subsequently in its aftermath for accountability purposes. Faced with clear potential for discursive pitfall it is not perhaps surprising that politicians (the principal, though not the only, focus of the accountability interview) become a byword for evasiveness. Indeed, we must at least entertain the possibility that evasion is on occasion a produced consequence of the discourse practices of the accountability interview, as much as a quality inherent in the interviewee's performance (or character).

7.3   The experiential/witness interview with an ordinary member of the public (− affiliation; + knowledge of; − agent/− active participant)

The experiential interview provides news programmes with personal reactions to issues or events and, where appropriate, with eyewitness accounts. As with the accountability interview there is a clear demarcation of roles between questioning and answering. One person asks the questions, the other answers them. The person who asks the questions also frames, focuses and closes the encounter. There are, however, particular differences in the way these actions are performed that mark the encounter as a case of the 'experiential' interview[1]. The interviewee is presented in the role of an observer, victim or survivor rather than as an active agent in relation to the news and is interviewed not to answer for the event but to answer about it – to give a viewpoint privileged by some kind of closeness to proceedings. There is a sense in these kinds of interview of the interviewee having been caught up in the news field involuntarily, not by choice but by accident. Questions tend to be of the kind: "What did it feel like when …?"; "And then what happened …?"; "Do you think that …?".

Some characteristics of the experiential interview may be illustrated in the following example from Channel 4 News which took place just prior to the interview with Baroness Symons, transcribed as Extract 7.2.1, and as part of the same *news item*. (Symons herself refers to it in her own interview as a very hh (.) moving er piece.) The interviewer is again the *presenter* (anchor) of the programme, Jon Snow.

Ext. 7.3.1

I	SNOW:	John Mosey lost his daughter Helga in the Lockerbie crash
2		he joins us now from Malvern (.) .hh
3		erm John Mosey (1.5)
4		d'you have every reason to believe Colonel Gaddafi now
5	JOHN MOSEY:	(2.5)
6		er to believe him (.)
7		erm well (.) we have to accept
8		that he's (.) jumped over all the hurdles that the United Nations
9		have placed in front of him (.).hh
10		and if your erstwhile enemy:: (.) says he wants to change
11		and shows (.).h verifiable (.).h er evidence of changing (.)
12		only a (.) fool I think would (.)
13		put their foot in his face at the last minute (.)
14	SNOW:	what will your thoughts be:: (.) tomorrow
15	MOSEY:	(2.5)
16		er I I can't see any negative side to this
17		erm I'm not sure about the timing (.).h
18		I'm not a politician (.).h
19		but it can only be a good thing only good can come out of it
20		erm when as I've said your enemy has done all
21		that's been demanded of him
22		by the United Nations (.).h
23		er surely we also have a responsibility
24		to keep our side (.).h of the bargain
25		and (.) and er (.) welcome these people
26		back into the:: community of nations
27		if we don't (.)
28		what sort of signal do we send
29		to the: (.) erm (.) dangerous world out there (.)
30		do we send a signal that says
31		don't do deals with the West (.).h they can't be trusted

```
32          they won't keep their side of the bargain (.)
33          we must maintain our integrity
34 SNOW:    d'you think he is the man who (.) ultimately killed your daughter
35 MOSEY:   (2.5)
36          I don't know (1.0)
37          I sat through the whole of the ten months trial (0.5)
38          I have some reservations (0.5) erm but we (.) said that
39          we would (.) accept the verdict of the: Scottish court
40          and that's what we (.) have to do (.)
41 SNOW:    and if you had to would you shake his hand
42 MOSEY:   (3.0)
43          huphh (.)
44          I'm not eager to become (.) a friend of his (.)
45          erm (.) but if I had to yes I wouldn't trouble me at all (.).h
46          er (.) thank God there's forgiveness for all of us (.)
47 SNOW:    John Mosey thank you so much for joining us
48          (2.5)
```

Although this example displays the standard question–answer structure of the interview this is clearly different from an *accountability interview*. For one thing John Mosey is *identified* in a very different kind of way to Baroness Symons.

```
1 SNOW:     John Mosey lost his daughter Helga in the Lockerbie crash
```

In contrast to Symons, who is addressed as a someone with an implied obligation to answer questions and who can represent an aspect of Government, Mosey is *identified* and addressed as an ordinary individual who has an entitlement to speak based upon a personal and particular connection with the news material, which the interview will provide an opportunity to develop. (As it happens, John Mosey is a retired clergyman and a leading member of the Lockerbie Victims Support group with some public profile[4]; but this is nowhere alluded to in the C4 news item.) John Mosey is not precisely a witness to an event. For one thing Blair has not yet met Gaddafi, so the event at the heart of the interview hasn't even happened. And, in any case, John Mosey will not be there when it does take place. At the core of his answers, nonetheless, we find some statement of personal experience:

```
16          er I I can't see any negative side to this
17          erm I'm not sure about the timing (.).h

36          I don't know (1.0)
37          I sat through the whole of the ten months trial (0.5)
38          I have some reservations (0.5)

44          I'm not eager to become (.) a friend of his (.)
45          erm (.) but if I had to yes I wouldn't trouble me at all (.).h
```

John Mosey is treated as speaking simply on his own behalf (as the father of a victim). Indeed, at the heart of the interview is quite simply an invitation to him to state his own personal views; and in offering his views (in the first person) he is responding to questions that are very different in kind from those of the accountability interview.

4 SNOW: d'you have every reason to believe Colonel Gaddafi now

14 SNOW: what will your thoughts be:: (.) tomorrow

34 SNOW: d'you think he is the man who (.) ultimately killed your daughter

41 SNOW: and if you had to would you shake his hand

These questions are directed to the personal beliefs, thoughts and feelings of the recipient rather than to issues of the interviewee's responsibility or liability. It is noticeable also that they are short and simple in construction. Indeed, Jon Snow's turns in the two interviews are quite different in character. Here they have just one turn-component. In the *accountability interview* they sometimes contain two or more. There is also no overlap between turns in this interview. Despite John Mosey's pauses there are no occasions where Snow speaks across his turn. It is not just that Mosey is not held to account for his views. They are treated as if they were by definition indisputable. This is an important point of difference between the *accountability interview* and the *experiential interview*. Indeed there is no suggestion in the *experiential interview* of answers being evasive or being treated as such. Whereas in the *accountability interview* interviewers routinely pursue a (satisfactory) response to questions by repeating or rephrasing them, in the experiential interview answers are rarely treated as unsatisfactory. Note, for instance, the way in which Snow moves from question to question, each of which represents a shift of topic.

If we examine Mosey's answers closely, however, it is not obvious that he has in each case answered the question which was put to him. In answer to the first question about whether he now believes Colonel Gaddafi he maintains that we should treat changes in behaviour at their face value. In answer to the question about what his thoughts will be tomorrow he says we should keep our side of the bargain. In answer to the question of whether Gaddafi killed his daughter he says we should accept the verdict of the Scottish court.

If Snow's questions are addressed to Mosey's thoughts, emotions and beliefs, the latter's answers invoke instead what might loosely be called 'principled bases for action' – Mosey says in effect that we should treat others' actions and words at face value, we should keep our side of a bargain, and we should remember that forgiveness is universal. And yet despite the apparent gap between the question and the answer there is little or no sense of any conflict of agendas here or of questions being evaded[5].

The two types of interview – the *accountability interview* and the *experiential interview* – are thus very different in character. The former is built upon questions designed to seek justifications from the recipient for their statements or lines of action and to challenge them. The latter is designed to elicit perspectives on an event or an issue. The most obvious kind of experiential interview is one involving a witness to an event or a survivor of it. But some kind of (non-responsible) connection to the event may be enough to warrant the interview.

The generic differences between these two types of interview are partly at the level of opening 'lead in' or introduction, partly at the level of question type and type of follow-up question from the interviewer. But they also invite a different kind of attention from their audience. The *accountability interview*, as currently practised, invites the audience to identify with the interviewer as their spokesperson: it proceeds as if the interviewer is asking questions on behalf of components of the public[6]. The *experiential interview*, however, occupies a quite different relationship to the audience. This kind of interview is shaped to give us the experiential flavour of the event and the audience is situated on the side of the interviewee, who has been invited to articulate a version of what we might think, see, or feel if we too were close up in some way to the event. Whereas in the *accountability interview* the interviewer speaks as if for us and the interviewee is presented as estranged from the audience ('an evasive politician')[7], in the *experiential interview* the interviewee is treated as one of us.

7.3.1 Witnessing and speaking from experience

A special class of experiential interview are those that depend upon having had a first-hand experience of an event or issue. For these interviews the entitlement is more direct even than that of John Mosey above in Extract 7.3.1 and may be seen as dependent upon an act of witnessing. This is particularly relevant in relation to a whole class of 'bad news' events such as accidents, disasters and emergencies. The irruption of the unexpected into everyday life, not least when fatalities and injuries are involved, provides a news frame for talking about survival and thereby places a premium on speaking from experience. In broadcasting bad news, the tales of survivors offer something similar to reportage[8]: they provide a significant counterweight to the core element of these news events – the accounts of death.

A significant component of news coverage of the London bombings of July 2005, for instance, was precisely this kind of witnessing. At the core of interviews with survivors – overwhelmingly pervasive across the domain of broadcast news – are accounts which routinely conform to Labov's description of narratives of personal experience (Labov, 1972b; Labov and

Fanshel, 1977; Labov and Waletsky, 1967). Indeed, a striking aspect of the London accounts is their sheer similarity: for all the unique awfulness of individuals' experiences, the forms through which this was mediated to the broadcast audience were highly uniform. This can be exemplified using the structural template identified by Labov for describing spoken narratives of personal experience. For everyday narratives Labov identified core elements of *orientation, complication, evaluation, resolution, coda*[9].

Orientation is Labov's term for the phase of the narrative devoted to establishing the context (e.g. time, place, persons, circumstances) in which the events of the narrative unfold. The orientation phase of these accounts in witness–survivor interviews following the London bombings is devoted to establishing the normality of the routine pre-existing the event. Thus:

Ext. 7.3.1.1

[Orientation]

1 INT'VIEWEE 1:	as usual I got on the train
2	travelled all the way to Kings Cross
3	went down the stairs as usual to the Piccadilly line
4	the first train came along
5	the platform was completely packed
6	erm and I was about to board the train
7	and a woman jumped in front of me
8	erm I kind of looked at the woman
9	and I usually would like . go past her
10	but I kind of tapped her on the shoulder and say "have a good day love"
11	and she kind of got on that train
12	the second train came which was also packed as well
13	and I thought "I gotta get to work" and so I boarded that train
14	erm and on that train I think I was in the first carriage
15	so I got on to there holding to the pole erm
16	and then the train started going along
17	ah don't know if it was about two minutes or five minutes

[Complication]

18	but (.) somefink happened

This is one of several interviewee narratives which set the scene broadly in terms of 'everything was proceeding as normal and then …' though this perhaps the most elaborated version[10]. Shorter, more straightforward, versions of this kind of *orientation* are as follows:

Ext. 7.3.1.2

[Orientation]

1 INT'VIEWEE 2:	well I was going to work
2	I was at Finsbury Park train station on the Piccadilly Line
3	and I got on at Finsbury Park

```
4          erm I was due to get off at Hammersmith
5          aand I don't really remember much really
6          until erm until actually it happened
7          which was I think we just left King's Cross
8          and su . I was just sitting there reading my book
```
[Complication]
```
9          and suddenly I just I heard a bang and it everything went black
```

Ext. 7.3.1.3
[Orientation]
```
I INT'VIEWEE 3:    so I was just sitting there
2          erm reading reading the Metro
3          about the:: erm about the Olympic games
4          an(d) reading the first two pages getting all excited
5          an(d) yeyyy fantastic
6          and everything was everything was going along really good
```
[Complication]
```
7          erm until all of a sudden (yeh)
8          (.) erm (.) some massive (.) massive bang (.)
```

These *orientations* are taken from fairly extended interviews. Remnants of this way of shaping the experience are traceable in vox-pop fragments such as the following:

Ext. 7.3.1.4
```
I VOXPOP WI:    we were on there like for thirty seconds
```
[Complication]
```
2          and then there was just an explosion in the carriage next door
3          and then there was just all smoke
4          and you couldn't breathe
```

Generally, therefore, *orientations* in these survivor–witness narratives set the scene in such a way as to emphasise a transition from the ordinary to the extraordinary – an irruption of something extraordinary into the humdrum continuum of the everyday. Note, however, that typically the accounts – especially the more elaborated ones – rehearse or recapture the 'naivety' of the experiencer: they emphasise, in other words, the raw immediacy of the experience, in its moment of unfolding, rather than anticipating later knowledge and packaging the event with the benefit of hindsight. For example:

Ext. 7.3.1.5
```
I INT'VIEWEE:    I was just sitting there reading my book
```
[Complication]
```
2 →        and suddenly I just I heard a bang
3 →        and it everything went black er
```

Ext. 7.3.1.6
1 INT'VIEWEE: everything was going along really good erm
[Complication]
2   until all of a sudden (yeh)[11] (.) erm
3 →   (.) some massive (.) massive bang (.)

Ext. 7.3.1.7
1 INT'VIEWEE: but (.) somefink happened
2 →   I don't know what happened erm
[Complication]
3 →   and my HEAD hit the pole that was in front of me
4   the blue pole that was in front of me
5 →   it SMACKED it kind of thing

By the time these interviews were broadcast, mostly on the following day, it was clearly established that the explosions had been caused by a series of bombs. But none of the interviewees draws upon this publicly available knowledge in producing their narratives. None of them, for instance, phrases it thus:

And then the bomb went off

Instead they treat the news interview not as an occasion simply to tell what happened but as an occasion to re-live the experience from the inside – to tell what it was like to have the event happen to them: they relate the fact of something happening while simultaneously remaining true to the sense of not knowing at that time **what** was happening.

In Labov's terms these crucial moments of extreme disruption in the ordinary lives of witness-survivors are clearly *complications* – described by him as hinge-points, crises or problems constituting the core event-line of narrative. However, although such elements are absolutely essential to the structure of narrative, their space in these accounts is quite truncated. Instead much greater attention is devoted to what Labov and Waletsky (1967) describe as *evaluation,* rehearsing, often in close detail, reactions to the immediate happening, not just of the interviewee but also of others in the scene. This is frequently done here in reported thought and reported speech, often coupled with verbs of cognition – "I remember", "I looked at my leg", 'I noticed", "I knew" "I felt really really faint", "the next thing I remember". The way in which these narratives are produced in broadcast interviews some time from the event significantly avoids what is already known about it (that a series of bombings had taken place) but emphasises instead precisely what the broadcast audience could not know – what it was like to experience it.

Ext. 7.3.1.8
[Evaluation]
     I thought, "this is the worst thing I have ever seen".

Ext. 7.3.1.9
[Evaluation]
> I thought "this is the end of the world, right here in this carriage"

Ext. 7.3.1.10
[Evaluation]
1   I remember holding on to it with my left hand and saying
2   "I've gotta keep focussed I've gotta keep focussed"

Ext. 7.3.1.11
[Evaluation]
1   a woman called Alison was saying to me
2   "Gary look calm down let's get on to the chair now"
3   and then at that moment a girl screamed
4   "I've lost my leg I've lost my leg"
5   and then I kind of looked at my leg
6   and I noticed that my leg was like hanging on my left leg
7   and I looked at at such funny angle I knew I lost my leg at that time
8   and then I pulled myself up with the strength of my arms onto a chair
9   and while I was on the chair Alison was saying to me
10   "Gary you've goto stay with me"
11   and blood was like oozing all over the place
12   and there was times I felt really really faint and fainted
13   and she kept on hitting me
14   and the next thing I remember is erm
15   I kind of like went down
16   cos I said "I couldn't stay on this seat no longer"

Ext. 7.3.1.12
[Evaluation]
1   erm the next thing I remember was
2   just the smell of just burning and smoke
3   and what not it's like burning rubber
4   and at that point I was
5   didn't really know what had happened
6   I was just afraid that there was a fire
7   and it was so busy
8   the train was so packed that I just
9   noone could move and noone could breathe
10   and I thought "well if there's a fire this is . this is it"

Ext. 7.2.1.13
[Complication]
1   I just couldn't breathe

[Evaluation]
2   I thought "this is not how I want to die (.)
3   I don't wanna die I erm (2.5) with smoke inhalation"
4   I (1.0) wuhdidn't want didn't want it to end erm (.) so I thought
5   "I need air I need air" (.)
[Resolution]
6   pushed the glass through
[Evaluation]
7   an(d) sort of stood there for a few minutes thinking
8   "oh my god this is it" (.)
9   by that stage (.) erm (1.0) people started screaming (.) erm (.)
10   yu you know sort of at the back carriages (1.0) erm (.)
11   you know I remember a lady saying "help me help me" (1.0)

Some surface features of these *Evaluations* are worthy of comment. It is noticeable, for instance, that they frequently rely on direct speech (or thought) and that these instances of direct speech and thought often involve *re-duplication*:

I thought "I need air I need air";
I thought "this is not how I want to die (.) I don't wanna die erm (2.5) with smoke inhalation";
saying "I've gotta keep focussed I've gotta keep focussed" ;
(myself) saying "look calm down calm down we're gonna get out";
(heard) a lady saying "help me help me";
a girl screamed "I've lost my leg I've lost my leg";
awful screaming of people like just "help help help".

Occurrences of *re-duplication* in the context of *Evaluation* typically seem to correspond to critical moments of particular intensity.

Evaluation in these narratives tends to be more elaborated than the *Complication* and tends to occur in reaction to it. As such *Evaluations* tend to intervene between the *Complication* and the *Resolution* (again in keeping with the classical structure outlined by Labov). For most of these narratives the *Resolution* typically involves 'the escape/rescue':

Ext. 7.3.1.14
[Resolution]
1   and all of a sudden we saw flashlights coming from like the driver's side
2   the ambulance and the police came in
3   and they took everyone out bit by bit bit by bit
4   and me and Alison was the last two to leave
[Evaluation]
5   erm the next thing I remember was waking up four days after that
6   in the Royal Free Hospi(ckle) still not knowing what's happened

7   and then my bruvver told me it was four bombs went off
8   and I was like "what?"
9   I couldn't believe it

Ext. 7.3.1.15
[Resolution]
1   eventually the:: er driver
2   "look just walk straight don't touch any of the:: er lines"
3   and we walked through the tunnel which (.)
4   I have no idea how long that was
5   er and eventually we got to Russell Square
6   erm the people helped us off the tracks onto the platform
7   and we walked up the steps up to Russell Square Station

After the *Resolution* and towards the end of these interviews we typically find a return to normality, corresponding to Labov and Waletsky's *Coda* (which in their account provides a way of moving from the time and situation of the narrative to the present time). Thus:

Ext. 7.3.1.16
[Coda]
1   it was just a case of just touching my body just to see if everything was ok
2   but I consider myself very fortunate ....
3   it's a bit weird because it doesn't seem like it happened
4   I'm just very grateful that I'm ok
5   erm but it's it's a bit strange and bit hard to deal with
6   but I'm determined to get to get to normal

Ext. 7.3.1.17
[Coda]
1   there's so many millions of (.) travellers so many trains going on (.)
2   the chance of it happening again at the same place the same time (.)
3   erm are pretty low
4   so (.) yeh I'm not going to stop my life you know
5   if anything I'm gonna enjoy my life more

Ext. 7.3.1.18
[Coda]
1   (.) but (.) that's about it wiff regards to detail
2   other than that I fink it's time for me now to move on

Ext. 7.3.1.19
[Coda]
1   I'm just going to get on with my life
2   because if ah have that malice or that anger or anyfink

3   it's only gonna hold me back an ah don't wanna be hold back
4   ah'm too positive and too strong to be held back
5   ah need to just go forward now

Ext. 7.3.1.20
[Coda]
1   I'm not going to be going that far as to be playing football
2   ah just wanna be mobile
3   to go to work come home do what ahm doing and then SING
4   cos ahm a singer
5   erm ah do a lot of music with Charles Bailey
6   as long as I can get along with doing that
7   my voice ain't gone anywhere
8   I'll still be happy
9   because like I say
10   I'm not being funny
11   but I feel like ah been blessed
12   God saved me for a reason

Several distinctive features may be found in these witness-survivor narratives from broadcast *experiential interviews*. Within the overall emphasis on the indescribable nature of the experience ("that was a scene I cannot describe") two complementary, almost contrapuntal, features stand out: what might be called respectively the *maximising generalisation* and the *minimising marker*. The maximising generalisation is, literally speaking, an overstatement. They typically deal with unqualified number, scope or extent:

everything went black; **everyone** was screaming; **no-one** could move and **no-one** could breathe; **no-one** could get **any kind of** communication out; **all** their clothes had been blown off; **everyone** started shouting; **everything** started getting like dusty; **everyone** was like literally couldn't breathe; **everyone** went down; **everybody** calmed down; **everything** went black er an(d) **everyone** was screaming; there was wreckage **all over** the track

Not all of these expressions can be exactly and literally true. But it is not in any case the business of these narratives to be forensically exact. They are better understood as fulfilling an obligation to render what it felt like; and if it felt like 'no-one could breathe', then that is the narrative truth.

In almost complementary distribution to the *maximising generalisation* is what might be called the *minimising marker*, most commonly realised in these examples by "just".

I was just didn't know what was going on an(d) I just touched my head an(d) I could just feel blood pouring an(d) it was just a case of just touching my body just to see if everything was ok so I was just sitting there erm reading reading the Metro

I just couldn't breathe

and then it was just screaming

I was just sitting there reading my book and suddenly I just I heard a bang

it was just chaos and panic

I was just afraid that there was a fire

the next thing I remember was just the smell of just burning

so packed that I just noone could move

I just just had no idea about what was happening at the time

We were on there like for thirty seconds
and then there was just an explosion in the carriage next door
and then there was just all smoke
and you couldn't breathe

there was awful screaming of people like just "help help help"
and it's just indescribable

I just wanted to see a friend or somebody new and give them a hug.

well like I say I've just gotta remain positive at the end of the day

ah just wanna be mobile to go to work come home do what ahm doing
and then SING

it's just for me to move on now.

I'm just naturally a bubbly person you know
in time they say I will have my down periods or whatever
but I'm just me I'm naturally a bubbly person

These examples of 'just' are in the main replaceable by 'simply'. Indeed they might be called 'simple-truth' markers. As such, they work in counterpoint to the *maximising generalisation*. They are a way of saying "here I am not making a special claim either for myself or the enormity of the event – it's just how it was". Thus "I'm just naturally a bubbly person" is a way of saying "this is simply the way that I am and I take no credit for it". They function to emphasise the truth of the statement being enunciated in the face of possible claims of exaggeration, self-promotion, special pleading, and so on[12].

As noted earlier, a striking aspect of these accounts is their sheer similarity, an observation that does not undermine the uniqueness and particularity of the event for the individuals who experienced it. Nonetheless, when these essentially private individuals are invited to tell what happened for a broadcast audience it is clear that they adopt strikingly similar forms of expression.

In part this is because they are occasioned discourses of a particular broadcast moment: they arise in the context of specific questions within the framework of a specific news agenda. These survivors' accounts are produced in response to specific types of question designed to display aspects of the experience to the public at large. Thus, there are questions designed as if to establish a chronology or to elicit the structure of the event:

```
1 INT'VIEWER:  so you came out of eventually got out of the front carriage
2              and then walked forwards towards Russell Square Station
```

But equally significantly there are questions designed to elicit the character of the experience:

```
1 INT'VIEWER:  well just what was it like to be on one of those trains
```

```
1 INT'VIEWER:  how d'you feel though today
2              you must still be in a bit shock I'd have thought
```

Thus, there is a dual focus to these interviews: to some extent they tell us what happened; but secondly – and perhaps more importantly – they tell us **what it felt like as it happened**. This dual focus gives a quite specific measure to the interviews. There is little sense of the interviewee being held accountable for their actions in the interview or even being made accountable for their knowledge – despite the evident effort that interviewees make to try and capture the detailed particularity of the event – the dialogue, the smell, the panic, the occasionally elaborate analogy, the appallingly gruesome injury, and so on. Their commitment to catching the unfolding of the experience is very strong ("the next thing I remember …").

In conclusion it is important to recognise that these interviews and their embedded narratives are conditioned by the contingencies of the broadcast moment and a sense of the appropriate sub-generic interview type at stake. In their narratives of personal experience, for instance, interviewees are not being required to achieve the forensic accuracy required by a court of law (though very occasionally they tip in that direction). Instead the interview format requires them to achieve some kind of simple 'truth to experience'.

There is a further dimension to the way in which these interviews are occasioned. They chime with a broader kind of public response. The sentiments of the individual speakers are treated as intersecting with a larger current of public opinion. They provide appropriate models for 'working things through' (Ellis, 2002). This can be seen especially in the closing of the interview.

Ext. 7.3.1.21
```
1 INT'VIEWER:  how d'you feel though today
2              you must still be in a bit shock I'd have thought
```

3 INT'VIEWEE: it's a bit weird because it doesn't seem like it happened
4 I'm just very grateful that I'm ok erm
5 but it's it's a bit strange and bit hard to deal with
6 but I'm determined to get to get to normal
7 INT'VIEWER: → good for you Mark Margolis
8 thank you very much for telling us about what happened to you
9 that's it from King's Cross ...

Ext. 7.3.1.22

1 INT'VIEWEE: NO: (.) probably not er probably yes tomorrow
2 probably won't go on the tube tomorrow (.) erm (1.0)
3 but saying that (.) I I prob I will next week you know (.)
4 erm there's so many millions of (.) travellers so many trains going on
5 (.) the chance of it happening again at the same place the same time (.)
6 erm are pretty low so (.) yeh I'm not going to stop my life you know
7 if anything I'm gonna enjoy my life more
8 INT'VIEWER: → it's a determination many other survivors will share

In each case the interviewer endorses the interviewee's expressed desire to return to normal. In this respect the interviews coincide with a larger framework of response that includes statements by public figures to the effect that 'life must go on'. Both of these interviews, for instance, were broadcast in the context of morning news programmes depicting Londoners returning to work (and an almost self-conscious normality) on the day immediately after the bombings. They offer compelling instances of individuals 'speaking from experience' but they also project a communal sense of solidarity articulated in collectively similar accounts of working things through. In voicing sentiments which are appropriate for public expression at that moment in that way, they provide an element of what John Ellis (2002) calls 'the private life of the public sphere'.

It is important to emphasise the distinctive character of this type of interview. These are not accountability interviews with 'public figures on the air' (Clayman and Heritage, 2002) Those who are interviewed in these interviews are not chosen or given an entitlement to speak because of their public prominence or their role in making the news or because of some responsibility for or complicity with the events of the news. They are not chosen because of accredited, specialised expert knowledge. They are not chosen as institutionalised correspondent, entitled to speak as a member of the broadcast institution itself. They are chosen and entitled to speak by virtue of the simple fact of witness. Rather than being recognisable public figures they are 'ordinary members of the public' who have by accident endured an experience that anyone could have endured but none would wish to have done and who have thereby acquired the self-deprecating burden of witness.

This is a curious kind of entitlement. For the public to know the nature of the event hidden from view and past in time, only those with first hand experience can tell them. And so these interviewees are obligated to describe the indescribable. These are witness-survivors who by a series of accidents have accidentally found themselves *in extremis* and who are shaping broadcastable public accounts of what it was that they survived and what it was that the audience, by an alternative set of accidents, escaped.

7.4　The expert interview (− affiliation; + knowledge about; − agency)

After the *accountability* and the *experiential* interview, the third main type of interview – the *expert interview* – is designed to elucidate the event or topic of the news by providing 'background' through eliciting supplementary information, elucidating unfamiliar concepts, spelling out the implications of a development or providing independent comment. They are most likely to be used when technical or semi-technical issues are involved – share price movements, adjustments to interest rates, announcements of scientific advances, health scares, changes to the law. Typically, though not invariably, they figure interviewees who are 'not affiliated' to the broadcast institution itself as a way of projecting a sense of the disinterested, non-partisan nature of the information, evidence or explanation being offered. Although not affiliated to the news organisation itself they do of course often have some kind of institutional affiliation or professional status – for instance "a pensions specialist with City firm Deloitte La Touche" – which confirms their expert credentials. As with other news interviewees this information will be referenced at the onset of the interview by the interviewer as part of the *identifier*.

Here is an example of an expert knowledge interview being used in order to cast light on an issue in the news – in this case whether or not to re-classify cannabis as a dangerous drug: the interview establishes a knowledge base from which to view the decision about re-classification. It is *focused* at the outset ("cannabis is not going to be re-classified as a more dangerous drug / even though many say that it is far more potent these days than it was / well is that true"). The interviewee is introduced not only by name ('Matthew Atha') but with a particular, topically relevant credential ('the director of the Independent Drug Monitoring Unit') which provides for his communicative entitlement in this particular context. And there are a series of factual questions about cannabis: 'what is skunk' …'is it more powerful' … 'how widely is it used' and so on.

Ext. 7.4.1: BBC Radio 4 *Today*

```
1 INT'VIEWER:  cannabis is not going to be re-classified
2             as a more dangerous drug
3             even though many say
4             that it is far more potent these days than it was
```

5		well is that true
6		Matthew Atha is
7		the director of the Independent Drug Monitoring Unit
8		and joins us from Liverpool
9		good morning
10	INT'VIEWEE:	good morning Sarah
11	INT'VIEWER:	(hhhen) first of all what is skunk
12	INT'VIEWEE:	skunk
13		well it depends how you define skunk
14		skunk technically is a trade mark variety
15		er supplied by a (hhhh) ho. a Dutch seed bank
16		but it has become come to be known
17		as any loose form of cannabis female flowering tops
18		erm grown indoors under lights
19		so which tend to be more potent than indeed cannabis resin
20		or imported cannabis bush
21		that's been carried half way round the world
22		and..er
23	INT'VIEWER:	and presumably also more likely to be grown at home
24	INT'VIEWEE:	yes in (0.5) the vast majority of cases
25		it is grown by by the users themselves
26		or by their friends etcetera
27	INT'VIEWER:	and is it more powerful
28	INT'VIEWEE:	(hhh) again it depends
29		erm in general it will
30		if we compare cannabis resin
31		the typical range of potencies of cannabis resin is about
32		three to seven per cent
33		the typical er potency range of skunk is
34		about eight to fifteen per cent
35		very occasionally up to twenty per cent
36		and on extremely rare occasions over twenty per cent
37		so it's on average about twice as as potent as as cannabis resin
38		but it's that's not the whole picture
39		cannabis resin has got other compounds in it
40		notably cannabidiol or CBD
41		which tends to take the edge off the high
42		whereas skunk doesn't have that
43		so it tends to intensify the high rather more
44	INT'VIEWER:	so so broadly it is a lot more powerful
45	INT'VIEWEE:	it is more powerful than can- cannabis resin
46		er commercial cannabis resin
47	INT'VIEWER:	and how widely is it used
48	INT'VIEWEE:	I would say
49		it is now the most common for(m)-

50   commonly used form of cannabis resin
51   in the UK by quite some margin
52   er ten years ago it er took up about ten per cent of the market
53   our figures for two thousand and four showed
54   it took nearly two thirds of the market
55 INT'VIEWER: and the way people smoke it
56   they don't put less in it because it's stronger
57 INT'VIEWEE: some do some don't
58   there are people who smoke
59   gargantuan quantities of the stuff you know
60   an ounce two ounces or even more than that a week
61 INT'VIEWER: so so should it have been up been re-classified
62   cannabis should have been re-classified
63   to be a more dangerous drug do you think
64 INT'VIEWEE: no can- no the class-
65   cannabis doesn't become more or less of a dangerous dr- drug
66   depending on its classification
67 INT'VIEWER: I I appreciate that
68   but the decision not to re-classify
69   was that the right one
70 INT'VIEWEE: no I think the decision not to reclassify was the right one
71   er primarily because so far re-classification
72   seems to have been an unqualified success
73   in that not only has usage not increased
74   it's actually seen to have decreased particularly among young people
75   and one could say that the forbidden fruit
76   when it's less forbidden loses much of its sweetness
77 INT'VIEWER: not cool any longer
78   Matthew Atha thank you

Two kinds of overlapping alternation of perspectives are apparent in this interview: (a) between a frame of reference derived from 'the life-world' (Schutz, 1973, Fairclough, 1995) and a framework of reference identifiable as 'scientific' – or, at least, one which is evidence-based; and (b) between the news frame of the interviewer and the expert frame of the interviewee. On several occasions during the interview a formulation offered by one party is re-formulated by the other.

So, for instance, when, the interviewer, Sarah Montague offers the formulation "more likely to be grown at home", Matthew Atha apparently concurs but reformulates it as "yes in ... the vast majority of cases it is grown by by the users themselves or by their friends etcetera". Another example is:

44 INT'VIEWER: so so broadly it is a lot more powerful
45 INT'VIEWEE: it is more powerful than can- cannabis resin er commercial
cannabis resin

The interviewee, rather than simply accept the unqualified comparative 'more powerful', supplies a precise term for the comparison. Indeed, there has up to this point been an alternation between 'potency' and 'powerful' in the interview, Sarah Montague offering 'powerful' twice in questions (though 'potent' when focusing at the outset) whereas Matthew Atha on the other hand offers 'more potent', 'range of potencies', 'potency range' and 'twice as potent'. At times, there are traces of ongoing re-formulation even within the turn of the interviewee. For instance, 'cannabis resin' becomes re-formulated as 'commercial cannabis resin' in the following: "it [skunk] is more powerful than can- cannabis resin er commercial cannabis resin". Likewise, "the most common for(m)" becomes re-formulated by the speaker as "commonly used form of cannabis".

However, whereas re-formulations in an accountability interview will typically be seen as 'evasive', and routinely treated as such by interviewers, here the overall effect might be described as one of 'striving for accuracy'. The selection and alternation of expressions or formulations is nuanced by the perspective of the speaker. Sarah Montague speaks on behalf of a common-sense perspective in which drugs are, broadly speaking, more or less powerful and more or less dangerous as a result. Her contributions mediate between that position and the informed perspective of the expert. Matthew Atha speaks instead on the basis of a set of (presumably) systematically gathered evidence underpinning statements of fairly precise proportions of potency –

Ext. 7.4.1

31	the typical range of potencies of cannabis resin is about
32	three to seven per cent
33	the typical er potency range of skunk is about eight to fifteen per cent
34	very occasionally up to twenty per cent
35	and on extremely rare occasions over twenty per cent
36	so it's on average about twice as as potent as as cannabis resin
37	but it's that's not the whole picture

Indeed, the interview as a whole elaborates and refines a distinction between 'skunk' and 'cannabis resin'.

Significantly, in its closing it moves away from the adducing of evidence (about potency) to the elicitation of an expert opinion on the merits of the policy of re-classification itself.

Ext. 7.4.1

70 INT'VIEWEE:	no I think the decision not to reclassify was the right one
71	er primarily because so far re-classification
72	seems to have been an unqualified success
73	in that not only has usage not increased
74	it's actually seen to have decreased particularly among young people
75	and one could say that the forbidden fruit

76   when it's less forbidden loses much of its sweetness
77 INT'VIEWER: not cool any longer
78   Matthew Atha thank you

One of the paradoxes of *expert interviews* is that while they are ostensibly about knowledge – data, evidence or science – they may well incorporate or build to a definite view in favour of one position on an issue or another. And positions may be advocated in ways quite immune from contradiction or interrogation. In other words, experts in the context of news are almost by definition not there to be held accountable by the broadcaster (unlike a fully public figure such as a politician). It is noticeable, for instance, that in moving to close the interview the interviewer reformulates in a manner that affiliates with the interviewee (ll. 65 and 66) rather than calls into question the inter- viewee's viewpoint. In a curious way, expertise – like experience in the expe- riential interview – is elicited in a manner which takes it beyond question.

Indeed, the expert knowledge rehearsed in the interview may be oriented as much to judgement as to elucidation. Here is an example of comment or judgement from an independent expert who has been asked to respond to a recently published government booklet '*Preparing for emergencies – What you need to know*'.

Ext. 7.4.2
BBC Radio 4: August 2004 *PM*
1 INTERVIEWER: well it's five fifteen just before the headlines
2   let's talk to Simon Turney an emergency planning consultant
3   good evening to you
4 INT'VIEWEE: (.) good evening=
5 INT'VIEWER: =waddyu think of this booklet
6 INT'VIEWEE: (.) I think generally it's an overstatement of the bleedin' obvious
7   an:: the (.) hhh criticisms that can be levelled at in ascending order are
8   that it's amateur (.) it's unrealistic (.)
          it's careless an' actually it's dishonest
9 INT'VIEWER: (1.0) justify all of that
10 INT'VIEWER: (.) hhh the: amateu::r bit is
11   the pretty pictures of fire officers and government doctors
12   now who on earth nee:ds (.)
13   photo (0.5) prints of (.) senior government officers
14   (.) hh in a domestic survival uh (.) leaflet
15   (.) hh the carelessness I think comes in the fact that here in Sheffield
16   all the fire engines have got the other nine nine nine number on
17   one one two
18   but you'd have to look very hard to find one one two
19   as the:: alternative to nine nine nine in the leaflet
20   because it it it isn't there (.) hh erm at all
21   (.) hh er as far as dishonesty's concerned two points

```
22          one is we are quite rightly advised
23          to take our mobile phones with us
24          but the first thing that happened to mobile phones
25          in any major disaster is
26          that under the government telephone preference sche-scheme
27          they get switched off (.)
28          they were switched off nearly twenty years ago at Hungerford (.)
29          when fourteen people were gunned to death
30          (.) hh erm and of course the arrangements for switching off (.)
31          both mobile and landline phones are far more sophisticated now
32          than they were ba-back in the eighties
33          (.) hhh the other major (.) issue I have with it is
34          actually about children and schools
35          that our instincts are obviously to go and collect our kids (.)
36          the leaflet tells us it may not be safe to do so
37          a::nd (.) get arrangements from (.) the local council
38          Sheffield Richmond wherever
39          (.) hh what arrangements they've made for letting parents know
40          when to collect their children from school
41          (.) hh well I'll be damned if I'd have any local council tell me
42          I couldn't collect my kids
43          and I'm sure that millions of people think think identically I=
44 INT'VIEWER:    =would they 'ave been better off not printing this
45 INT'VIEWEE:    (.) hh phew for eight million quid I think
46          they could have got something a lot more concrete
47          and a lot more pragmatic out
48          I agree with one point that erm Caroline Flint said
49          that yes it's good that they've actually managed to do it
50          they've had nearly three years since nine-eleven
51          and heightened public awareness
52          (.) hhh erm phh if I was marking a GCSE paper I think
53          I'd refer this one back and make them resit in the Autumn
54 INT'VIEWER:    Simon Turney thank you
55          here are the headlines
```

Again an *identifier* ("Simon Turney an emergency planning consultant") is used to introduce the expert by name and to specify his credentials to speak. He is then asked without preliminaries "waddyu think of this booklet?" He is asked, that is, for a statement of opinion rather than to elucidate some background. His answer is a particularly trenchant kind of comment.

```
6 INT'VIEWEE:    (.) I think generally it's an overstatement of the bleedin' obvious
7          an:: the (.) hhh criticisms that can be levelled at in ascending order are
8          that it's amateur (.) it's unrealistic (.)
9          it's careless an' actually it's dishonest
```

Although the speaker is *identified* as an emergency planning consultant, the opening question goes straight to the issue of judgement. The interviewer's second turn at line 9 asks him simply to justify the judgement. And the interviewer's third turn at line 41 ("would they 'ave been better off not printing this") is a conducive question: although it is framed as a polar interrogative, it is not an open 'yes/no' question. Instead, there is a preference for agreement with the proposition, 'they would have been better off not printing the pamphlet'. In effect, the expert's ('independent') position external to the broadcast institution facilitates the rehearsal of criticism: expertise is invoked here in the service of criticism which is located as sourced from without[13]. (It is not offered as the BBC's position but as the position of experts.)

Indeed, the interviewee's presented entitlement to speak is based upon privileged knowledge over and beyond the assumed ordinary knowledge and experience of the audience. Interviews of this type are designed to mediate between the assumed 'lifeworld' of the broadcast audience and the technicalities of the issue/event at hand. Where they involve an outside expert, not affiliated to the broadcaster, there is usually some attempt to ground them iconically – the economist or financial expert against the background of the dealing room, the medical expert in the hospital or lab, or the academic framed by book-lined shelves.

Just as there are gradations of affiliation, there is also some ambiguity at times about the relation of the expert to the event or topic at hand. On defence, intelligence or police issues, for instance, it is not uncommon for the expert to be a retired member of the police, intelligence services or the armed forces[14]. This gives the interviewee an entitlement to speak from the basis of privileged knowledge, though one in which their neutrality may not necessarily be guaranteed.

7.5   The interview fragment

Extended interviews with political or public figures are an important feature of in-depth, analytic, background news programmes, such as *Newsnight, Today, Panorama, Channel 4 News* in the UK and *ABC 20/20, CBS 60 Minutes, CBS Evening News* and *NBC Nightly News* in the United States. In bulletin programmes, however, the news interview as a complete, live speech event is a diminishing element. Increasingly interviews are used instead – throughout news output – as inserted fragments in other elements such as reports. Here, for instance, part of a report about drink-driving includes three fragments of speech from sources other than the reporter – two customers in a pub, and a senior police officer (see pp 107–108 and 112–113 above).

REPORTER: But what happens if your wine comes in a large glass
or the lager you're drinking happens to be a strong

continental type. Each of these on their own will put you over the limit and merely adds to the confusion.

CUSTOMER 1: "This a Stella Artois which ah know is quite strong. It's heading towards a whole one and half to two units. So again it's probably a pint is as much. But the best thing is not to do it."

CUSTOMER 2: "Everybody is different innit they? (....) It's what ye limitations are, I suppose, or what ye think are yer limitations."

REPORTER: Every year government sponsored adverts ram home dangers of drink driving. It works for many motorists but for others the police are the deterrent.

POLICE OFFICER: "The core message is 'don't drink and drive'. You can see the results behind me. If ye are gonna drink and drive, we're gonna do our damnednest to catch ye."

The practice here amounts to a form of direct quotation. The main and framing discourse is that of the reporter. But embedded seamlessly within it are utterances from members of the public and from a police officer. These speakers are not introduced by the reporter using a reporting clause or by a caption but are presented directly by video-clip extract, edited into the body of the report. Thus we see each speaker saying their piece – presumably in response to questioning by the reporter. It is difficult to make sense of these elements except as embedded fragments of larger interviews conducted by the reporter in preparing the report.

In running news, especially when dominated by a single major event, short on-the-spot interviews amongst bystanders – vox pops – play an important role in offering a range of emotional reactions to the event. Here, for instance, are some fragments from the coverage of the funeral of Diana, Princess of Wales.

1 REPORTER:	You were saying earlier
2	some of what Earl Spencer had to say
3	you thought might be a bit political
4 CLAIRE:	yes
5	and I felt when I was listening to it
6	it didn't feel like er er a speech I expected at a funeral

Reactions to the Queen's televised speech, broadcast earlier, had been solicited in similar fashion in vox pops with bystanders in public spaces outside Buckingham Palace:

1 REPORTER:	do you think the Queen struck a chord
2 BYSTANDER 1:	she sounded very sincere
3	and she looked as though she were very moved
4	and I think that will satisfy everyone

5 BYSTANDER 2: I thought she said everything that she should have said
6   can't think of anything that she left out at all

The focus of these vox pops is clearly on the personal reactions – the thoughts and feelings of an interviewee who has heard or witnessed something. In these cases, what gives the interviewee their entitlement to speak is simply their capacity to provide in a reasonably fluent and articulate manner some kind of personal experience of something which has happened in the public eye – one that will be seen as representative of what anyone might feel or think in those circumstances. In some cases there may be a range of possible responses (grief, anger, sadness, shock, courage). If so, the broadcaster will be aiming to catch and dramatise the range. Notice in the extracts above how central to these interviews is the statement of speaker's personal point of view or opinion:

"**I thought**", "(I) can't **think**", "I **think** that will satisfy everyone", "**I felt**" "it didn't feel like a speech I **expected** at a funeral".

Of course these statements of opinion come in response to particular kinds of question, such, for instance, as "do you think the Queen struck a chord?" Interviewees are being asked to offer a view, their view. But there is no sense that they are going to be held accountable for it, asked to justify it, or have their view forensically disproved. Indeed, in marked contrast to the accountability interview these interviews are presented to the audience in a way that offers possible points of identification (or dis-identification), along the lines of – 'yes: that is how I felt, or how I might feel in their position', or even 'that is not how I felt'.

7.6   Conclusions

In previous work on the news interview, considerable attention has been devoted to its role as an instrument for holding politicians to account, with studies of evasion (Harris, 1991), of challenges to questions by interviewees (Heritage and Greatbach, 1991), of how neutrality is performed (Clayman and Heritage, 2002; Hutchby, 2006) and of how issues are pursued by interviewers (Clayman and Heritage, 2002). Apart from Clayman, 1991, and Ekström, 2001, however, few accounts of the news interview place it within the overall economy of news discourse. The aim of this chapter has been to establish that news interviews are of more than one type and to show that it is a mistake to regard the accountability interview with a public figure as the principal or defining type, despite their public salience and despite the way in which broadcasters themselves routinely regard them as the cornerstone of their public-service remit.

Leading news presenters or news anchors may pride themselves on holding political figures evenly to account in a 'no-nonsense', non-deferential manner.

And the history of political interviewing from the 1960s onwards may well show a clear line of development from deference through to confident adversarialism (see Clayman and Heritage, 2002, and Chapter 8 below). A classic discussion of the BBC in the 1970s described it as 'holding the middle ground' – as situating itself as close as possible to the central positions of the post-war political consensus in Britain (Kumar, 1975). And it is not difficult to show that this kind of apparent neutralism has shifted over the intervening decades into a more populist stance in which interviewers – like tribunes of the people – ventriloquise on behalf of a presumed sceptical public.

But this is only one kind of history of the news interview – one that relies heavily on the relation of politicians to the public and how broadcasters mediate between them. Another way of considering the news interview is as part of a different history in which broadcast news constantly seeks to discover appropriate forms of discourse for a mass audience who are mostly watching or listening the news at home (or on the commute). The prevalence of the news interview and changes to its forms can be as well understood as part of what commentators have called variously the personalisation, informalisation or conversationalisation of public discourse (Scannell, 1996; Cameron, 2000; Fairclough, 1992). It is no longer appropriate for news to be delivered (if ever it was) in the form of a single-voiced monologue by a man dressed in a dinner suit. It has become a thing of many voices – orchestrated by the institution admittedly – but often presented in dialogue with each other. In this process, the news interview itself is the primary mechanism for dramatising or making palpable the news as an interactional, dialogic discourse.

In this respect changes in news discourse and in the role of the interview within the news can be considered as part of more general processes of discursive, communicative and socio-cultural change. This is undoubtedly true. But the more general history has a particular inflection within broadcast news. It is worth recalling that the first uses of the term 'interview' in the modern sense (in the mid-nineteenth century) emerge in journalistic contexts. As pointed out at the beginning of this chapter, it is in the journalistic domain that the first specialisation of the term began. Thus, from its earliest adoption within journalism, 'interviewing' as a practice has lent itself to forms of quotation. In this respect the news interview remains true to its roots. It is still about quotation. Even in the special case of the political interview the goal – as Blum Kulka (1983) notes – "is not necessarily to corner the politician (that would be appropriate in the courtroom) but to get him to state his opinions and analysis of political issues, in a *manner that is quotable* – i.e. in a manner that has news value beyond the program itself" (p. 146).

Although the notion of 'quotability' is most at stake in the context of the accountability interview, as we noted above, it also applies to some extent across the range of interview types – especially in the context of hybrid cases. Martin Bashir's well-known interview of Princess Diana took place on BBC's flagship current affairs programme, *Panorama*; but the form adopted was much closer to the experiential interview than to the accountability type. It involved Bashir asking questions such as the following:

what were the expectations that you had for married life?

how aware were you of the significance of what had happened to you?

it's been suggested in some newspapers that you were left largely
to cope with your new status on your own
do you feel that was your experience?

had you always wanted to have a family?

but did you feel that you had to maintain
the public image of a successful Princess of Wales?

The questions are addressed to the recall of the interviewee's mental states – her thoughts, attitudes and feelings – and cover a range of topics including her health, her attitude to, and experience of, fame, and her marriage. In this way the interview proceeds very much in experiential terms, constructing the interviewee, we might almost say, as a witness-survivor. So there is little attempt by Bashir, despite the status of the programme, to expose contradictions in accounts, to reformulate in search of a different answer, or to pursue a point in the face of apparent evasion. The measure of the impact of the interview, however, is the way in which it yielded quotable quotes such as

well there were three of us in this marriage
so it was a bit crowded

(this in answer to the question: "do you think Mrs Parker-Bowles was a factor in the breakdown of your marriage?").

Or

I'd like to be a queen of people's hearts
in people's hearts
but I don't see myself being Queen of this country

The interview thus had considerable news value, with segments and quotations from it widely disseminated across the media[15].

News in general, as currently understood, depends upon sources. Every news item is sourced in some way from a variety of outlets – press releases, briefings, court proceedings, 'tip-offs', publicists, political speeches and debates, and agency wire feeds. A crucial tool in the process of gathering and assembling the news from a range of sources is the interview. The role of the fully fledged extended interview may be reduced to brief inserts or quotations in the smooth surface of a broadcast news report. But it will survive by quotation into the report or even as the news item itself. The broadcast news interview, and the practices of direct quotation derived from it, takes us – the news public or audience – closer to the sources of the news. The incorporation or embedding of interviews, or fragments from them, into the news displaces news discourse away from the single-voiced enunciation of the event and draws us closer to the event itself and to a range of typical reactions to it and opinions about it. The practice of interviewing and the derived practices of quotation represent a shift from narration to dramatisation, in which what is dramatised is in part the making of the news itself but also in which a society or community can be seen in conversation with itself about matters of the moment.

8   The changing discourses of broadcast news

8.0   Broadcast news as an order of discourse

Broadcast news as an order of discourse rests upon a tacit compact between the broadcaster and the audience about the nature of news, in which it is constituted in terms of particular values and qualities (such as relevance, facticity, scale or significance, clarity, interest, credibility, authoritativeness, event-ness and recency) and for the delivery of which an appropriate formal-structural machinery has been evolved. This machinery involves a structured arrangement of elements composed of discourse genres such as *News Headline, News Presentation, News Report* and *News Interview*; and the structural norms of broadcast news govern the chaining of these discursive elements within the routine sequences of news discourse. The constitutive sequence for a *News Bulletin Programme* has been described in Chapters 4, 5 and 6, and may be recapitulated as follows.

1. News Programme ➡ Signature + Headline + Signature + Opening + News Item 1-n + Closing

The core of the *News Programme* is the *News Item*. The structure of the *News Item* may be stipulated as follows.

2. News Item ➡ News Kernel {+ News Report {+ News Interview (Correspondent^1/Expert)$^{(1-n)}$}}

Variant structures here are: (1) *News Kernel* on its own; (2) *News Kernel* followed simply by *News Report*; or (3) *News Kernel* followed by *News Report* followed by *News Interview* with either the *Correspondent* or an *Expert* (or both).

Occasionally a live two-way with a *Correspondent* may be used to bracket or frame the *News Report*. (In other words it is possible for the *News Kernel* to introduce the *Correspondent* on location by means of a live two-way who then introduces a pre-recorded *News Report* which in turn leads in to a resumed live two-way – the whole package being known inside the industry as 'a doughnut'.)

Significantly, there are structural constraints on the placing of most elements. Headlines, almost by definition, and unsurprisingly, occur very near, or at the onset, of the programme. Less obviously, a *News Report* must be preceded by the presentation of a *News Kernel* in front position in the structure of a *News Item*. It is also highly unusual for a two-way interview to occur without a preceding *News Report*, unless it is to 'top and tail' it. In this way the structural backbone of the *News Bulletin Programme* is a sequence of *News Items* that could consist simply of studio presentation of *News Kernels*. In practice this 'pure sequence' is usually elaborated (unless in very short bulletins) by the use of *News Reports* and *News Interviews* which build upon *News Presentation* and are structurally dependent upon it.

At the same time we should note the increasing use of what might be called 'free elements' within the structural chain. Headlines in their prototypical form must occur at or very near the beginning of the bulletin programme. Increasingly, however, headline-like objects are repeated – with variations – between *News Items* at intervals within the overall sequence of the programme. In this role they are prefaced with expressions such as "coming up next ...", "later in the programme ...", "after the break ..." and at the end of the programme "our top stories today ...". If headlines – on the analogy with print journalism – are designed to grab initial attention, then these trailers and resumes for *News Items* are designed to sustain attention within the unfolding programme.

8.1 Stylistic, sub-generic norms of broadcast news discourse

Although there is an interlocking unity about these elements and the way in which they constitute the news as an order of discourse, it is also the case that these various constitutive elements, when considered in themselves, display sub-generic distinctiveness. The *News Interview*, for example, as a component of the news is quite different from the *News Report*. Furthermore, as we saw in Chapter 7, it surfaces in various guises in the news: it works differently in form and structure when doing accountability, providing expert knowledge or offering first-hand experience. Equally, *News Kernels* are typically done in *News Presentation* from within the studio to studio camera(s), in direct visual address to audience and in perceived 'transmission time'. *News Reports* are typically done by voice-over to edited actuality footage in recorded time (prior to transmission time), though it is common also to include instances of direct-to-camera elements – 'stand-uppers' – in which the reporter speaks discernibly 'on location' from a non-studio space relevant to the item – i.e. from within the perceived field of the news item. Thus, each of the different structural elements within broadcast news discourse is expounded or realised in different ways, reflecting the different sub-generic statuses of the elements within the whole.

The structuring of broadcast news in its totality as an order of discourse provides a stable discursive machinery for the routine production of news programmes and a settled horizon of generic expectations to guarantee their easy intelligibility. On the other hand, however, the very normativity of this order of discourse, its predictability and its reliability, its well-worked set of familiar practices, provides a platform for piecemeal innovation and change.

8.2   Broadcast news and pressures for change

Indeed, a major challenge in writing about broadcast news at the present time is the accelerating rate of change in the overall news environment. One kind of pressure for change comes from the relation of news to its audience. There are, for instance, well-recognised changes in the demographic composition of the available audience for news: in Western industrialised countries, extended life expectancy and falling birth-rates are leading to ageing populations. At one end of the demographic spectrum those who watch mainstream evening news programmes are growing older, while at the same time there is evidence that younger audiences are finding different sources for their news, relying less on print and broadcast media and drawing more of their news from the web and dedicated news channels or through genre-mixing formats such as *Have I got news for you?* in the UK or *The Daily Show* in the USA. In addition, some studies have shown that changing life-styles and patterns of work have encouraged different preferences in the way news is attended to: the working day, for instance, has grown longer, leading to a growing preference for 'morning' or 'breakfast news' over 'evening' or 'late-night news'.

Second, the move from analogue to digital transmission has consequences for notions of broadcasting. Particularly with the advent of digital transmission we are moving from an era of 'spectrum scarcity' to 'spectrum abundance' (Ellis, 2002). As more channels carry news to households the range of choice for individual viewers increases, both in terms of new channels carrying news bulletins and news programmes (for instance, Channel 5 in the UK), as well as in terms of more channels dedicated exclusively to 24 hours of running news coverage (such as, for instance, BBC News 24, Sky News, or Al-Jazeera). The proliferation of platforms or outlets for the news intensifies competition for the already changing audience, encouraging broadcasters to review and experiment with existing modes of address and with ways of accentuating the immediacy of their material.

Third, there are pressures on the forms of broadcast news from the interaction between and convergence of different news platforms – radio, television, print and the internet. Audiences for broadcast news now have available to them news in a variety of formats from a variety of alternative platforms. Radio and television news may be streamed to a laptop computer or downloaded as a file or podcast, and email responses to a live news programme may be incorporated into the bulletin pro-gramme itself. Web-based 'blogs' that incorporate responses to specific news programmes or to aspects of broadcast news coverage may be quoted in newspapers. These interactions between and convergence of news platforms are reshaping the habitual news formats in the different media. Rolling broadcast news tends to undercut the news-reporting function of news-papers; and this, combined with the success of blogs on the internet, has increased the presence (perhaps temporarily) of comment and opinion sections in print.

Because of these manifold pressures some widespread assumptions have developed about changes taking place within the order of discourse of broadcast news articulated in terms of concerns about its possible tabloid-isation, about 'dumbing down' and about a possible draining of content through the demands of continuous news coverage. In order to examine what changes may be taking place in broadcast news the next section will compare a bulletin news programme from over 20 years ago with an exam-ple of current practice. More specifically, the comparison will feature the main lunchtime news bulletin programme from the UK's main Independ-ent Television channel, sometimes described as Britain's third terrestrial channel.

8.3 Illustrating some changes in the discourse of broadcast news: two bulletin news programmes

The first programme dates from 27th July 1985. Here is the opening of ITN News at One on that day.

Ext. 8.3.1:   News at One 1985[2]
Signature music + Graphics

1	ANNOUNCER:	this is the news at one from ITN	
2		with Leonard Parkin	[PRE-OPENING]
3	PRESENTER:	hello good afternoon	[GREETING]
4		after the coup in Uganda	[NEWS ITEM 1: KERNEL]
5		General Tito Okello	
6		a man in his seventies is being sworn in as head of state	
7		the toppled president Milton Obote is in exile in Kenya	
8		and Kampala is said to be quiet after the weekend's looting	
9		when as one diplomat said the beer was in charge	
10		we've been talking about the new leader in Uganda	
11		with the former president Godfrey Binaisa	
12		and the leader of the SDP and former foreign secretary	
13		Dr David Owen is here in the studio	
14		among today's other stories	[HEADLINES]
15		a national identity card for soccer fans	
16		the F.A. secretary calls it an expensive red herring	

17	and a political safari in Kenya for the leader of the opposition
18	the head of Uganda's armed forces [NEWS ITEM 1 continues]
19	General Tito Okello
20	is been sworn-in as the country's head of state about now
21	Radio Kampala made the announcement this morning
22	ending the:: uncertainty in Uganda
23	since Saturday's military coup deposed President Milton Obote
24	General Okello who's in his seventies
25	helped topple Idi Amin in 1979
26	and was chief of defence in Obote's government
27	the radio broadcast said he would become head of state
28	and rule over a military council
29	an executive prime minister would be appointed
30	to form a broad-based government
31	before a general election in twelve month's time
32	and top civil servants would keep their jobs
33	no mention was made of brigadier Basilio Okello
34	no relation of the new leader
35	who played a major part in the coup
36	at the same time it was announced that General Okello
37	has taken over power in Kampala
38	it was reported that former President Obote
39	had been granted asylum in neighbouring Kenya
40	he was reported to be in Nakuru ninety miles from Nairobi
41	Kampala itself is reported quiet
42	after two days of riots and looting
43	armed soldiers and police are patrolling the streets
44	and a night-time curfew has been imposed
45	Uganda is virtually sealed off
46	with its airport and borders closed
47	although some refugees have fled into Kenya
48	from there Glyn Mathias has sent us this report

49 REPORTER: Kampala is reported to be quiet so far today...[REPORT(voice over)]
{ report, delivered as voice-over to single fixed image, continues for 1' 10" }

50	... unlikely it would be re-opened today
51	Glyn Mathias / News at One / Nairobi

52 PRESENTER: the former Ugandan President Godfrey Binaisa [INTERVIEW 1:]

53	who is in exile in London
54	says he's ready to serve the new administration
55	he was in charge for a year in 1979
56	between the regimes of Amin and Obote
57	before being forcibly removed in a palace coup
58	earlier I asked him
59	if a government national of unity now made sense

60 INT'VIEWEE 1: yes from the point of view of who will be willing

61   to go and and er assist
{ Interview 1 continues for 2'30", comprising 5 question and answer exchanges}
62 PRESENTER: well I'm joined now by the leader of the SDP   [INTERVIEW 2:]
63   and former Labour foreign secretary Dr David Owen
64   well that was a picture of a shambles in in Uganda
65   is Okello the man to lead them out of it
66 INT'VIEWEE 2: I don't know I somewhat doubt it I don't know him
67   but er he's very much associated with the: old regime
68   but of course never been in a political position before
69   on the other hand
70   the army is the:: crucial ingredient of er reconciliation
71   and it's been divisions within the army that have been perhaps
72   the most worrying thing that's developed
73   so if he COULD restore unity in the army
74   a::nd then law and order and then political unity
75   and keep to the timetable of going to elections
76   that would be a formidable achievement
77   but er I don't envy him the task
78   it's a Uganda's in a very very dangerous situation at the moment
79 PRESENTER: then . it would be an enormous achievement
80   but as Godfrey Binaisa said
81   they've had military rule now fo:r for eight years
82   and they don't like it any more than when they started
83 INT'VIEWEE 2: well they had military rule under Idi Amin
84   I mean Obote was in a sense er
85   more of a genuinely democratic leader
86   the trouble was he was always very controversial
87   from the:: earlier time that he: was (the) leader of the country
88   and the human rights record of er Uganda
89   has slipped in the last few years very badly
90   I don't think it's got ever got quite as bad as under Idi Amin
91   but er . Obote's rule is a genuine disappointment
92   on the other hand before we all rejoice and say
93   er this is bound to be better
94   I think we've got to be very cautious
95   my own feeling was that Obote (is) better than Idi Amin
96   and I'm not yet sure that
97   this has got the coherence and the stability
98   to govern Uganda effectively
99 PRESENTER: is there any way:: in which the west
100   and more particularly us with our long relationship with Uganda
101   can do anything
102 INT'VIEWEE 2: well there may be ...
{ Interview 2 continues for a further 2'30" with Answer, Question, Answer}
103   then further and much more savage economic sanctions

104	will be forced on us	
105 PRESENTER:	uhhh Dr Owen .	[INTERVIEW CLOSING]
106	thank you very much for joining us uhhh	
107	well we move on now	[NEWS ITEM 2]
108	to the latest news from South Africa	
109	where . another black has been shot	
110	after reportedly driving his car	
111	at high speed at an army foot patrol ...	

This transcript covers the first news item, including headlines for the programme, and lasts 10'42". The first item itself contains a news report lasting 1'10" as well as two interviews lasting 2'30" and 4'00" respectively. The programme in its entirety lasts 22'03".

Compare this opening with one from an equivalent programme broadcast over 20 years later. Once again this is lunchtime news from the UK's third terrestrial channel, broadcast at 1.30 p.m. on Tuesday 19th September 2006.

Ext. 8.3.2: ITV Lunchtime News 2006[3]

1 PRESENTER 1:	Hungary's Prime Minister admits:	[MAIN HEADLINE]
2	"we lied; we screwed up"	
3	his voters run riot through the streets of Budapest	
{Signature music and graphics }		[SIGNATURE]
4 PRESENTER 2:	it was a secret recording and a staggering admission	
5	he's simply lied to win a general election	
6	and he's been doing it for years	
7 PRESENTER 1:	he says he won't resign	
8	despite thousands protesting on the streets	
9	and hundreds taken to hospital	
10	we'll have the very latest live from Budapest	
11 PRESENTER 2:	also this lunch time	[HEADLINES]
{Bong}		
12	underestimated by Britain	
13	underestimated by NATO	
14	the Defence Secretary's frightening admission about the Taliban	
{Bong}		
15 PRESENTER 1:	and coming home the successfully separated twins	
16	starting their new lives / apart	
{Signature music}		
17 PRESENTER 1:	hello / welcome to Tuesday's lunchtime news	[GREETING]
18	I quote: "We lied; we screwed up	[NEWS ITEM 1: KERNEL]
19	not a little a lot"	
20	it's an extraordinary admission for any leader	
21	but for a Prime Minister it's tantamount to political suicide	
22 PRESENTER 2:	the Hungarian Prime Minister Ferenc Gyurcsany	

23		was recorded telling his M.P.'s
24		that he had misled the country just to win the election
25		and he went on: "No European country has done something like this
26		as bone-headed as we have"
27	PRESENTER 1:	his frank admission was leaked to the press last night
28		and it provoked a furious reaction from his people
29		thousands marched in protest
30		within minutes things turned violent
31		(an) demonstrators firebombed cars
32		and stormed the state television station
33		police reacted with water canons
34	PRESENTER 2:	well this morning Mr Gyurcsany warned
35		he'd crack down on any more protests
36		saying it had been the longest and darkest night
37		well in a moment we'll be getting the latest live
38		from the capital Budapest
39		but first Romilly Weeks reports
40		on a night of violent conflict in Hungary
41	REPORTER:	it looked like [NEWS ITEM 1: REPORT]
42		a scene from the Communist past
43		mass protests rioting and fires on the streets of Budapest
44		the people's anger fired by an astonishing admission
45		from their Prime Minister that in order to get elected
46		his party had lied morning evening and night
47	TRANSLATOR:	"There is not much choice there is not
48		because we screwed up not a little a lot
49		no European country has done something
50		as bone-headed as we have
51		as simply we have lied
52		throughout the last year and a half for two years
53		it was totally clear that what were saying is not true
54		you cannot quote any significant government measure
55		we can be proud of
56		other than at the end
57		we managed to bring the government back from the brink nothing"
58	REPORTER:	reaction to the Prime Minister's honesty
59		in that leaked recording was swift
60		protesters tried to storm the state television building
61		and in a stand-off with riot police
62		over one hundred and fifty were injured
63		the worst unrest since the uprising against Soviet rule in fifty-six
64		now there are demands for Mr Ferenc Gyurcsany to go
65	P. M.:	I'm staying er an and I'm doing my job
66		er I'm extremely committed er to fulfill my programme
67		( ) and reforms

68   I know its (.) very difficult
69 REPORTER: Mr Ferenc Gyurcsany party won the election
70   on the promise of tax cuts
71   apparently this is what happens if taxes then go up
72   and you reveal you've lied all along
73 AMBASS'DOR: er what the Prime Minister
74   wanted to achieve i::s for everybody
75   er to understand that the moment of truth has come
76   that is to say er we have er spent and overspent
77   er for very very long er we have delayed
78   er necessary reforms necessary decisions
79   not for two or four years but for sixteen years
80   and this has to come to an end
81 REPORTER: this is what Budapest looked like
82   after what even the Prime Minister called
83   the longest and darkest night of the Republic
84   as police cleared the damage
85   Mr Gyurcsany must be reflecting
86   on the wisdom of telling the truth about lies
87   Romilly Weeks / ITV news

88 PRESENTER 2: this popular uprising [NEWS ITEM 1: KERNEL CONTINUES]
89   against the government
90   is just the latest challenge facing Hungary
91   whose path to democracy has been slow and painful
92   after the second world war Hungary a once proud empire
93   was firmly under communist rule and in the grip of the Soviet Union

94 PRESENTER 1: the nineteen fifty-six   [NEWS ITEM 1: ELABORATION]
95   Hungarian uprising
96   saw the first attempt to throw off the Soviet yoke
97   but it was brutally crushed by Russian tanks
98   after hand-to-hand street-fighting.
99 PRESENTER 2: but in the nineteen eighties Communism across Europe
100   began to crumble as the Iron Curtain fell
101 PRESENTER 1: the nineteen nineties saw the dawn of a new era
102   democracy was restored
103   and Hungary joined NATO and later the EU

104 PRESENTER 2: well I'm joined now   [NEWS ITEM 1: LIVE 2-WAY]
105   from Budapest by Andras Pustay
106   who's from the Hungarian TV station MTV
107   erm Andras thank you very much indeed
108   for joining us this lunchtime
109   extraordinary pictures overnight
110   what's happening right now
111 WITNESS/EXPERT: (1.0) well tell me about those pictures
112   actually although there's a big damage

113	er by early morning (.) everything got back on track(s)
114	so both channels of the Hungarian television er worked properly
115	and it's er basically thanks for our supporters our viewers
116	who. who er sent us emails and and and phone calls as well
117	hundreds of them to express their sympathy
118	and er actually that means much more for them er for us now
119	than if it was financial aid
120	because er we are . actually experiencing a small nine eleven
121	er (.) er because it's for us a big shock
122	and and if I look around amongst my colleagues that what I see
123	nothing's going to be the same again afterwards
124	so now that ( )
125 PRESENTER 2:	people at home Andras
126	sorry just to interrupt to let you know that
127	people at home are watching those pictures from overnight
128	water canon dancing in the street fire blazing
129	I mean reminiscent of the Ukraine
130	which did leave lead to a change of government
131	is your Prime Minister going to survive this
132 WITNESS/EXPERT:	(1.0) well er don't make me comment on political issues
133	because I am actually in charge of er a TV programme
134	but er as far as I know the Prime Minister announced that
135	he's going to remain in power
136	and that's his er (.) that's his er goal er at the moment
137	to to stay in power
138 PRESENTER 2:	alright Andras /
139	sorry for putting you on the spot there about the political questions
140	I know just how you feel
141	thanks for joining us this lunchtime [LIVE 2-WAY CLOSING]
142 PRESENTER 1:	now then [NEWS ITEM 2]
143	economic migrants

This transcript, like the previous one, covers the first news item, including headlines for the programme, and lasts 6'30". Included in the first item is a news report lasting 2'00" as well as a live two-way interview lasting 1'40". The overall bulletin programme lasts 20'35".

In comparing news across a 20-year interval the question of parameters of change naturally arises. A common theme of some commentary (Langer, 1998; Barnett and Seymour, 1999) has been the possible softening and parochialising of the news agenda. Barnett and Seymour (1999), for instance, claim that the TV news and current affairs agenda devotes increasing space to human-interest stories and topics such as sport, scandals, crime, celebrity gossip and entertainment to the neglect of foreign and political news-in brief, that TV news has been tabloidised! Not all share this view[4]. Winston's (2002) study of television news set out to review the tabloidisation thesis by comparing a sample of UK TV news output from 1975 with 2001. And his results did not confirm a drift towards tabloidisation. Overall he concludes:

> The television news services reflected the broadsheet news agenda in 1975 and, arguably, with the one exception of Channel 5, they still did in 2001. Foreign coverage apart, such diminution of seriousness as has occurred would appear to be no more severe on television than it has been in those broadsheets ... [This] is not tabloidization. The British television news agenda has simply not moved sufficiently for that charge to be sustained ...
>
> (Winston, 2002, pp. 18–19)

The comparison offered in this chapter between programmes from 1985 and 2006 similarly lends little support to the specifics of the tabloidisation thesis. Although at the level of discourse presentation and structure we can show significant differences between the discourse of the two programmes, at the level of content there are some surprising similarities. Here, for instance, is the running order in terms of news items for the two programmes.

ITN 1985 (average length of item, 2'12")

1.	Coup in Uganda	10'42"
2.	South African shot by an army foot patrol	01'41"
3.	Bomb explosion in Belfast	00'26"
4.	Home secretary seeks to ban BBC programme which includes an interview with top IRA man	00'40"
5.	New move in teacher's pay dispute	00'25"
6.	Government proposes identity cards to combat football hooliganism	01'47"
7.	Disturbance outside court at trial of child rapist	00'27"
8.	Opposition leader Neil Kinnock visits aid projects in Kenya	01'57"
9.	Summer recess of Parliament: assessment of state of three main parties	03'41"
10.	Banks reduce lending rate to 11.5%	00'17"
	TOTAL:	22'03"

ITV 2006 (average length of item, 2'16")

1.	Hungarian Prime Minister admits: "We lied"	06'30"
2.	The government is proposing to restrict migrants from Bulgaria and Romania from entering the UK	00'32"
3.	Resistance to NATO forces in Afghanistan is stronger than anticipated. Speech from UK Defence Secretary	03'56"
4.	Trial of those accused of fertilizer bomb plot continues at Old Bailey	01'52"

COMMERCIALS

5.	Mother of new-born complains at shortage of midwives	02'09"
6.	Liberal Democrat leader Sir Menzies Campbell wins important vote at Liberal Democrat Party conference	02'15"
7.	Metropolitan police plead not guilty to breach of health and safety regulations	00'16"
8.	The Royal Mail introduces stamps for online purchase	01'45"
9.	Twins joined at birth return home after operation to separate them	01'20"
	TOTAL:	20'35"

The average length of items at 2'12" in 1985 and 2'16" in 2006 is similar. And the news agendas seem broadly comparable. Both bulletin programmes lead on an international story and contain a significant international element. With topics such as politics, high-profile court cases and public services included in both programmes and with no particular coverage of entertainment, sport or scandal, there are no signs of a predilection for a tabloid news agenda. In some ways this finding is all the more noteworthy since these are lunch-time news programmes where any anticipated shift to a 'lighter' or tabloid news agenda would most likely be more evident.

Despite the passage of time, then, there are strong continuities between the two programmes. However, although there is little sign of tabloidisation, there are some notable differences. In visual design, for instance, there is both continuity and difference. The programme in 1985 uses a staple semiotic resource of news programmes then and now – a spinning globe (see Chapter 3 above, Figures 3.1 and 3.2) – to emphasise the global reach of its interest, while both graphics and voice-over place emphasis on the time of the bulletin. In 2006 the graphics are more three-dimensional, animated, with the emphasis now wholly on clock-time.

In 1985 the studio is merely a flat backdrop to news presentation. By contrast, the studio spaces of 2006 are highly elaborated: they have been made into a specialised mise en scène for the delivery of the news. This is not simply an exercise in 'branding'[5]. The studio space has now been constituted as an arena for dynamic presentation using complex forms of depth – sometimes with illustrative graphics for individual news items and sometimes with visual backdrops emblematic of the process of news gathering and editing itself. So the studio itself has become a space opening onto other spaces either depicting the larger organisation devoted to gathering and delivering the news or bringing the world of the news into the studio.

In 1985 the presenter is depicted seated and viewed in close up (head and shoulders) and there is little variation either in movement by the speaker

Figure 8.1 Opening signature graphic: ITN *News at One*, 1985.

Figure 8.2 Opening signature: ITV *Lunchtime News*, 2006.

Figure 8.3 ITV *Lunchtime News*, 2006. Moving from opening signature graphic to headlines: the dual presenters are depicted poised for opening headline. The news-room is discernible in left background.

Figure 8.4 ITN *News at One*, 1985. Single presenter beginning headlines.

Figure 8.5 ITN *News at One,* 1985. Presenter: "the head of Uganda's armed forces General Tito Okello" (ll. 16–17).

or in the angle from which he is viewed – almost invariably from head-on with camera at eye-level. News presentation is static and fixed. There is greater use of prestige forms of pronunciation (contributing to a greater sense of formality in the delivery) and the mode of visual address is perceptibly less direct, with the presenter switching, sometimes uneasily, between autocue and paper script. By contrast ITV in 2006 uses two presenters (see Figures 8.6 and 8.7) who move within the studio setting and who are seen sometimes standing in full view in long shot and sometimes at a curved table/console in mid-shot, sometimes from eye-level and sometimes from a high angle, with the transitions managed by panning and zooming as well as by switching from one camera to another. The style of presentation has shifted from relatively 'closed' and static to 'open' and dynamic – especially in the opening section of the programme. Pronunciation in 2006 is less oriented to prestige forms and there is not only greater use of postural shift throughout a news programme but also a wider range of kinesic expressiveness. Presenters – especially when standing – use their hands more and there is a greater range of facial movements around the eye and mouth. There is a tendency to greater naturalism and informality in delivery as well as an attempt to create out of simple alternation between two speakers a sense of counterpoint or dialogue between the presenters.

Figure 8.6 ITV *Lunchtime News*, 2006. Presenter 1: "... thousands marched in protest /within minutes things turned violent ..." (ll. 29–30). Extending right forearm to indicate relevance of back-projection.

Figure 8.7 ITV *Lunchtime News*, 2006. Presenter 1: "he says he WON'T resign." (l. 7). Raised eyebrows for additional emphasis. Presenter 2 in responsive listening mode.

The structure of the opening has also changed. In 1985 the sequence is

Signature Music and Graphics + Pre-Opening + Greeting + News Item 1 <Headlines>

In other words, after signature music, graphics and the continuity announcement in voice-over, the programme opens with a greeting from the presenter who then moves directly to the lead item – the coup in Uganda. The headlines are buried inside that first item and are delivered by the presenter straight to camera.

By contrast current news practice front-places the headlines to form the onset of the whole news bulletin – even before the graphics – and these may occur using an illustrative clip from each item, with voice-over from the presenter, to give the following sequence.

Headlines + Signature Music and Graphics + Greeting + News Item 1

By giving the headlines greater prominence (and visual focus) in the later programme as opposed to the earlier, a quite different sense of opening pace is created. In addition, in 1985 ITN devoted approximately half of the 20-minute programme to the first item – the ongoing coup in Uganda. And more than half of this item, in turn, is devoted to 'talking heads' in

Figure 8.8 ITV *Lunchtime News*, 2006. First headline: Presenter 1 "Hungary's Prime Minister admits: 'we lied; we screwed up'" (ll. 1–2).

the studio (interviews with Binaisa, a former Ugandan President, and Owen, a former UK Foreign Secretary). In 2006, by contrast, although the total scheduled length of the programme is 24 minutes, it is interrupted by commercials and no item in itself lasts longer than 6'30". There is more explicit signposting of direction using headlines at the outset and trailers within the flow of items ('coming up in the rest of the programme ...').

In some respects the first item in 1985 may look superficially similar to current practice, but its realisation is in one particular respect markedly different. A fully elaborated news item may well take the form:

News Item ➡ News Kernel + News Report + News Interview 1 + News Interview 2

And on the face of it this is precisely the structure of the first item in 1985, except for a crucial difference. It is now unusual for political public figures to be interviewed live within the confines of a news bulletin programme[6] (although segments from pre-recorded interviews may well be inserted into reports, as happens in the 2006 extract with the Hungarian Prime Minister, and also with the Hungarian ambassador to London). When a news interview occurs in a bulletin news programme, the interviewee will most likely be a correspondent (or 'editor'), who will be invited to give an assessment (or, maybe, an explanation) of the significance of the news material, or an expert. In further contrast with present practice, the 1985 interviews of two public figures are used, not for accountability purposes, but to shape assessments of the news event – the role now offered more commonly to correspondents/editors.

Owen, for instance, is asked by Parkin if the new head of state in Uganda will be able to restore order: "Is Okello the man to lead them out of it?". To which Owen replies: "I don't know I somewhat doubt it I don't know him" (Extract 8.3.1: ll. 58–59). Generally, Owen's turns are full of evaluation, markers of personal point of view and marked modality and he elaborates his views over extended turns without interruption from the interviewer.

Ext. 8.3.1: (ll. 73–78)

73	so **if** he **COULD** restore unity in the army
74	a::nd then law and order and then political unity
75	and keep to the timetable of going to elections
76	that **would be** a formidable achievement
77	but er **I don't envy** him the task
78	it's a Uganda's in a very very dangerous situation at the moment

These are some of the very features identified earlier in the discussion of live two-ways between *presenter* and affiliated member of the institution – reporter, correspondent or editor. Like contemporary interviews with correspondents, this interview with Owen seems designed to construct a collaborative (though, given his former position as Foreign Secretary, authoritative) assessment of the news material. Between 1985 and 2007 a significant tendency can be observed in which evaluative assessments are brought 'in-house' to the affiliated correspondent/editor, whose affiliated status is then treated as if ambiguous or attenuated.

Other kinds of change noticeable in current bulletins when compared with 1985 include the greater use of graphics, often involving moving images or as backdrop in the studio to support news stories, and more use of live feeds, not only to reporters at the site of a news story, but also to presenters themselves – sometimes now split for especially dominant events to one presenter in the studio and one on location[7]. All these dramatise the broadcasting of news, with the studio no longer merely a conduit with a simple backdrop but a dynamic arena for its performance.

8.4   Changes in presentational style: towards conversation

Thus, despite continuities of news agenda and content, there are signs of significant shifts though mostly in what could be called presentational style – in delivery, mode of address, and discourse structure. Change in television news is not so much 'towards tabloidisation' of the news agenda but in the direction of the informalisation or the conversationalisation of discourse[8]. Admittedly, this movement towards the conversational, or the informal, has been noted in other areas of public life. Fairclough (1995), for instance, notes "an apparent democratisation of discourse which involves the reduction of overt markers of power asymmetry between people of unequal institutional power ... This tendency", he continues, "is manifested in a great many different institutional domains" (1995, p. 79). Related to the democratisation of discourse is a phenomenon that he describes as 'synthetic personalisation'[9] – "the simulation of private, face-to-face, person-to-person discourse in public mass-audience discourse – print, radio, television" (p. 80). And Fairclough also remarks upon "the 'conversationalization' of public discourse", which he says is "a striking and pervasive feature of contemporary orders of discourse". Generally, Fairclough, in noting these developments, tends to view them in a critical light.

> On the one hand, [conversationalization] can be seen as a colonization of the public domain by the practices of the private domain, an opening up of public orders of discourse to discursive practices which we can all attain rather than the elite and exclusive traditional practices of the public domain, and thus a matter of more open access. On the other hand, it can be seen as an appropriation of private domain practices which are needed in post-traditional public settings for the complex processes of negotiating relationships and identities.
>
> (p. 138)

As he notes elsewhere: "informalized and conversationalized relations in public may be spaces of more penetrative forms of power" (1996, p. 8).

There are two kinds of problem with this approach. First, it tends to see the changes as of fairly recent origin, stemming particularly from marketising and consumerist pressures. Sociolinguists, however, have charted shifts in formality from 'power' to 'solidarity' – especially, for example, in terms of address – in 17th century England (Francis, 1988), 18th century France (Brown and Gilman, 1960), 19th and early 20th century Russia (Friedrich, 1972) or 20th century Iran (Ardehali, 1990) (all of them cases where there seems to be an incidental relationship with revolutionary social change) that suggest that the unfolding of these changes may have begun earlier and with a more extended aetiology. Second, developments around informalisation and the democratisation of discourse may not only long pre-date marketising and consumerist pressures but also have a history which is uneven and discontinuous. Elias's (1996) encyclopaedic study of informalisation and civilisation in Germany draws attention to the ways in which extreme forms of both formality **and** informality can exist side by side within the same society (as was the case, he suggests, in 18th century Salzburg).

Fairclough tends to view such changes in the round with suspicion, as a form of disguise for the real relations of power. Scannell (1996), by contrast, makes a persuasive case that, inasmuch as such changes may be traced within broadcasting itself, they stem from its own particular conditions and history and should be viewed as a positive contribution to its communicative ethos. Indeed, they conform to a discernible trajectory in the history of broadcasting in which the distinctive form of the social relationship imbricated in broadcasting has been foregounded from the outset. As Scannell puts it:

> Sociability is the most fundamental characteristic of broadcasting's communicative ethos ... To describe the communicative manner and style of radio and television as conversational means more than chatty mannerisms and a personalized idiom ... It means orienting to the normative values of ordinary talk in which participants have equal status and equal discursive rights ... The communicative task that broadcasters faced was to find forms of talk that spoke *to* listeners, modes of address which disclosed that listeners were taken into account in the form of the utterance itself ... [R]adio and television's communicative style was first found in the development of friendlier forms of address, a more informal discursive style as markers of a general sociable intent that showed itself in most areas of programme output'.
>
> (1996, pp. 23–24)

The very fact that, in broadcasting, audiences may easily disengage places a considerable onus on the broadcaster to sustain their interest. "The character of broadcasting as *necessarily* sociable", says Scannell, "lies in the form of its communicative context, and the broadcasters' lack of control over their audiences. The relationship between broadcasters, listeners, and viewers is an *unforced* relationship because it is unenforceable" (Scannell, 1996). In a multi-channel environment these pressures can only have increased: the kinds of change in the discourse of the news we have noted above seem part and parcel of a situation in which broadcasters seek to find a way of communicating to people who have no particular reason for switching on the television or radio and who can easily switch off or switch over.

8.5   Uneven rates of change

Although it is possible to see a trajectory of change in comparisons of news programmes separated by time, this change is not necessarily even and continuous. It may, indeed, be possible to show, as Scannell argues, that

> communicative ethos on radio and television has – over 70 years – shifted from distant and authoritative relationships between broadcast-ers and audiences to more equal, open and accessible relationships.
> (1996, p. 20)

Nonetheless, "communicative ethos, even dominant communicative ethos is ... not some simple unitary thing. It not only changes in time, but at any one time it will vary across different areas of programme output ... and within particular areas" (op. cit. p. 20).

In this respect news is no exception. As an order of discourse it might best be viewed as a fragile attainment, an arena of discursive innovation com-peting with sedimented discursive practices. When the current discourses of broadcast news are viewed in comparison with those of the past it is possible to detect tension between opposing norms at different points in the chain of discourse structure, with some subgenres of the news displaying emergent practices in uneasy competition with dominant or residual ones (Williams, 1973). In the following four sections we will examine some significant areas of competing norms in the discourse practices of the news where an emerging norm is not fully stabilised or sits uneasily alongside an established practice. The first section considers some aspects of news presentation, the second and the third examine contradictory tendencies in news interviewing, while the fourth section examines some of the implications of the use of the live two-way.

8.6   Discursive change and normative tension: news presentation and the limits of conversationalism

Dual presenters have become an increasingly common feature of many types of news programme, from running news to bulletin news, from 'soft' news programmes (such as Breakfast News) to 'harder' news programmes such as BBC Radio 4's *Today*. It is easy to understand the impetus behind the introduction of dual presenters: it offers greater variety of voice within one programme; and in the alternation from one voice to another it also opens up the possibilities of a sense of conversational interchange, even of banter. In its televisual manifestation, however, dual presentation can become inherently contradictory. In conversation, typical dialogic behaviour is governed by the norm – 'attend to your interlocutor': if you are the hearer attend to the speaker – it helps you to follow what they are saying and to time the onset of your contribution. If you are the speaker, on the other hand, attend to the hearer: it helps to see if you've gained uptake. However, in televisual news presentation involving alternation between presenters there are two severely complicating factors – the script and the audience. The active presenter must address the audience while simultaneously reading the script on autocue; and this rules out attending to their inactive co-presenter. The inactive presenter, on the other hand, also needs to follow the autocue while occasionally attending to their co-presenter (who meantime is ignoring them in favour of the audience/autocue). This produces intermittently peculiar configurations in which one presenter seems to be attending to a speaker/interlocutor who is clearly not attending to her; or occasions where, conversely, the hearer – the inactive presenter – seems to ignore the speaker. Two norms are in conflict – natural dialogue versus public dual monologue[10]. The direction of discursive change towards increasing 'conversationalism' is at odds with and is unable to overcome the inherently monologic character of news presentation. Some of these tensions may be seen illustrated in Figures 8.9–8.11 from the opening of ITV Lunchtime News given in Ext. 8.3.2: ll. 21–24.

8.7   Discursive change and normative tension: accountability interviewing and the limits of adversarialism

Standard histories of the broadcast news interview in both the USA and the UK tend to characterise early interviews as diffident. They display what seems, by later standards, marked deference on the part the interviewer towards the interviewee. Here is a well known example, an interview in 1951 with the then British Prime Minister, Clement Atlee (adapted from Clayman and Heritage, 2002, p. 189):

Ext. 8.7.1

1	INT'VIEWER:	good morning Mister Atlee
2		we hope you've had good journey (0.2)
3	INT'VIEWEE:	ye::s excellent (0.2)
4	INT'VIEWER:	can you: (.) now you're back hhh
5		having cut short your lecture tou:r (.)

Figure 8.9 Presenter 1: "... is tantamount to political suicide ..." Presenter 2, with his turn to speak imminent, seems to be following the autocue (compare his orientation here with Figure 8.7 above).

Figure 8.10 Presenter 2: "... that he had misled the ..." l. 24. Presenter 1 in listening mode.

Figure 8.11 Presenter 2: "… was recorded telling his M.P.s" (l. 23). Presenter 1 scanning autocue for her upcoming turn.

6		tell us [something of how you vie:w the=
7	INT'VIEWEE:	[mm
8	INT'VIEWER:	=election prospects (0.2)
9	INT'VIEWEE:	oh we shall go in to give them a good fight (0.2)
10		very good (0.4) very good chance of winning
11		we shall go in confidently
12		we always do (0.7)
13	INT'VIEWER:	er and on what will Labour take its stand (0.4)
14	INT'VIEWEE:	we:ll that we shall be announcing shortly (0.2)
15	INT'VIEWER:	what are you're immediate plans Mister Atlee
16	INT'VIEWEE:	[my
17		immediate plans are to go down to a committee
18		to decide on just that thing hhh (.)
19		soon's I can get away from here (0.2) hh
20	INT'VIEWER:	um hh (.) anything else you would care to say
21		about (.) the coming election (.)
22	INT'VIEWEE:	no: (0.6)
23	INT'VIEWER:	erm (0.4) erm

The interview lasts only about a minute and is treated by the interviewee as if it were an unwanted imposition. The questions are answered in cursory, almost minimalist, fashion and the final invitation to add anything further is simply declined. The distance between this exchange and current practice is marked.

The evolution of a more forceful, adversarial style of broadcast interview in the years that followed this example is traced in the British context to the advent of commercial television (ITV) in 1955 (see Clayman and Heritage, 2002). One ITV interviewer in particular, Robin Day, came to broadcasting with a background as a courtroom lawyer and adopted a much more forensic, adversarial approach to the interview. For him the relevant generic model came not from the BBC but from altogether another institutional sphere than broadcasting (though he may have been influenced by the less deferential approach of American counterparts such as Ed Murrow of CBS). His more aggressive approach soon became established as the dominant model and became normative not only at ITN/ITV but was soon also adopted by the BBC. Well-known practitioners in British broadcasting such as Jeremy Paxman and John Humphrys (both BBC) conduct interviews firmly within that tradition and their practice underpins the typical approach to what was described in Chapter 6 as the accountability interview. A similar history can be traced in the USA, culminating in figures such as Dan Rather.

Studies by academics have often favoured the trajectory followed by developments in practice. Harris (1991) for instance, assumes that interviewees should answer the question that they are asked (rather than attempt to talk to a hearably different topic) and that interviewers should seek to pursue the answer that their questions implicate. Indeed, histories of the British television interview (e.g. Clayman and Heritage, 2002) celebrate moments where interviewers (Robin Day and Jeremy Paxman usually) asked and persisted with the difficult, sometimes unanswerable question[11]. Recent examples of this kind of approach may be found in interviews of party leaders, conducted by Paxman prior to the 2005 general election.

Ext. 8.7.2

```
 I PAXMAN:   this evening I'm in Leeds with the Prime Minister Tony Blair
 2          Prime Minister (.) is there anything you'd like to apologise for (2.0)
 3 BLAIR:    well if (.) if you want (.) me to apologise for the:: (.) war in Iraq
 4          I'm afraid I can't say that I'm (.) sorry we:: removed Saddam no
 5          if ( ) if you're asking me are there things
 6          that I've (.) got wrong over the past eight years (.)
 7          I've already said there are certain things:: (.)
 8          that any government gets wrong (.) hh
 9          I suppose I've had my share of those (.)
10 PAXMAN:  but do you accept that there is a trust issue
11          and that the reason opposition parties can talk about
12          wiping the smirk off your face (.) hh
13          is because you can't any longer say
```

14   look at me I'm a pretty straight kind of guy (.)
15 BLAIR: well (.) (i)trust is an issue (.)
16   but then people are going to have to decide (1.0)
17   you know (0.5) are we to be trusted when we say
18   we've run a strong economy and we'll continue to do so
19   with low interest rates and low unemployment and low inflation

Similar moments occur in the interview with the Liberal Democrat leader, Charles Kennedy.

Ext. 8.7.3
1 PAXMAN: have you er (.) changed your lifestyle
2   I mean is your doctor happy about how much you smoke and drink
3 KENNEDY: (.) yes my doctor is actually rather approving
4   he would like to see me not smoke at all (.) er
5   but I have drastically come down since the turn of the year hhh
6   and I'm determined that it's going to be (.) phased out altogether
7   particularly with the arrival of the new one
8 PAXMAN: (1.5) you talk about the arrival of the new one
9   (and) of course it changes everybody's life [d'you
10 KENNEDY: [sure
11 PAXMAN: (.) you must look at your life
12   and you think you've been what 20 years at this game
13   you've never really done anything else (.)
14   Tony Blair has decided he's not going to go on and on and on (.)
15 KENNEDY: yeh
16 PAXMAN: (.) are you
17 KENNEDY: (.) I hope so
18   that's my intention.

Some of these questions are difficult in part because they verge on matters of personal fitness rather than public policy, even though couched in oblique terms.

Ext. 8.7.2: l. 2
2 PAXMAN: Prime Minister (.) is there anything you'd like to apologise for (2.0)

Ext. 8.7.2: ll. 10–14
10 PAXMAN: but do you accept that there is a trust issue
11   and that the reason opposition parties can talk about
12   wiping the smirk off your face (.) hh
13   is because you can't any longer say
14   look at me I'm a pretty straight kind of guy (.)

Ext. 8.7.3: l. 2
2 PAXMAN: I mean is your doctor happy about how much you smoke and drink?

In the last case, for instance, merely to ask about personal consumption of tobacco and alcohol in this context is to imply a problem. To frame this concern inside a question about medical assessment ("is your doctor happy") only compounds the difficulty. In Kennedy's case it may not have been widely noticed at the time that his answer referred only to tobacco and not to alcohol. But in less than a year he was forced to resign as leader of the Liberal Democrats after admitting to a drink problem. Questions of this kind are a long way from the opening of the Atlee interview:

Ext. 8.7.1: ll. 4–9

```
4 INT'VIEWER:    can you: (.)
5                . . . . .
6                tell us [something of how you vie:w the=
7 INT'VIEWEE:            [mm
8 INT'VIEWER:    =election prospects (0.2)
9 INT'VIEWEE:    oh we shall go in to give them a good fight
```

Nor is it enough, it seems, to pose the difficult question. In his accountability interviews with political leaders Paxman would not only ask the difficult question but would seek also to demonstrate that the politician cannot (or will not) answer it. Here is Paxman questioning Kennedy about his party's proposal for a local income tax.

Ext. 8.7.4

```
 1 PAXMAN:    I mean let's take one of your top target seats Cardiff Central (.)
 2 KENNEDY:   right (.)
 3 PAXMAN:    er (.) would (.) the: nurse and the fireman living there
 4            be worse off or better off
 5 KENNEDY:   well as you say and as we say ourselves on our own figures
 6            hh they will pay a net (.) er increase in their contributions.
 7 PAXMAN:                                              [so they will be
 8            worse off.
 9 KENNEDY:   but (.)
10 PAXMAN:    do you know by how much=
11 KENNEDY:   =but but do remember plea::se
12            and you take Cardiff Central as an example of this
13            an awful lot of students there
14            an awful lot of students are going to benefit by our proposals
15            for scrapping top-up fees and tuition fees=
16 PAXMAN:    =yes but the (.) this couple (.) a nurse and a fireman (.)
17            average earnings (.) band D house
18 KENNEDY:   yes
19 PAXMAN:    d'you know by how much they will be worse off
20 KENNEDY:   well (0.8) by definition a local income tax is precisely that
21            we've given (the range of the things)
22 PAXMAN:                       [do you know by how much they'd be worse off=
```

23 KENNEDY: =it will depend on the local circumstances
24 PAXMAN: [well
25   (th) actually yes they do depend precisely upon local circumstances
26 KENNEDY: [yes   [yes
27 PAXMAN: and indeed there's a very helpful calculator on your website
28 ((fast))   which enables you to work out
29 ((fast))   whether you'd be better or worse off (.)
30 ((slow))   and they would in fact (.)
31 ((slow))   be four hundred and twenty nine pounds (.) worse off
32 ((fast))   that's enough to take a holiday

Paxman here recyles the same or similar questions over successive turns:

Ext. 8.7.4: ll. 3–4
3 PAXMAN: er (.) would (.) the: nurse and the fireman living there
4   be worse off or better off
Ext. 8.7.4: l. 19
19 PAXMAN: d'you know by how much they will be worse off
Ext. 8.7.4: l. 22
22 PAXMAN: ((overlaps)) [do you know by how much they'd be worse off=

His repetition of the same or related questions over separate turns treats any intervening answer as not adequate to the purposes of the question and thereby contributes to an impression of the interviewee avoiding the question. This impression is further reinforced by turns in which Paxman either reformulates an interviewee's answer (as if it were unsatisfactory) or supplies his own answer in the terms of his own question.

Ext. 8.7.4: ll. 7–8
7 PAXMAN: ((overlaps))   [so they will be worse off.
Ext. 8.7.4: ll. 30–32
30 ((slow)) and they would in fact (.)
31 ((slow)) be four hundred and twenty nine pounds (.) worse off
32 ((fast)) that's enough to take a holiday

A similar discursive practice can be discerned at work in his interview with Blair.

Ext. 8.7.5
1 PAXMAN: do you accept any responsibility at all
2   for the death of Dr David Kelly
3 BLAIR: (2.0) (hhh) (1.5) it was a terrible (.) terrible thing to have happened
4   (2.0) I don't believe we had any option however (1.0)
5   but to disclose (1.0) his name (.)
7   because I think had we failed (.) to do so (.)
8   that would have been (1.0) seen (.)

```
9          as attempting to conceal something from the committee (.)
10         that was looking in to this (.) at the time
11         and again (.)
12 PAXMAN: do you accept any responsibility at all
13 BLAIR:               [in relation to this (.) no I I I I've said
14         what I've said (.)
15         and I feel desperately sorry for his family
16         and indeed (.) for the terrible ordeal that they were put through
17         but as I said at the time
18         and again this has been gone into time and time again (1.0)
19         I (.) if we had concealed the fact (.)
20         cos this whole row was about (.) erm the information that
21         as as you know we've been over this many many times
22         had been given to the BBC reporter (1.0)
23         he had then come forward (.) and said to his superiors (1.5)
24         this is me (.)
25         I think it's me who's responsible for having given this story
26         there was a Foreign Affairs Select Committee
27         (.) Report going on at the time
28         I think if we'd concealed that from people
29         we would have been subject for a different
30         to a different (type of allegation)
31 PAXMAN:           [so the short answer to the question is
32         you don't accept any responsibility
33 BLAIR:  well it's a a it's not a question of not accepting responsibility
34         it is a question of simply explaining the circumstances
35 PAXMAN:                                    [it's a question to which
36         you could give a yes or no answer Prime Minister
37 BLAIR:                              [yeh but it's maybe not (.)
38         a question (.) you need to give a yes or no answer to
```

Here again the question is recycled through successive exchanges.

Ext. 8.7.5: ll. 1–2
```
1 PAXMAN: do you accept any responsibility at all
2          for the death of Dr David Kelly
```

Ext. 8.7.5: l. 12
```
12 PAXMAN: do you accept any responsibility at all
```

And then one of Blair's answers is reformulated by Paxman (in overlap with Blair) as a direct answer to the terms of the question:

Ext. 8.7.5: ll. 31–32
```
31 PAXMAN:           [so the short answer to the question is
32         you don't accept any responsibility
```

Indeed, Blair continues this exchange by resisting the terms offered by Paxman for answering his question.

Ext. 8.7.5: ll. 33–38
33 BLAIR: well it's a a it's not a question of not accepting responsibility
34   it is a question of simply explaining the circumstances
35 INT'VIEWER: [it's a question to which
36   you could give a yes or no answer Prime Minister
37 BLAIR: [yeh but it's maybe not (.)
38   a question (.) you need to give a yes or no answer to

This way of doing accountability in the news interview exemplifies the claim made by Clayman and Heritage that "the *interactional* accountability of answering questions is the fundamental basis for the *public* account-ability of public figures" (Clayman and Heritage, 2002, p. 235) – but only because these interviews are conducted and designed for broadcast-ing (and, additionally, within the public sphere of a general election). In other words the public display of 'being treated as not having answered the question' is produced within the discursive practice of the interview for the benefit of the overhearing audience. Paxman may be a fairly extreme example of this interviewing style: he is on record as saying that "why is this lying bastard lying to me?" provides a sound basis from which to operate when interviewing politicians (see Clayman and Heritage, 2002, p. 31).

In general this dominant model for the accountability interview may be seen as contributing to – or even defining – what has been described by Tolson (2005) as 'sceptical pragmatics'. For instance, if a politician notice-ably fails to answer a question, the inference that follows is that it is because they have something to hide and 'sceptical pragmatics' becomes part of a generally recognised problem of trust in the public sphere. The accountability role of media institutions in modern public life has been pur-sued with such assiduousness that it becomes flattened into a generalised perception in which the public can no longer trust any public figure – regardless of their credentials. Paxman's declared background assump-tion, "why is this lying bastard lying to me", becomes produced in the interview as if it were the habitually assumed alignment of the public itself.

But significant sections of the wider public feel less than completely comfortable. One commentator at least has asked whether or not there has been a general erosion of the democratic process by corrosive journalism.

[The] access to the media which is granted to politicians is on increas-ingly harsh terms. We have become accustomed to interviews with politicians and other public figures being constructed around the interviewees' most neuralgic points: we don't, in the main, expect a discussion in the round about the field of problems in which the public figure has to operate ... Both sides assume bad faith: the interviewer assumes evasion, at worst deceit; the interviewee assumes concentration on sore points, at worst a fight from which the interviewer would normally emerge the winner. The irony here is increasingly obvious: a technique to elicit information and increase clarity produces the smoke of battle and the fog of war.

(Lloyd, 2004, p. 14)

Indeed, what had become almost a taken-for-granted premise of interviewer behaviour has come increasingly to be called into question not just by 'victims' of it – the interviewees – but also by sections of the audience and even by some practitioners. The main presenter of Channel 4 *News*, Jon Snow, had remarked not long before the Paxman interviews that "I don't think we are very deferential on television any more. Paxo has seen to that. We could do with a bit more of it [deference?]". The Paxman interviews, cited above, themselves generated controversy amongst the audience when they were first broadcast in April 2005, as the BBC was forced to acknowledge on its website, noting that the majority of viewers who contacted them were unimpressed.

Can you ask Jeremy Paxman not to put on that 'I am God' look on his face when he is in the chair?" wrote viewer Ivan Wain. A BBC spokesman replied "It is the job of interviewers such as Jeremy Paxman to put the questions and ... to press for answers". But viewer Andrew Lashbrook said: "Please BBC, don't use Paxman at the next election to do these questions – he's arrogant, smug and rude. I wanted to hear what Charles Kennedy had to say, not hear Mr Paxman constantly interrupt him". According to Randall Northam, Paxman showed his "ego and power complex". He added: "Please stop Jeremy Paxman from being so offensive. I'm not a Liberal Democrat supporter but to ask Charles Kennedy if his doctor approved of his drinking and smoking was going too far.

(Matt Holder, "Paxman special sparks backlash".
BBC *NewsWatch*, 19th April 2005[12])

So while the broad trajectory of change may chart a path from deference to adversarialism, there are signs that there are limits to its further development. It is not just that the discursive practices themselves may change; but changes also take place in the way these practices are regarded. Increasingly aggressive interviewing begins to attract negative comment. Conflicting norms of validity come into play so that although it is justified by some practitioners and a segment of public opinion as necessary for the pursuit of truth it is increasingly perceived as inappropriately rude.

8.8   Discursive change and normative tension: the accountability interview and the limits of neutralism

An important aspect of accountability interviewing in the news is the performance of neutrality. Clayman and Heritage pose it as perhaps the key interactional problem: "how do interviewers manage to assert themselves in an adversarial manner while maintaining a formally impartial or neutralistic posture?" (op. cit. p. 151). In answer they cite a range of discourse practices that cluster particularly in the broadcast accountability interview. These include the use of third-party attributed statements in interview questions. Paxman's interview of Blair contains a prime example.

Ext. 8.7.2: ll. 10–14
```
10 PAXMAN:  but do you accept that there is a trust issue
11          and that the reason opposition parties can talk about
12          wiping the smirk off your face (.) hh
13          is because you can't any longer say
14          look at me I'm a pretty straight kind of guy (.)
```

Paxman's reference to 'wiping the smirk off your (Blair's) face' is potentially highly face-threatening[13] on at least two counts: (1) it presupposes that Blair smirks (with all its negative connotations); (2) it presupposes that others have the power at a stroke to curtail Blair's smirking and are in a position to exercise this power (or at least talk about exercising it). But these presuppositions are presented as if separate from the views of the interviewer by being embedded within a third-party attributable statement: it is not Paxman talking about wiping the smirk off Blair's face but "opposition parties"[14]. Further practices include referring to the public or the audience on whose behalf the interviewer questions. "You have to be frank with people don't you?" says Paxman to Kennedy, following up later in the interview with "That is being frank with the electorate is it?", thereby highlighting that the questions are designed to elicit answers for the audience at large (here "people" and "the electorate") on whose behalf the interviewer speaks. Other practices underpinning interviewer 'neutralism' include the withholding of in-turn feedback by the interviewer (noted in Chapter 7 above) and, perhaps most crucially, maintaining the questioning role. As long as interviewers restrict their role in accountability interviews to asking questions (on behalf of 'the public') it is difficult to associate them with holding a particular personal 'line' on a particular issue.

In the context of accountability interviews we may say that the cluster of discourse practices around neutralism (so well identified in Clayman and Heritage, 2002) amounts to a normative order in this dimension of the overall order of discourse of the news. However, there are growing signs of disturbances to this normative order or, at least, that the rigour and consistency of its application is variable. Increasingly, the account-ability interview verges on argument as views are expressed no longer as embedded within interviewer questions and no longer formally separated through devices such as the third-party attributable statement from those of the interviewer. Instead, the structure of questions and answers is replaced by assertion and counter-assertion. Here, for instance, is the opening of an interview on Radio 4's *Today* programme between John Humphrys – one of the programme's presenters – and a protester, Abu Izzadeen,

Ext. 8.8.1: Radio 4 *Today* programme, September 22nd, 2006
1 HUMPHRYS: the home secretary John Reid experienced at first hand
2   a taste of Muslim anger this week (.)
3   he was talking to a group of Muslims
4   urging them to do more to tackle extremism (.) (hhh)
5   when he was shouted down by one of his audience Abu Izzadeen (.)
6   he told Mr Reid he was a tyrant (.)
7   who had no right to come to a Muslim area (.) (hh)
8   Mr Izzadeen was bustled out of the room
9   since when he's avoided the media (.)
10   but he's with me now good morning to you (.)
11 A. IZZADEEN: g(ood) morning (.)
12 HUMPHRYS: you said to Mr Rei::d
13   how dare you come to this area
14   I suppose I should say to you (.)
15   how dare you suggest that he shouldn't (1.0)
16 A. IZZADEEN: erm (.) my address to Mr Reid was (.) primarily to do with
17   hi::s (.) behaviour in the past year (.) erm (.)
18   and his previous position (h)as e::r Defence minister
19   he's been killing Muslims abroad (hh) (.) in Iraq and Afghanistan (.)
20   and (he) (h)as Home Secretary he has been (.) presiding
21   over arrest of many Muslims (.) (hhh)
22   and that in that (.) light how dare he come to address the Muslims
23 HUMPHRYS: he's been carrying out the law of the land
24 A. IZZADEEN: which is completely oppressive
25 HUMPHRYS: in your view
26 A. IZZADEEN: definitely
27 HUMPHRYS: does he is he not allowed to express his own view (.)
28 A. IZZADEEN: his his view is nothing more than to ask the Muslim community
29   (.) to:: turn in on itself (.) and spy and do the police's job (.)
30 HUMPHRYS: no he's
31 A. IZZADEEN: [(that's what'll) happen
32 HUMPHRYS: what he's saying to Muslim people of this country (.)
33   (hhh) i::s that if they know (.) of a crime
34   that may be committed (.) by a Muslim or by anybody else (.)
35   then they should inform the authorities

36   isn't that everybody's responsibility including yours=
37 A. IZZADEEN: =I think it's much more (.) wider than that
38   we're facing in the UK a complete attack (.)
39   a crusade by the British government (.) over a thousand arrests (.)
40   many houses been raided in the daytime in the night time
41   women have been arrested taken away from their homes
42   with no evidence whatsoever

The normal pattern of Interviewer-question and Interviewee-answer is hardly in evidence. Humphrys's first turn in the interview (ll. 12–14) is structured not so much as a question but as an assertion and counter-assertion: 'you said X; I suppose I should say Y'. And this becomes the pattern that underlies the opening exchanges between Humphrys and Abu Izzadeen. The assertion by the latter that John Reid has "been killing Muslims abroad ... and has been presiding over arrest of many Muslims" (ll. 19–21) is countered by Humphrys with the claim that in doing so Reid 'has been carrying out the law of the land' (l. 23), which in turn is countered by Abu Izzadeen with the claim that the law of the land "is completely oppressive", which is countered by Humphrys with the claim that this is Abu Izzadeen's view.

There are increasing signs that, when faced with views considered to lie outside the mainstream of political and social life[15], interviewers feel absolved from strict adherence to the normal background norms of interviewing – doing neutralism behind the question-and-answer format. This is the opening 'question' by Jon Snow in an interview with the Deputy Israeli Ambassador to the UK, Zvi Ravner:

Ext. 8.8.2: Channel 4 News July 2006
1 SNOW: . . Zvi Ravner who's the:: er Deputy Israeli Ambassador to London
2   he joins us now (.) (hh)
3   Zvi Ravner (.) this is collective punishment (.)
4   you've cut off the water you've cut off the petrol
5   you've cut off the electricity (.)
6   and you're starving the hospitals out (.)
7 ZVI RAVNER: (this is) not a:: collective punishment (.)
8   this is a cul this is not just about a soldier
9   it's a culmination of er about one year long since we ...

The statements "you've cut off" X, Y, Z (ll. 4–5) share some formal similarities with requests for confirmation[16]. But they are not heard as such in this context where they expound the grounds for the assertion with which Snow begins the interview: "this is collective punishment" (l. 3). Indeed, the interviewee hears Snow's turn as built around that assertion and uses it to build his own response which takes the form of a counter assertion or denial based upon simple reversal of the initial polarity from positive to negative: "(this is) not a:: collective punishment (.)" (l. 7). Snow's initial turn, therefore, is not a question; nor, indeed, is it a third-party attributable statement used to distance the claim from his own viewpoint. Instead, the interaction here opens – rather like the *Today* extract earlier – as claim and denial.

There are two ways of understanding this movement away from the discursive practice of neutralism. One challenge to neutralism may come from the erosion of areas of consensus in significant areas of social and political life (particularly around questions of value). Or to put this point differently, there is a clearer recognition of the multiplicity of viewpoints in many areas, this coupled with what the philosopher MacIntyre has described as "the incommensurability of moral positions" (MacIntyre, 1997). Quite simply, more positions are contestable, fewer taken for granted. A second (and perhaps related) challenge to neutralism may come from an evolution in how the role of the interviewer is understood. Moral positions may seem at one moment incommensurable but in an incommensurable moral world the accountability interviewer increasingly finds it difficult to insulate him or herself from every position. Instead, they assume the role not just of 'tribune of the people' simply pursuing the truth on behalf of the audience through question and answer, but also on occasion the role of 'arbiter of truth'. Examples of this tendency increasingly abound. Here is Paxman with Blair.

Ext. 8.8.3: The Paxman Interviews, April 2005
```
I PAXMAN:   alright, let's look at Iraq (0.5) (hh)
2           when you told parliament that the intelligence
3           was (.) extensive (.) detailed a::nd authoritative (.)
4           that wasn't true was it (.)
5 BLAIR:    no it was true (.) (hhh)
6           there was no doubt about it
7 PAXMAN:                          [it wasn't extensive
8           it wasn't detailed and it wasn't authori[tative
9 BLAIR:                                          [I'm I'm sorry
10          it it was
```

Whatever the underlying reasons for the shift from question and answer as a way of doing accountability, it seems clear that neutralism as a formal local practice performed within the accountability interview is increasingly compromised.

Overall the accountability interview as a generic component of the order of discourse of the news is in an unsettled period of change.

8.9   Discursive change and normative tension: the live two-way and the limits of informality

A final example of discursive change in play is the increasing resort to the live two-way (discussed at length in Chapter 6) as a way of elaborating the news previously presented from the studio in a news kernel. This innovation was, according to Winston (2002), almost unknown in 1975. As he comments: "the news might well have left the studio",

> but, as often as not, one can well ask, "To what purpose?" Moreover, there is often very little to justify an update; for instance, if the reporter is abroad in the East and all about him or her are asleep. Broadcasting's fetishizing of "liveness" is driving these links rather than journalism.
>
> (p. 15)

As we suggested in Chapter 6, however, liveness is an incomplete explanation of the use of the live two-way: its emergence may equally be related to a shift towards informality, unscriptedness and conversation in the delivery of the news – aspects also recognised by Winston.

> Visually, these conversations between news personnel had the interviewee (i.e. the correspondent) looking directly at the lens – in effect addressing the audience while seemingly talking to the studio-based newscaster ... This interview technique allows for an informality of language which was not heard in 1975.

As we saw in Chapter 6, however, increasing use of the two-way highlights competing sets of norms about 'truth-validity' in the overall discourse of the news, confirming that the discourses of the news are neither homogeneous nor static but amount to an evolving system of discourses in the process of change with corresponding alterations in the alignments of discourse around the validity claims of truth, sincerity and appropriateness. As Scannell argues persuasively in *Radio Television and Modern Life*, the media have aspired in the broadcasting of talk as much to entertainment and sociability as to truth and the correspondence to fact (Scannell, 1996). In its increasing emphasis on the person, on dialogue and on conversation as a mode of delivery, news discourse has registered and projected those changes discernible in many areas of broadcasting as well as in public life more generally. In the live two-way we can see a quite particular instance of those broader changes at work. But like all change it produces uncertainty about its status and most particularly about what kinds of validity claims most properly apply to it.

8.10   Discursive change and the validity claims of broadcast news

The news is often considered in terms of a problem of fit between the words of the broadcaster and the world being reported. Quite apart from critical academic commentary, practitioners themselves are intensely aware of possible problems. For one thing they are regulated by civil laws relating to libel, defamation or the invasion of privacy and professional codes that encourage them to be impartial and objective, to educate and to inform, to hold powerful figures to account but at the same time to practice 'fairness'.

In general, therefore, broadcast news as an order of discourse attracts attention under the claim to truth. Of course, a discourse that projects the claim to truth is not necessarily true; it simply stands or falls by the claim. However, although the generalised 'claim to truth' is the default or axiomatic claim for news discourse, this claim does not (and cannot) work uniformly across all its sub-genres. In *news presentation* and *news report* the claims to truth are strongly projected. But, as we have noted, in certain kinds of interview, including the two-way with correspondent or the experiential interview with a member of the public, the claims may be less to do with correspondence to reality and more to do with sincerity, authenticity and fidelity to emotion or experience.

In short, the variable sub-generic properties of the different structural elements of the news offer different kinds of claim to validity. Indeed we may, following Habermas (1979, 1990), distinguish at least three principal kinds of claim that discourse in general may be subject to: a claim to truth, a claim to sincerity and a claim to appropriateness[17]. Thus, a trigonometric proof may prioritise or foreground the claim to truth (or correspondence to reality) whereas a compliment or a declaration of love may foreground the claim to sincerity (correspondence to the emotional state of the speaker). Appropriateness (or 'taste') may be only a subsidiary claim in each of these instances but in selected cases it may become particularly salient: humour (cartoons, for instance) often raises questions of appropriateness. Habermas distinguishes only three kinds of validity claim; but a fourth kind of claim could be added to account for those kinds of discourse which rest principally on a claim to special well-formedness: a poem, for instance, may be judged not by its sincerity or its truth or even by its appropriateness but by the degree to which it successfully projects a satisfying form. Under certain conditions it is quite possible for a discourse or utterance to manifest all claims to validity simultaneously[18]. But in most cases discourse or utterance projects predominantly a claim of a particular type.

The use of categorical assertion, the absence of marked epistemic modality in *news presentation* may project the validity claim of truth; and this claim to validity may be extended across the other sub-genres, reinforced by professional codes and institutional provisions relating to bias, impartiality, accuracy and fairness. However, the different genres of broadcast news do not project identical claims to validity; and change within the normative tendencies of one sub-genre compared with another may exert contradictory pressures: for instance, closer identification with the audience within certain sub-genres of news interview, such as the witness or experiential interview, may be seen as running counter to the pre-eminence of the unqualified claim to truth. Accordingly, especially in the wake of social and discursive change, some degree of tension between opposing norms may arise both within and across the genres of news.

Moreover, appropriateness or even aesthetic criteria are undoubtedly at stake, particularly in areas of television news where certain kinds of image may be subject to judgement on grounds of taste. European television news agencies, for instance, are generally more reluctant than equivalent Arabic channels to screen available footage of the dead or the mutilated in Iraq. Televising the execution of Saddam Hussein posed powerful tensions between, in this case, the rival claims of truth and appropriateness. Broadcasters, on the other hand, were more likely to screen examples of the offending Danish cartoons of the prophet than were print outlets (certainly in the UK) inclined to publish them. So appropriateness may well be a subsidiary and additional focus in the broadcasting of the news. Indeed, recent debates about aggressive, adversarial news interviewing, noted above, may also be understood in these terms.

8.11 Towards an ethics of the discourse of broadcast news

Broadcast news is a highly particularised order of discourse. The news, perhaps more than any other area of contemporary social and institutional life, is instantiated in discourse and is conducted exclusively through it. Unlike areas such as law, politics, medicine, education it offers little in the way of specialised goods and services beyond the complex proliferation of statements about the world. It is highly salient; and comments on its efficacy, power, declining standards and quality are routine. Indeed, there is probably no major institutional area of modern life where a highly particularised order of discourse is so pervasive, so widely available, so endlessly referred to, and so much the subject of comment and reaction. As Ekström (2002) comments, in his discussion of TV journalism, it is "clearly among the most influential knowledge-producing institutions of our time" (p. 259).

As an order of discourse it is constituted in a complex interplay of genres and sub-genres; and it is sometimes overlooked that the projected "knowledge claims vary somewhat between different journalistic genres" (Ekström, 2002, p. 274). There are, across the genres, "different forms of knowledge, produced under different conditions and with different claims" (Ekström, 2002, p. 263). It may, admittedly, be difficult not to regard the claim to truth as axiomatic. As Ekström himself observes:

> Characteristic of journalism is its claim to present, on a regular basis, reliable, neutral and current factual information that is important and valuable for citizens in a democracy.

And in this respect Ekström is close to the position advanced by O'Neill (2001): that "truth telling is an internal and constitutive end of journalism" (p. 303). But as O'Neill points out

> Truth telling in the context of journalism involves more than simply the presentation of accurate information. Two points are of particular significance here. First the journalist works within certain norms of communication. Some of these are particular to the practice, for example, those governing that very particular genre, the newspaper headline. Others are general norms of communication.
>
> (op. cit. p. 304)

Much of this book has stressed the communicative character of broadcast news. Broadcast news, and the journalism that informs it, may well aspire to truth-telling as its constitutive end. But it is about much more than this. As an ensemble of interlocking genres it is oriented to its audience, which it must engage with and hold, as much as to 'storyable events'. For this reason other virtues must cohere around the truth-telling virtues of honesty, integrity, objectivity – virtues such as clarity, accessibility, engagement (both with the topic and the audience). These virtues and others constitute forms of excellence that inform the practices of broadcast news both as broad excellences and technical ones.

Discussions of journalism as an ethical practice often prioritise one dimension over all others – basically the need to achieve literal correspondence to the world. The worst opprobrium is reserved for cases where stories or facts were fabricated; the second for where they were wrong. And, inasmuch as truth-telling is *the* constitutive end of journalism, it is clear why this should be so. But journalism – the news – has to be more than this. There is little to be gained by telling truths that are not of much concern to its audience.

There are, of course, well-developed critiques of the news for paying too much attention to the audience. It has been criticised as infotainment, as populist, and for dumbing down. And, undoubtedly, weak journalism is sometimes defended behind the excuse of 'giving the audience (the public) what it wants'. Nonetheless, genres of news exist within the public sphere as part of a compact between the producers and the audience; and the enactment of the contract requires continuous assessments by producers of likely audience response in relation to complex interlocking editorial decisions. The material needs to be true to the world but appropriate to the audience.

In view of this, it is not sufficient to arrive at an ethics of broadcast news that relies primarily on the claim to truth and that applies only to its producers. A comprehensive ethics of news as an order of discourse needs to recognise the significance of other kinds of claim and also to include the audience within its range of application. After all, audiences are active in relation to the news and increasingly so. Through email, blogs and 'citizen journalism' audiences increasingly assert themselves within 'the community of practice' (Wenger, 1998) which is the evolving institution of the news. But, if there are virtues in terms of whose excellence we judge producers of the news, then are there equivalent virtues to honesty, courage and integrity that apply to the audience? Aristotle's original account of virtue in *Nicomachean Ethics* identified virtues by reference to a *via media* – a golden mean between extremes: thus, courage, for example, is defined as a golden or virtuous mean between cowardice and recklessness. Aristotle's *via media* provides a way of defining virtues for audiences: a mean somewhere between trust and scepticism; between compassion and indifference; between engagement and withdrawal; between curiosity and prurience. A precise vocabulary for these mid-points is lacking: but the space between extremes is where we need to be.

These *viae mediae* could be seen as constituting the space of witnessing. The news presents to us a world layered with significances, as a place of interests and concerns. Of course, news is a succession of snapshots, of course these are highly selective, and of course at times the focus could better be described as determined by prurience than by the public interest. But broadcast news – the pre-eminent genre of the audiovisual media – has in the words of John Ellis (2002) introduced a particular modality of perception to contemporary societies – "that of witness ... confronting us with much more about the wider world than previous generations encountered ... The essence of this sense of witness is that 'we cannot say that we do not know'".

Unlike much work on the language of news, the aim of this book has been not so much to arbitrate on the truth validity of broadcast news but to explore how it works as an order of discourse to produce accounts of the world in relation to its audience. Deliberating on the truthfulness of news is undoubtedly a responsibility of those who produce it; and it is right that they should be held accountable for it. At the same time, however, the determination of truth is equally as much a task for audiences – one which depends upon an understanding of how news works as an order of discourse.

Notes

2 Broadcast news and discourse analysis

1 Sinclair and Coulthard (1975), Coulthard and Montgomery (1981), Labov and Fanshel (1977), Van Dijk (1988a,b), Cameron (2001), Levinson (1983), Swales (1990), Eggins and Martin (1997), Eggins and Slade (1997).
2 Sacks (1992), Schegloff (1988), Drew and Heritage (1992), Boden and Zimmerman (1991), Clayman and Heritage (2002), Hutchby and Woofit (1998), Hutchby (2006)
3 Scannell (Ed.) (1991), Tolson (Ed. 2001)(2006), Matheson (2005).
4 Fairclough (1992, 1995), Chouliaraki and Fairclough (1999), Wodak and Meyer (2001).
5 "It is because genres exist as an institution that they function as 'horizons of expectation' for readers and as 'models of writing' for authors" (Todorov, 1990, p. 18).
6 The case of the BBC correspondent, Andrew Gilligan, discussed in Chapter 6 is interesting in this respect. His report on the government's dossier about Iraq's weapons of mass destruction, which he said had been 'sexed up', was criticised by subsequent inquiry. As a result, Gilligan himself resigned from the BBC, as also did the Director General and the Chair of the BBC board of governors. But none of the editorial team associated with the programme – including its presenter – resigned or were disciplined.
7 "Dead air is a phenomenon whereby a broadcast which normally carries audio or video unintentionally becomes silent or blank (also known as unmodulated carrier). The term is most often used in cases where programme material comes to an unexpected halt, either through operator error or for technical reasons, although it is also used in cases where a broadcaster has 'dried up'. In many parts of the world 'dead air' is considered to be one of the worst crimes a broadcaster can commit... Under British broadcasting laws, any radio station which transmits dead air for more than ten minutes without rectifying the situation, broadcasting an announcement, or warning its listeners can be penalised or fined up to £25,000 per minute." Wikipedia.
8 The British regulatory body for broadcasting, *Ofcom*, includes in its code for broadcasters provisions for 'fairness'. This contains rules about informed consent for people appearing on programmes. "Where a person is invited to make a contribution to a programme (except when the subject matter is trivial or their participation minor) they should normally, at an appropriate stage:

* be told the nature and purpose of the programme, what the programme is about and be given a clear explanation of why they were asked to contribute and when (if known) and where it is likely to be first broadcast;

* be told what kind of contribution they are expected to make, for example live, pre-recorded, interview, discussion, edited, unedited, etc.;
* be informed about the areas of questioning and, wherever possible, the nature of other likely contributions" [Rule 7.1 of the Broadcasting Code.]

9 Deontic modality relates to the coding of obligation and permission – usually by the speaker towards the hearer (for example: "You may borrow my book"). Although notions of obligation and permission are a significant dimension of a comprehensive treatment of modality they are not a prominent feature of news discourse and so are not discussed here.

3 The discourse structure of broadcast news

1 This way of stating the structure of the programme is drawn from linguistics where it has most application as a notation for stating grammatical structure at the level of sentence. Used in this context it is tantamount to suggesting that there is a grammar of broadcast news, an idea which finds some support in the work of Bentele (1985) and Van Dijk (1988a,b).
2 Not all programmes with presenters who address the camera/audience adopt the practice of greetings and farewells. History and fine art commentary, for instance, quite frequently use direct visual address to camera but do not typically greet the audience in the manner of gardening or cookery programmes – or in the manner of the news.
3 Although the term 'package' is sometimes used in the industry for these pre-recorded video or audio clips, the term *report* is preferred here in order to emphasise its discourse-generic characteristics.
4 Other news values relating to 'elites', 'conflict', and so on are at stake here. The ones under discussion here, however, are perhaps the most generalised, abstract and underlying.
5 There is more to structure than punctuation. These changes are in their own way as profound as the tendencies produced by the telegraph – economy, precision and objectivity.

4 News presentation

1 Of course, tactical advantage can be derived from the use of spokespersons such as press secretaries. They can speak for the president or prime minister and on most occasions their words will be taken as expressing the views of their *principal*. But there is still scope for denying the connection when things go wrong.
2 Unless, that is, the accent is Scottish or Welsh. Even here, however, any Scottish, Welsh or indeed English accent tends *not* to be one of those strongly associated with the major urban areas such as Glasgow, Cardiff, or for that matter Birmingham. They carry not the marks of a well-defined locale (Crosby, Sparkbrook, Maryhill or Splottlands) but project a neutral national ethnicity.
3 Two of the provisions of UK's Ofcom *Broadcasting Code of Standards* reinforce the tendency to restrict the role of newspresenters: "5.3 No politician may be used as a newsreader, interviewer or reporter in any news programmes unless, exceptionally, it is editorially justified. In that case, the political allegiance of that person must be made clear to the audience.....5.8 Any personal interest of a reporter or presenter, which would call into question the due impartiality of the programme, must be made clear to the audience." In short, roles outside those of broadcasting the news that may cause any conflict of interest or might compromise due impartiality are discouraged by the regulatory body.

4 The teleprompter screen is in front of the lens of the camera, and the words on the screen are reflected to the eyes of the speaker using a one-way mirror. As the speaker does not need to look down to consult written notes, he or she appears to have memorised the speech or be speaking spontaneously, and can look directly into the camera's eye.

5 Occasionally, traces of an earlier, pre-autocue, style can be caught at the beginning or end of a programme. The news reader, for instance, may be seen shuffling their notes as the credits transit up the screen at the end of the programme. And they sometimes look up to camera from their notes at the beginning of an item or a programme.

6 Otherwise, however, newsreaders occupy an oblique relationship to the words that they use and through those words to us. Apart from the examples of greetings and farewells just mentioned there is little or no verbal direct address to the audience – nothing to correspond, for instance, to the Radio DJ's patter: "for any of you recovering from Christmas, here's ..." or "Hello to Cynthia from Ruislip who's requested 'The Lark Ascending' for her husband Norman who is recovering from flu. Hope you're feeling better Norman".

7 Zelizer (1990) makes a further distinction – between what she calls the 'place of the reporter' and the 'place of the event' – in what is called here 'the space of the news field'. She uses this to make the interesting point that reporting from the site of the news can be seen as an indication of the report's authenticity. Conversely, however, she notes that the place of the reporter and the place of the event do not always exactly match in news reports, the reporter only seeming to report from the place of the event. This enables a spurious authenticity to be lent to them. One problem with her account, however, is that it interprets news as being literally about events which take place in locales, these being necessarily determinate and highly specific. But if, for example, the Bank of England Monetary Policy Committee raises interest rates so that both the value of shares and the price of houses fall, from where should the reporter report the news: from the Bank of England, the stock exchange or an estate agent's office or the representative house of a vendor?

8 Finding the right vocabulary to name these elements is problematic. In some ways 'subsidiary' as term for elements such as reports and interviews does less than full justice to their significance. Frequently, they provide important elaborations to the kernel. In structural terms, however, whether they elaborate on material provided in the kernel or not, they are dependent on it. For this reason, the term subsidiary was chosen, even though they may fulfil a significant elaborative role.

9 Admittedly, it is enunciated for us by the presenter but, as section 4.2 suggests, this does not make the presenter the narrator of the account or the author of the kernel.

5   The discourse of television news reports: narrative or commentary?

1 As Caldas-Coulthard (1997) puts it: "One of the explanations for the domination of news in the discourse of the media is that news is **narrative** or story telling and therefore the most attractive and vivid representation of experience through language ... Like any other narrative text news is centrally concerned with past events which develop to some kind of conclusion" (Caldas-Coulthard, 1997, p. 45).

2 A rather different argument, though one that still involves issues of realism, is suggested by Scannell (1996), who sees radio and television news as the successors to great historical novels of the 19th century as exemplified by Scott, Stendhal or Tolstoy. Radio and television bring to fulfilment a process begun with the daily

press in which the two worlds of everyday life and public events are brought together (Scannell, 1996, pp. 160–164).

3 As Kuhn makes clear, the 'staging' of scenes for the camera/audience and the construction of character as a point of subjective identification are perhaps the two most important constraints on cinematic codes: "The conventions of classical editing constitute a particular mode of address to the spectator. In accepting a certain kind of verisimilitude in the spatial and temporal organisation of the film narrative the spectator becomes witness to a complete world, a world which seems even to exceed the bounds of the film frame. In looking at the faces of characters in close-up, and in identifying with characters in the text through taking on their implied point-of-view, the spectator identifies with the fictional world and its inhabitants, and so is drawn into the narration itself. Consequently, a resolution of the narrative in which all the ends are tied up is in certain ways pleasurable for the spectator" (Kuhn, 1985, pp. 214–215). It is the absence of character as a point of identification and the purported avoidance of staging as a way of suggesting a world in its fictional totality that most marks out television news as quite different from the narratives of mainstream cinema.

4 These figures deliberately exclude major transitions within the news between, for example, studio intro and report or between report and interview.

5 The two exceptions are interesting as both involve a delayed cut to a shot of a speaker (and a move away from voice-over). In each case we hear the voice of the speaker before we see them on camera. The change in voice-quality prepares for the cut.

6 Sky News, for example, suffered a major crisis of credibility over a news report during the Iraq war which apparently featured a Royal Navy submarine engaged in firing a cruise missile in support of the invasion. The report failed to make clear that the footage was archive material gathered during exercises and did not feature the submarine in action at the time. Sky News held an internal inquiry, the reporter lost his job and subsequently took his own life.

7 Further analysis of this report, including the matching of still images from the visual track with referring expressions in the verbal track, may be found in Edginton and Montgomery (1996), pp. 98–104.

6 The discourse of live, two-way affiliated interviews

1 To be more precise, the concern here is with **epistemic** rather than with deontic modality. Epistemic modality is variously understood in terms of ways of limiting or increasing the strength of an assertion, ways of limiting or increasing the amount of commitment to the truth/accuracy/probability of the proposition, or ways of signalling the degrees of knowledge regarding factuality. Deontic modality by contrast is concerned with the encoding of obligation. See: Perkins, 1983; Coates, 1982; Stubbs, 1996.

2 And this despite the way in which the BBC's Producers' Guidelines have long counselled against this outcome when interviewing correspondents. The 2005 version of the guidelines (unchanged since at least 1996) stipulates:

It is entirely right to call upon correspondents to express their judgement based on their knowledge of a subject, but entirely inappropriate to ask them about things of which they cannot be sure, or on which they can only speculate. Producers should establish in advance exactly how much a correspondent will be able to move a story on or clarify it.

(BBC Producers' Guidelines Online, p. 183)

The examples discussed here suggest that this advice is honoured more in the breech than in the observance.

3 I am indebted to conversations with Fabio Crestani for the terms 'push' and 'pull', which are drawn from the field of Information Science, where they are generally used to describe different ways of managing information in relation to a user (see Agosti, M., Crestani and Pasi (eds) (2001)). A search engine such as Google allows a user to 'pull down' information. More sophisticated mechanisms will be able to offer or 'push' information to a user on the basis of previous searches. The usage in this paper, applied to modality choices, is somewhat different. It seeks to capture what at first sight seems a less than rational aspect of certain kinds of speech performance in which a speaker will first raise, then lower, the strength of an assertion in the course of making it. (The reverse is also possible.) I think it is a feature of the public performance of un-scripted speech. The tension between overstatement and understatement lends colour and interest to the performance. Live two-ways often sound more interesting than informative. A related phenomenon has been noted by Anne-Marie Simon-Vandenbergen (1996) in relation to responses in political interviews. She distinguishes on the basis of modality choices between the confident politician and the non-committal politician but she also notes that 'upgrading' (overtone) and 'downgrading' (undertone) can occur within the same turn.

4 The underlying propositions are not always easy to recover because of a crucial characteristic of live speech in this sub-genre, namely, intermittent 'vagueness' (see Channell, 1994).

5 Alasdair Milne in an interview in the London *Standard* during the Falklands War, May 12th, 1982. Cited in Harris, 1994.

6 In 2007 at the end of a lengthy round of negotiations between the BBC and the British Treasury, the BBC were awarded a 4-year funding settlement but at a rate of increase less than inflation, which could thus be regarded as a cut in funding in real terms. Some commentators speculated that this was a punishment for the Gilligan affair, though the Government emphatically denied this.

7 In September 2003, for example, the then leader of the Tory Party, Iain Duncan Smith, in his conference speech to the party faithful accused the Prime Minister of lying about his role in the Dr Kelly affair: this did not provoke demands by Blair for a retraction or threats of a libel action. And opinion pieces in newspapers similarly may be allowed to pass without reaction. But the claim that the government was lying in a generic news discourse type that purports to be about rhetorically unadorned facts rather than opinion could not easily pass off simply as a 'contribution to political debate'.

8 In May 2004 Britain's *Daily Mirror* newspaper published photographs, thought to have been obtained from British soldiers who had served in Iraq, which purported to show scenes of Iraqi detainees being abused by soldiers of the Queen's Lancashire Regiment. These photographs were subsequently proven to be fakes, the story was hopelessly compromised and the editor of the newspaper, Piers Morgan, resigned as a result. However, a year later eleven soldiers of the same regiment were put on trial after an Iraqi detainee was beaten to death in custody in 2003. One of the soldiers pleaded guilty to a charge of inhumane treatment, was jailed for a year and dismissed from the army. It is clear therefore that the prisoner abuse by members of the Queen's Lancashire Regiment did occur in Iraq; and in this essential respect the story in the *Daily Mirror* was true. The story was undermined, however, by inaccuracies in the evidence adduced in support of its claim. Some would see similarities in the journalistic failures at the BBC and the *Daily Mirror*.

9 In the event the BBC published the Neil report, which made a number of recommendations about journalistic practice and the training of its own journalists.

7 The broadcast news interview

1 There is a complicated history of ideas behind Fairclough's usage. His source for the notion of discourse technologies is the work of Foucault – particularly *Discipline and Punish* – where a blurring takes place between physical means of containment (for example, the asylum, the prison and the panopticon) and strategies or techniques of containment including examination, interrogation and confession. Prison and interrogation for Foucault are closely related sides of the same coin. Each operates as a device for constituting subjects in a determinate way with determinate effects. As in much of his work, surprising insights flow from drawing together hitherto unrelated practices and displaying previously undernoted connections between them. In this case his emphasis on the productivity of form draws together what Marx might have separated out as 'means of production' and 'relations of production'. Raymond Williams in *Television, Technology and Cultural Form* follows Marx more closely in describing television as a technology but emphasising the historically specific social relations of use that it evolves and is adapted to serve. His view of technology is closer to the sense of 'configuration of technical means for a social purpose'.

2 Bell and van Leeuwen (1994) suggest that the first published newspaper interview in question–answer format was by James Gordon Bennett of a possible witness to the murder of a prostitute, published in the *New York Herald* in 1836. Historians of journalism, they say, also refer to Bennett's interview of President Martin van Buren, again in the *New York Herald*, published in 1839.

3 One of Garfinkel's (1984) 'breach experiments' required his graduate students to reveal to an everyday interlocutor that their conversation had been audio-recorded without permission. The generally negative reactions that this provoked encouraged Garfinkel to formulate the principle that most 'naturally occurring' talk took place under the presupposition of not being overheard.

4 He has been quoted by media organisations such as BBC and CNN on several occasions, including the outset of the Lockerbie trial, its conclusion, and after 9/11. In those contexts the following kind of format would be used: "The Reverend John Mosey, speaking on behalf of the British victims, said: 'I'm surprised the verdict is so soon but glad from a personal point of view … we waited over eight years for a trial and have been out here at the trial for nearly a year. It will be a relief to finally know'" (*Independent*, 31/01/01). In other words, a representative status was granted to him and he himself adopted a spokesperson's position. This is not the line followed in the C4 interview.

5 Strictly speaking, of course, Snow's questions in any case are almost impossible to answer. How can one have **every** reason to believe anyone? How can anyone know what their thoughts will be tomorrow? The last question ("if you had to would you shake his hand") looks tautological.

6 A role sometimes described as that of 'tribune of the people'.

7 "This was nothing like the breakfast times I'd left behind – hurriedly eating a bowl of cornflakes while listening to John Humphries (sic) fighting to get a straight answer from a slippery politician on Radio 4": Biscay Adventure, Sarah Button, *Yachting World* June 2004. The reference is to BBC Radio's flagship current affairs programme broadcast daily between 6 and 9 a.m. and to the adversarial interviewing style of its presenter, John Humphrys. The writer clearly identifies

with Humphrys and although she may not speak for every member of the audience she undoubtedly sums up how Humphrys and the BBC would like the programme and his interviews to be experienced: "renowned as a tough and tenacious interviewer" (BBC profile).

8 Carey (2003) says of reportage that it "endlessly feeds its reader with accounts of the deaths of other people, and therefore places him (sic) continually in the position of a survivor – one who has escaped the violent and terrible ends which, it graphically apprises him, others have come to. In this way reportage, like religion, gives the individual a comforting sense of his own immortality." In broadcast news the survivor role, where appropriate, is incorporated into the news itself.

9 An additional element described by Labov is the 'abstract', which – coming in first position in his story grammar – may signal transition to the story and encapsulate its point, perhaps by brief summary. These do feature in the data here, presumably because the point of the story is obvious and is presupposed by the context and the previous discourse. The element is therefore redundant.

10 There is a case for regarding this orientation as incorporating its own mini-narrative featuring a complication (unable to board train) and resolution (finally boarded train). This mini-narrative projects forward to the later narrative complication of the bomb and its aftermath: if the narrator had been able to board an earlier train he might have escaped unscathed. This seems a quite deliberate implication of the orientation and one which carries forward right through to the narrative's concluding coda, though the implication is never exactly spelt out.

11 This is an interesting case of a news interviewer affiliating with an interviewee through the production of a receipt or acknowledgement token inside the interviewee's turn. It seems to indicate that for the purposes of this (experiential) material the performance or preservation of formal neutrality – so much a feature of the accountability interview – is simply not relevant.

12 Myers (2000) citing Woofit (1992) notes a similar pattern, "I was just doing X when Y happened", in interviews about supernatural events.

13 Interviews with correspondents are sometimes used to cover similar kinds of ground to *expert interviews*. But here, when the interviewee is a specialist correspondent from within the broadcast institution, the presentation of background tends to be done neutrally and impersonally as a guarantee of the authoritativeness of the information.

14 The 'emergency planning consultant', Simon Turney, was formerly Director of Emergency Planning for South Yorkshire Fire and Civil Defence Authority.

15 There were echoes of these words in Blair's reference to Diana as "the people's princess" in the statement he made about Diana on the day after her death – a statement in itself that was widely quoted.

8 The changing discourses of broadcast news

1 The term 'correspondent' is used here to embrace what news institutions may variously designate Reporter, Editor or Correspondent, as noted in previous chapters. The crucial defining characteristics of a Correspondent are that they are usually contracted employees of the institution, affiliated exclusively or primarily with it and subject to its codes of practice.

2 Timings for this programme are as follows. Overall length of bulletin, 22'03"; news item 1, 10'42"; news item 1 report, 1'10"; news item 1, interview 1, 2'30"; news item 1, interview 2, 4'00".

3 The timings for this programme are as follows. Overall programme length, 20'35"; News Item 1, 6'30"; News Item 1 Report, 2'00"; News Item 1 Live Two-way, 1'40".

4 For instance, Ofcom's report on Public Service Broadcasting, 2005, found no evidence of declining 'seriousness' in TV current affairs.

5 The studio space of CNN, BBC, Sky News and others is similarly complex and multi-layered.

6 By 'public figure' here is meant simply a person with accredited responsibility for action in relation to the news event. The most obvious public figures are politicians, trades unionists, members of the professions, office holders in associations, etc. There is thus a difference between an ordinary 'member of the public' and a 'public figure', though there remain problematic instances. Sven-Goran Eriksson as manager of the English Football team, for example, was clearly considered a public figure, as were chosen members of his team. Whether the wives and girlfriends of players were public figures in the same sense was a matter of some debate. Set-piece interviews of public figures are not uncommon, of course, but are now usually reserved for extended news magazine programmes, examples of which in the UK are BBC2's *Newsnight,* or Channel 4's *Channel 4 News.* The *Today* programme on BBC Radio 4 has a slot at 8.10 daily devoted to the interview of a public figure. Interviews of this kind in these slots tend to be adversarial and accountable (see Chapter 7).

7 During the 2006 fighting in Lebanon, Jon Snow presented UK Channel 4's News from outside the UN in New York running the programme from the location of the lead story when it's very big.

8 This trend is borne out by Winston's (2002) comparison where he notes the increased use of stand-uppers and live two-ways with correspondent/editors and the reduced use of presenter in direct address to camera.

9 See also Horton and Wohl's (1956) concept of 'intimacy at a distance'.

10 Another dimension in which tension between opposing norms can be detected is in the area of increased expressivity in news presentation: a wider range of 'keying' is now favoured in reading the news. When news presenters preserve a strictly neutral emotional orientation to what they present, it can lead to a flat delivery overall. When, however, an emotional orientation is allowed to colour the delivery of a particular item this may lead to a discrepant orientation, or keying, in the transition from one item to another.

11 The most famous of these moments is perhaps the interview in which Paxman asked the Conservative Home Secretary Michael Howard thirteen times in succession whether he had overruled the Director General of Prisons. See Clayman and Heritage, 2002, pp. 256–257, where they refer to it as a 'landmark of aggressive interviewing'.

12 Nonetheless, they also published on the following day a strong defence of Paxman, citing better viewing figures for Paxman than for Snow. See "The BBC and the 'Paxman problem' ", by Roger Mosey, Head of Television News, *NewsWatch,* 20th April 2005.

13 See Brown and Levinson (1978): 'face' is "the public self-image that every member wants to claim for himself", including "the positive consistent self-image or 'personality'... including the desire that this self-image be appreciated and approved of" (1978, p. 61).

14 The proposition itself, of course, (that opposition parties do so talk) may be considered contentious or, in Labov and Fanshel's and Blum Kulka's terms, 'disputable'; but an interviewee risks 'not answering the question' if they spend interview time taking issue with propositions buried as presuppositions in the preface to a question.

15 Abu Izzadeen was later arrested on February 8th 2007 by counter-terrorism officers under Section 1 of the Terrorism Act 2006 on suspicion of inciting terrorism.

16 See Labov: "when A makes a statement about a B-Event it is heard as a request for confirmation".

17 A fuller treatment of Habermas's proposals with respect to validity claims may be found in Montgomery (1999) and Simpson (2003).

18 Thus, a love poem addressed singularly and in private to a beloved may provoke reactions along the axes of all four claims to validity. (And the beloved might, for instance, reject the poem as simultaneously untruthful, insincere, tasteless and clumsy in form.)

References

Agosti, M., Crestani, F. and Pasi, G. (eds.) (2001) *Lectures on Information Retrieval: Lecture Notes in Computer Science*. Heidelberg: Springer-Verlag.

Aitchison, J. and Lewis (2003) *New Media Language*. London: Routledge.

Allan, S. (1999/2004) (2nd edn) *News Culture*. Buckingham: Open University Press.

Altman, R. (1986) Television/Sound. In Modleski, T. (ed.), *Studies in Entertainment: Critical Approaches to Mass Culture*. Bloomington: Indiana University Press, pp. 39–54.

Ardehali, P. (1990) Pronoun exchange as a barometer of social change. In *Dialectical Anthropology*, Volume 15(1), pp. 82–68.

Arendt, H. (1958) *The Human Condition*. Chicago: Chicago University Press.

Aristotle (2004 edn) (Hugh Tredennick (ed.), J. Barnes (Introduction), J.A.K. Thomson (translator)) *Nicomachean Ethics*. Harmondsworth: Penguin Classics.

Atkinson, J.M. and Drew, P. (1979) *Order in Court: the Organisation of Verbal Interaction in Judicial Settings*. London: Macmillan.

Atkinson, J.M. (1992) Displaying neutrality: formal aspects of informal court proceedings. In Drew, P. and Heritage (eds.), *Talk at Work*. Cambridge: Cambridge University Press.

Auslander, P. (1999) *Liveness*. London: Routledge.

Austin, J.L. (1962) *How to Do Things with Words*. Oxford: Clarendon Press.

Barnett, S. and Gabor, I. (2001) *Westminster Tales: the Twenty-First Century Crisis in Political Journalism*. London: Continuum.

Barnett, S. and Seymour, E. (1999) *A Shrinking Iceberg Travelling South …. Changing Trends in British Television*. London: Campaign for Quality Television.

Bednarek, M. (2006) *Evaluation in Media Discourse: Analysis of a Newspaper Corpus*. London: Continuum.

Bell, A. (1991) *The Language of News Media*. Oxford: Blackwell.

Bell, A. (1994) Telling stories. In Graddol, D. and Boyd-Barrett, O. (eds.) (1994) pp. 119–136.

Bell, A. and Garrett (eds.) (1989) *Approaches to Media Discourse*. Oxford: Blackwell.

Bell, M. and van Leeuwen (1994) *The Media Interview: Confession, Contest, Conversation*. New South Wales University Press.

Bennett, T., Boyd-Bowman, Mercer and Woollacott (eds.) (1981) *Popular Television, and Film*. London: BFI.

Bentele, G. (1985) Audio-visual analysis and a grammar of presentation forms in news programs: some mediasemiotic considerations (pp. 159–184).

In Van Dijk (ed.) *Discourse and Communication: New Approaches to the Analysis of Mass Media Discourse and Communication*. Berlin: Walter de Gruyter.

Berger, P. and Luckmann (1971) *The Social Construction of Reality*. Harmondsworth: Penguin.

Biber, D. (2003) Compressed noun-phrase structures in newspaper discourse: the competing demands of popularization vs. economy. In Aitchison and Lewis (eds.), *New Media Language*. London: Routledge, pp. 169–182.

Blum Kulka, S. (1983) The dynamics of political interviews, *Text*, 3(2), 131–153.

Brown, P. and Levinson, S. (1978) *Politeness: Some Universals in Language Usage*. Cambridge: CUP.

Brown, R. and Gilman, A. (1960) The pronouns of power and solidarity. In Sebeok, T.A. (ed.) (1960) *Style in Language*. Cambridge, MA: MIT Press, pp. 253–276.

Boden, D. and Zimmerman (eds.) (1991) *Talk and Social Structure*. Berkeley: University of California Press.

Boltanski, L. (1999) *Distant Suffering: Politics, Morality and the Media*. Cambridge: CUP.

Bordwell, D. (1985) *Narration in the Fiction Film*. London: Methuen.

Bordwell, D. and Thompson, K. (1979) *Film Art: an Introduction*. Reading Massachusetts, Addison-Wesley.

Bondi Paganelli, M. (1990) Off-air recordings: what interaction? The case of news and current affairs. In Favretti (ed.) (1990) *The Televised Text*. Bologna: Patron Editore.

Bourdieu, P. (1992) *The Logic of Practice*. Cambridge: Polity.

Caldas-Coulthard, C. (1997) *News as Social Practice*. Florianopolis: ARES.

Cameron, D. (1995) *Verbal Hygiene*. London: Routledge.

Cameron, D. (2000) *Good to Talk*. London: Sage.

Cameron, D. (2001) *Working with Spoken Discourse*. London: Sage.

Carey, J. (ed.) (2003) *The Faber Book of Reportage*. London: Faber.

Carter, R. and Simpson, P. (eds.) (1988) *Language, Discourse and Literature: Introductory Reader in Discourse Stylistics*. London: Routledge.

Chafe, W.L. and Nichols, J. (eds.) (1986) *Evidentiality: The Linguistic Encoding of Epistemology*. Norwood, NJ: Ablex.

Channell, J. (1994) *Vague Language*. Oxford: OUP.

Chouliaraki, L. (2006) *The Spectatorship of Suffering*. London: Sage.

Chouliaraki, L. and Fairclough (1999) *Discourse in Late Modernity – Rethinking Critical Discourse Analysis*. Edinburgh: Edinburgh University Press.

Clayman, S. (1991) News interview openings: aspects of sequential organisation. In Scannell, P. (ed.), *Broadcast Talk*. London: Sage.

Clayman, S. (1992) Footing in the achievement of neutrality: the case of news interview discourse. In Drew, P. and Heritage (eds.), *Talk at Work*. Cambridge: Cambridge University Press, pp. 163–198.

Clayman, S. and Heritage (2002) *The News Interview: Journalists and Public Figures on the Air*. Cambridge: CUP.

Coates, J. (1982) *The Semantics of Modal Auxiliaries*. London: Croom Helm.

Cohen, S. and Young (eds.) (1965?) *The Manufacture of News*. London: Constable.

Cole, P. and Morgan, J.L. (eds.) (1975) *Syntax and Semantics 3: Speech Acts*. New York: Academic Press.

Cook, P. (ed.) (1985) *The Cinema Book*. London: BFI.

Conboy, M. (2002) *The Press and Popular Culture*. London: Sage.

Conboy, M. (2003) Parochializing the global: language and the British tabloid press. In Aitchison, J. and Lewis (eds.), *New Media Language*. London: Routledge.

Corner, J. (1995) *Television Form and Public Address*. London: Arnold.

Coulthard, M. (1985) *An Introduction to Discourse Analysis*. London: Longmans.

Coulthard, M. and Montgomery (eds.) (1981) *Studies in Discourse Analysis*. London: Routledge and Kegan Paul.

Coulthard M. and Brazil (1992) Exchange structure. In Coulthard, M. (ed.), *Advances in Spoken Discourse*. London: Routledge.

Crisell, A. (2nd edn) (1994) *Understanding Radio*. London: Routledge.

Davis, H. and Walton, P. (eds.) (1983) *Language, Image, Media*. Oxford: Blackwell.

Drew, P. and Heritage (eds.) (1992) *Talk at Work: Interaction in Institutional Settings*. Cambridge: CUP.

Edginton, B. and Montgomery, M. (1996) *The Media*. London: The British Council.

Eggins, S. and Martin (1997) Genres and registers of discourse. In Van Dijk, T. (ed.), *Discourse as Structure and Process*. London: Sage.

Eggins, S. and Slade (1997) *Analysing Casual Conversation*. London: Cassell Academic.

Ekström, M. (2001) Politicians interviewed on television news in *Discourse and Society*, 12(5), 563–584.

Ekström, M. (2002) Epistemologies of TV Journalism: a theoretical framework. *Journalism*, 3(3), 259–282.

Elias, N. (1996) *The Germans*. New York: Columbia University Press.

Ellis, J. (1982) *Visible Fictions*. London: Routledge.

Ellis, J. (2002) *Seeing Things: Television the Age of Uncertainty*. London: I.B. Tauris.

Fairclough, N. (1992) *Discourse and Social Change*. Oxford: Blackwell.

Fairclough, N. (1995) *Media Discourse*. London: Arnold.

Fairclough, N. (2003) *Analysing Discourse: Textual Analysis for Social Research*. London: Routledge.

Fetzer, A. (2002) 'Put bluntly, you have something of a credibility problem': Sincerity and credibility in political interviews. In Politics as Text and Talk, Chilton, Paul and Christina Schäffner (eds.), pp. 173–201.

Fetzer, A. and Weizman, E. (eds.) (2006) Pragmatic aspects of political discourse in the media. Special Issue of *Journal of Pragmatics*, 38(2).

Feuer, J. (1983) The concept of live television: ontology as ideology. In Kaplan, E.A. (ed.) pp. 12–22.

Firth, J.R. (1957) *Papers in Linguistics (1934–51)*. London: Oxford University Press.

Fiske, J. (1987) *Television Culture*. London: Methuen.

Flowerdew, J. and Gotti (eds.) *Studies in Specialized Discourse*. Bern: Peter Lang.

Foucault, M. (1966/1970/2001) *The Order of Things*. London: Routledge.

Foucault, M. (1969/1972/2002) *Archaeology of Knowledge*. London: Routledge.

Fowler, R. (1991) *Language in the News: Discourse and Ideology in the Press*. London: Routledge.

Francis, G. (1988) In Carter, R. and Simpson, P. (eds.) *Language, Discourse and Literature: Introductory Reader in Discourse Stylistics*. London: Routledge.

Frank, Russell (2003) Folklore in a Hurry: The community experience narrative in newspaper coverage of the Loma Prieta earthquake. *Journal of American Folklore*, 116(460), 159–175.

Friedrich, P. (1972) Social context and semantic feature: the Russian pronominal usage. In Gumperz, J. and Hymes, D. (eds.) (1972) *Directions in Sociolinguistics*. New York: Holt, Rinehart and Winston, pp. 270–301.

Galtung, J. and Ruge (1965a) The structure of foreign news: the presentation of the Congo, Cuba and Cyprus crises in four Norwegian newspapers. *Journal of Peace Research*, 1, 64–91.

Galtung, J. and Ruge (1965b) Structuring and selecting news. In Cohen, S. and Young (eds.) (1965/1981) *The Manufacture of News*. London: Constable.

Gans, H. (1979/2004) *Deciding What's News: a Study of CBS Evening News, NBC Nightly News, Newsweek, and Time*. Evanston, Illinois: Northwestern University Press.

Garfinkel, H. (1967/1984) *Studies in Ethnomethodology*. Malden MA: Polity Press/ Blackwell Publishing.

Garton, G., Montgomery, M. and Tolson, A. (1991) Ideology, scripts and metaphors in the public sphere of a general election. In Scannell, P. (ed.) *Broadcast Talk*. London: Sage, pp. 100–119.

Gitlin, T. (1980) *The Whole World is Watching: Mass Media in the Making and Unmaking of the New Left*. Berkeley: University of California Press.

Gitlin, T., Glasgow University Media Group (1976) *Bad News*. London: Routledge and Kegan Paul.

Glasgow University Media Group (1980) *More Bad News*. London: Routledge and Kegan Paul.

Glasgow University Media Group (1985) *War and Peace News*. Milton Keynes: Open University Press.

Goffman, E. (1981) *Forms of Talk*. Oxford: Blackwell.

Golding, P. and Elliott, P. (1979) *Making the News*. London: Longman.

Graddol, D. (1994) The visual accomplishment of factuality. In Graddol, D. and Boyd-Barrett, O. (eds.) (1994) pp. 136–160.

Graddol, D. and Boyd-Barrett, O. (eds.) (1994) *Media Texts: Authors and Readers*. Clevedon: Multilingual Matters.

Greatbatch, D. (1998) Conversation analysis: neutralism in British news interviews. In Bell, A. and Garrett, P. (eds.) *Approaches to Media Discourse*. Oxford: Blackwell.

Grice, H.P. (1975) The logic of conversation. In Cole, P. and Morgan (eds.) *Syntax and Semantics 3: Speech Acts*. New York: Academic Press, pp. 41–58.

Gumperz, J. and Hymes, D. (eds.) (1972) *Directions in Sociolinguistics: The Ethnography of Communication*. New York: Holt, Rinehart and Winston.

Haarman, L. (1999) Television talk Ch. 3. In Lombardo, L. et al. (eds.) (1999) *Massed Medias: Linguistic Tools for Interpreting Media Discourse*. Torino: LED, pp. 157–245.

Haarman, L. (2004) 'John, what's going on?': some features of live exchanges on television news. In Partington, A., Morley and Haarman (eds.), *Corpora and Discourse*. Bern: Peter Lang.

Haarman, L. (2006) The construction of stance in BBC television coverage of the Iraqi war. In Flowerdew, J. and Gotti (eds.), *Studies in Specialized Discourse*. Bern: Peter Lang.

Habermas, J. (1979) What is universal pragmatics? In *Communication and the Evolution of Society*, Boston, MA: Beacon, pp. 1–68.

Habermas, J. (1989) *The Structural Transformation of the Public Sphere*. Cambridge Massachusetts: MIT Press.

Habermas, J. (1990) *Moral Consciousness and Communicative Action*. Cambridge MA: Harvard University Press.

Hall, S. (1981) The determinations of news photographs. In Cohen, S. and Young (eds.), *The Manufacture of News*, revised edn. London: Constable.

Halliday, M.A.K. (1978) *Language as Social Semiotic*. London: Arnold.

Halliday, M.A.K. (1985) *An Introduction to Functional Grammar*. London: Arnold.

Harcup, T. and O'Neill, D. (2001) What is news? Galtung and Ruge revisited. *Journalism Studies* 2(2), 261–280.

Hargreaves, I. and Thomas (2002) *New News Old News*. London: ITC/BSC

Harris, R. (1994) *The Media Trilogy*. London: Faber.

Harris, S. (1991) Evasive action: how politicians respond to questions in political interviews. In Scannell, P. (ed.), *Broadcast Talk*. London: Sage, pp. 76–99.

Hartley, J. (1982) *Understanding News*. London: Routledge.

Hartley, J. (1996) *Popular Reality: Journalism, Modernity, Popular Culture*. London: Edward Arnold.

Hartley, J. and Montgomery, M. (1985) Representations and relations: ideology and power in press and TV news. In Van Dijk, T. (ed.), *Discourse and Communication: New Approaches to the Analysis of Mass Media Discourse and Communication*. Berlin: Walter de Gruyter.

Helm, J. (ed.) (1967), *Essays on the Verbal and Visual Arts*. Seattle: University of Washington Press.

Heritage, J. and Greatbatch, D. (1991) On the institutional character of institutional talk: the case of news interviews. In Boden and Zimmerman (eds.), *Talk and Social Structure*, University of California Press, pp. 93–137.

Horton, D. and Richard Wohl, R. (1956) Mass Communication and Para-social Interaction: observations on intimacy at a distance. *Psychiatry*, 19, 215–229.

Housley, W. and Fitzgerald, R. (2002) The reconsidered model of membership categorization analysis. *Qualitative Research*, 2, 59–83.

Hunston, S. and Thompson, G. (2000) *Evaluation in Text*. Oxford: OUP.

Hutchby, I. (2001) *Conversation and Technology: From the Telephone to the Internet*. Oxford: Polity.

Hutchby, I. (2005) News talk: interaction in the broadcast news interview. In Allan, S. (ed.) (2005), *Journalism: Critical Issues Maidenhead*, Open University Press, pp. 210–224.

Hutchby, I. (2006) *Media Talk*. Maidenhead: Open University Press.

Hutchby, I. and Woofit, R. (1998) *Conversation Analysis*. Cambridge: Polity Press.

Hutton (2004) *Final Report of the Hutton Inquiry*. www.the-hutton-inquiry.org.uk/content/report/index.htm extracts reprinted in Coates, T. (ed.)(2004) *The Hutton Inquiry 2003*. London: Tim Coates.

Hymes, D. (ed.) (1977/2001) *Foundations in Sociolinguistics: an Ethnographic Approach*. London: Routledge.

Kaplan, E.A. (ed.) (1983) *Regarding Television: Critical Approaches – An Anthology*. Los Angeles: The American Film Institute.

Kuhn, A. (1985) History of Narrative Codes. In Cook, P. (ed.), *The Cinema Book*. London: BFI.

Kumar (1975) Holding the Middle Ground: The BBC, the public and the professional broadcaster. *Sociology*, 9(1), 67–88.

Labov, W. (1972a) *Language in the Inner City*. Philadelphia: University of Pennsylvania Press.

Labov, W. (1972b) The transformation of experience in narrative syntax. In *Language in the Inner City*, Philadelphia: University of Pennsylvania Press, pp. 354–398.

Labov, W. (1972) *Sociolinguistic Patterns*. Philadelphia: Univeristy of Pennsylvania Press.

Labov, W. and Fanshel, D. (1977) *Therapeutic Discourse: Psychotherapy as Conversation*. New York: Academic Press.

Labov, W. and Waletsky, J. (1967) Narrative analysis: oral versions of personal experience. In Helm, J. (ed.), Seattle, WA: Washington University Press, pp. 12–44.

Lakoff, G. (1972) Hedges: a study in meaning criteria and the logic of fuzzy concepts. *Papers of the Chicago Linguistic Society*, 8, 183–228.

Lerman, C.L. (1983) Dominant discourse: the institutional voice and control of topic. In Davis, H. and Walton, P. (eds.) (1983) *Language, Image, Media*. Oxford: Blackwell, pp. 75–103.

Levinson, S. (1983) *Pragmatics*. Cambridge: CUP.

Lloyd, J. (2004) What are the Media Doing to our Politics? London: Constble and Robinson.

MacGregor, B. (1997) *Live, Direct and Biased? Making Television News in the Satellite Age*. London: Arnold.

MacIntyre, A. (1997) *After Virtue*. London: Duckworth.

Malinowski, B. (1946) The problem of meaning in primitive languages. In Ogden, C.K. and Richards, I.A. (8th Ed.) *The Meaning of Meaning*. London: Routledge and Kegan Paul.

Marriott, S. (2007) Journalism, evidentiality and broadcast reports of the U.S. Election. *Journalism: Theory Practice and Criticism*, 8(2).

Matheson, D. (2005) *Media Discourses*. Maidenhead: Open University Press.

Meinhof, U.H. (1994) Double encoding in news broadcasts. In Graddol, D. and Boyd-Barrett, O. (eds.) (1994) *Media Text: Authors and Readers*. Clevedon: Multilingual Matters, pp. 212–223.

Mills, S. (2004) (2nd edn) *Discourse*. London: Routledge.

Modleski, T. (ed.) (1986) *Studies in Entertainment: Critical Approaches to Mass Culture*. Bloomington: Indiana University Press.

Montgomery, M., Garton, G. and Tolson, A. (1989) Media discourse in the 1987 general election: ideology, scripts, and metaphors. *English Language Research Journal*, 3, 173–204.

Myers, G. (2000) Entitlement and sincerity in broadcast interviews about Princess Diana. *Media, Culture & Society*, 22, 167–185.

Ogden, C.K. and Richards, I.A. (1923) *The Meaning of Meaning: Study of the Influence of Language Upon Thought and of the Science of Symbolism*. London: Routledge and Kegan Paul.

O'Neill, J. (2001) Truth telling as constitutive of journalism. In Chadwick (ed.), *The Concise Encyclopedia of Ethics in Politics and the Media*. London: Academic Press.

Park, R.E. (1940) News as a form of knowledge: a chapter in the sociology of knowledge. *American Journal of Sociology* 45, 669–686. Extracts reprinted in Tumber, H. (1999) *News: a Reader*. Oxford: OUP.

Partington, A., Morley and Haarman (eds.) (2004) *Corpora and Discourse*. Bern: Peter Lang.

Pearce, M. (2002) *Informalization in UK General Election Propaganda*. Unpublished Ph.D. thesis: University of Leeds.

Perkins, M.R. (1983) *Modal Expressions in English*. London: Frances Pinter.

Peters, J.D. (1999) *Speaking into the Air: a History of the Idea of Communication*. Chicago: Chicago University Press.

Philo, G. (2002) Television news and audience understanding of war, conflict and disaster. *Journalism Studies*, 3(2), 173–186.

Philo, G. and Berry, M. (2004) *Bad News from Israel*. London: Pluto Press.

Richardson, John E. (2006) *Analysing Newspapers: an Approach from Critical Discourse Analysis*. London: Palgrave Macmillan

Sacks, H. (1992) *Lectures on Conversation*. Oxford: Blackwell.

Saeed, J.I. (1997) *Semantics*. Oxford: Blackwell.

Sancho, J. and Glover (2003) *Conflict Around the Clock: Audience Reactions to Media Coverage of the 2003 Iraq War*. London: ITC.

Saville Troike (2003) *The Ethnography of Communication: an Introduction*. Oxford: Blackwell.

Scannell, P. (ed.) (1991) Broadcast Talk. London: Sage.

Scannell, P. (1996) *Radio, Television and Modern Life*. Oxford: Blackwell.

Scannell, P. (1998) Media-Language-World. In Bell, A. and Garrett (eds.), *Approaches to Media Discourse*. Oxford: Blackwell.

Scannell, P. (2000) For-anyone-as-someone structures. *Media, Culture & Society*, 22(1), 5–24.

Scannell, P. and Cardiff (1991) *A Social History of British Broadcasting: 1922–39 – Serving the Nation*. Oxford: Blackwell.

Schegloff, E. (1972) Notes on a conversational practice: formulating place. In Sudnow, D.N. (ed.), *Studies in Social Interaction*, pp. 75–119.

Schegloff, E. (1988) From interior to confrontation: observations on the Bush/Rather encounter. *Research on Language and Social Generation*, 22, 215–40.

Schegloff, E. (1997) Whose Text? Whose Context? *Discourse & Society*, 8.

Schlesinger, P. (1978/1992) *Putting 'Reality' Together*. London: Routledge.

Schudson, M. (2003) *The Sociology of News*. New York: W.W. Norton.

Schutz, A. (1973) *Structures of the Lifeworld: Vol. 1*. Northwestern University Press.

Scollon, R. (1998) *Mediated Discourse as Social Interaction: a Study of News Discourse*. London: Longman.

Simon-Vandenbergen, A. (1996) Image-building through modality: The case of Political interviews. In Discourse and Society. Vol. 7(3), 389–415.

Simpson, P. (2003) *On the Discourse of Satire*. Amsterdam: John Benjamins.

Sinclair, J. and Coulthard (1975) *Towards an Analysis of Discourse*. Oxford: OUP.

Stubbs, M. (1996) *Text and Corpus Linguistics*. Oxford: Blackwell.

Stubbs, M. (1983) *Discourse Analysis: The Sociolinguistic Analysis of Natural Language*. Oxford: Blackwell.

Swales, J. (1990) *Genre Analysis: English in Academic and Research Settings*. Cambridge: CUP

Tester, K. (2001) *Compassion, Morality and the Media*. Milton Keynes: Open University Press.

Thompson, J.B. (1995) *The Media and Modernity*. Oxford: Polity Press.

Thomborrow, J. and Coates (eds.) (2005) Studies in Narrative 6: The Sociolinguistics of Narrative Amsterdam: John Benjamins.

Titunik, I.R. (1973) The formal method and the sociological method (M.M. Baxtin, P.N. Medvedev, V.N. Volosinov) in Russian theory and study of literature. In Volosinov, V.N. (ed.) *Marxism and the Philosophy of Language.* London: Academic Press.

Todorov, T. (1990) *Genres of Discourse.* Cambridge: CUP.

Tolson (2005) Sceptical pragmatics in television news: coverage of the two budget speeches in BBC television news. Paper given at the 2005 Ross Priory International Seminar in Broadcast Talk.

Tolson, A. (1991) Televised chat and the synthetic personality. In Scannell, P. (ed.) *Broadcast Talk.* London: Sage, pp. 178–201.

Tolson, A. (1996) *Mediations.* London: Arnold.

Tolson, A. (ed.) (2001) Television Talk Shows: Discourse, Performance, Spectacle. London: Lawrence Erlbaum Associates.

Tolson, A. (2006) *Media Talk.* Edinburgh: Edinburgh University Press.

Tuchman, G. (1978) *Making News: a Study in the Construction of Reality.* London/New York: the Free Press.

Tumber, H. (ed.) (1999) *News: a Reader.* Oxford: OUP.

Van Dijk, T. (1988a) *News as Discourse.* London: Lawrence Erlbaum Associates.

Van Dijk, T. (1988b) *News Analysis.* London: Lawrence Erlbaum Associates.

Van Dijk, T. (ed.) (1985) *Discourse and Communication: New Approaches to the Analysis of Mass Media Discourse and Communication.* Berlin: Walter de Gruyter.

Van Dijk, T. (1991) *Racism and the Press (Critical Studies in Racism and Migration)* London: Routledge.

Ventola, E. (ed.) *Discourse and Community: Doing Functional Linguistics.* Tübingen: Gunter Narr Verlag.

Volosinov, V.N. (1973) *Marxism and the Philosophy of Language.* London: Academic Press.

Wenger, E. (1998) *Communities of Practice.* Cambridge: CUP.

White, P.R.R. (1997) Death, disruption and the moral order: the narrative impulse in mass-media 'hard-news' reporting. In Christie, F. and Martin, J.R. (eds.), *Genre and Institutions: Social Processes in the Workplace and School.* London: Cassell, pp. 101–133.

White, P.R.R. (2000) Media objectivity and the rhetoric of news story structure. In Ventola, E. (ed.), *Discourse and Community: Doing Functional Linguistics.* Tübingen: Gunter Narr Verlag, pp. 379–397.

Widdowson, H.G. (2004) *Text, Context, Pretext: Critical Issues in Discourse Analysis.* Oxford: Blackwell.

Williams, R. (1973) Base and superstructure in Marxist cultural theory. *New Left Review,* 82, 3–16.

Willis, D. (1992) Caught in the act: using the rank scale to address problems of delicacy. In Coulthard, M. (ed.), *Advances in Spoken Discourse.* London: Routledge.

Winston, B. (2002) Towards tabloidization? Glasgow revisited, 1975–2001, *Journalism Studies,* 3(1), 5–20.

Wodak, R. and Meyer (eds.) (2001) *Methods of Critical Discourse.* London: Sage.

Wooffit, R. (1992) *Telling Tales of the Unexpected.* Brighton: Harvester.

Woolfson, N. (1979) The conversational historical present alternation, *Language,* 55, 168–182.

Woolfson, N. (1982) *CHP: the Conversational Historic Present in American English Narrative*. Dordrecht: Foris.

Zelizer, B. (1990) Where is the author in American TV news? *Semiotica,* 80, 37–48.

Index